HUMOROUS INTRODUCTIONS FOR EMCEES

HUMOROUS INTRODUCTIONS FOR EMCEES

A COMPILATION OF PRACTICAL SPEECHES AND STORIES TO BE USED IN INTRODUCING TALENT OF ALL TYPES.

By

LAWRENCE M. BRINGS, M. A.

Formerly, Director, Department of Speech, Teachers College, Aberdeen, S. D.; Instructor in Speech, the University of Minnesota; President, Northwestern College of Speech Arts; professional lecturer and entertainer.

PUBLISHERS

T. S. DENISON & COMPANY

MINNEAPOLIS, MINNESOTA

First Printing, September 1955
Second Printing, October 1956
Third Printing, February 1957
Fourth Printing, January 1958
Fifth Printing, March 1959
Sixth Printing, February 1960
Seventh Printing, April 1961
Eighth Printing, January 1962
Ninth Printing, February 1963
Tenth Printing, March 1964
Eleventh Printing, May 1965
Twelfth Printing, December 1965

Printed in the U. S. A.
By THE BRINGS PRESS

Library of Congress Catalog Card Number: 55-11067

PREFACE

Many emcees, amateur and professional alike, fail many times to introduce talent properly. How often, as a member of an audience or a group, have you been bored by the fumbling attempts of the emcee to introduce the talent scheduled to appear on the program? If your observation is similar to mine, it occurs more often than necessary. The weakness of his presentation can be attributed to a lack of preparation or simply because he hasn't had a reliable source of information. In many instances he doesn't know the formula.

As a result of many years experience as a professional emcee and entertainer, I have decided to do something about this problem by providing source material for the emcee who wishes to make a success of his appearance on a program.

To meet the demand for practical assistance, I have assembled a wide variety of material that has been contributed by many successful professional emcees. Credit has been given to each contributor. Practically all this material has been tested in actual use. Nevertheless it is impossible for me to vouch for the originality or newness of all the stories and anecdotes that are included in the introductions.

To enhance the value of this book, almost two hundred different types of talent and situations requiring the presence of an emcee are included. In addition, the last section of the book contains a variety of short bits and general material that any emcee can dovetail into his line of patter.

I do not recommend that users of this book follow these written introductions verbatim. To do so would eliminate the spontaneous adaptation to the specific situation and the talent that is so all-important. After all, these introductions are merely suggestive of a treatment to be followed. Secure all the necessary data about the talent's background and work out your own presentation. Be sure that any stories you use are appropriate. Although there is much material assembled in this book that the professional emcee can use, I fully recognize that these guideposts will be of greater aid to the inexperienced emcee. The underlying formula will give him courage to face a task that he usually considers an ordeal.

Even the experienced emcee, I believe, can profit by making a careful study of the many types of introductions contained in this book. Regardless of what evaluation he may give to this material, at least he must agree that the treatment is practical and realistic. There is something significant about a statement made to me by a professional emcee after he had examined this manuscript: "If I find one joke or one new idea on one page of any book of this type, it will be easily worth the price of the entire book to me."

I do not claim that this collection of suggested introductions is so perfect, however, as to meet the requirements of all emcees in all situations. At least I have made an attempt to meet a need and I hope that the users of this book will find it a valuable prop in time of stress. I shall appreciate your reactions and your constructive criticism.

—Lawrence M. Brings.

CONTENTS

SECTION ONE

The Master of Ceremonies

SECTION TWO

Introducing Talent

SECTION THREE

The Emcee at Special Occasions

SECTION FOUR

Novelty Treatments

SECTION FIVE

Short Bits for the Emcee

SECTION ONE

Chapter One

THE MASTER OF CEREMONIES OR TOASTMASTER

Few of us are so calloused to our inherited traditions that we can cross the path of a black cat without a feeling either of foolhardy bravado or informed superiority. We all know the basic superstitions that accompany certain of our customs. Yet none of us are fully aware of the extent to which our reactions to everyday situations are determined by centuries of tradition.

The subject of this book, for example, is probably seldom considered a traditional thing. The organization of a banquet or other programs necessitates the appointment of a Master of Ceremonies simply to see that the program progresses smoothly and orderly. We feel it is a logical thing, and the fact that the chairman of this function is called the master of ceremonies is merely a case of—well, we have to call him something. Yet the master of ceremonies has a history no less venerable than the above-mentioned cat.

The Origin of the Emcee

It was soon after his accession to the English throne in 1603 that James I appointed Sir Lewis Lewknor as the first "Master of Ceremonies" in the English speaking world. We know little about this worthy man or about the office he filled, except that it was his duty to arrange the receptions and departures of all visiting foreign ministers. As a symbol of his office he was to wear a medal attached to a gold chain around his neck. On one side of the medal was an emblem of peace with the motto, "Beati Pacifi," and on the other side an emblem of war with the motto, "Dieu et mon droit." What significance may be attached to this two-faced medal is lost to us today.

This first master of ceremonies died in 1627 and Sir John Finett accepted the appointment from that ill-fated monarch Charles I in which capacity he served until the latter was beheaded in 1649. Sir John apparently took a much greater interest in posterity than had his predecessor because he wrote a diary, which is quite rare today, describing his functions and daily activities in the Royal Household. It was published in 1650 under the quite esoteric title, **Finetti Philoxensis.**

The seventeenth century was an age of punctilio in extreme. Ambassadors and great ladies vied with each other for the doubtful honor of being seated first at state banquets. It was Sir John's obligation to satisfy everyone's desire to be seated ahead of his peers in such a way as to not precipitate some grave international incident. He was a walking copy of a royal-type Emily Post. He describes some of the problems he had to solve as "a **clash** between the Savoy and Florence ambassadors for precedence;" "questions betwixt the Imperial and Venetian ambassadors, concerning **titles** and **visits;**" and "the Frenchman takes **exceptions** about **placing.**"

In these and many other such sensitive diplomatic near-crises our seventeenth-century master of ceremonies had to produce some sly and clever solutions. For example, Sir John tells us how he solved a question of precedence between the Russian ambassador on one hand, and the French and Spanish on the other. The master of ceremonies, with all the condescension of an undertipped head-waiter, placed the Russian in a seat where he had a fine view of the king's face but from whence he could see nothing of the entertainment itself. On another occasion the same Muscovite complained that there had been but one lord in waiting at the head of the stairs when he arrived at a reception at Whitehall. The wily Sir John assured him that in England it was considered a greater honor to be received by one such lord than by many.

How the Emcee Entered Everyday Affairs

It is not known precisely when or under what circumstances the title of master of the ceremonies was applied to some lesser dignitary than a member of his Majesty's household. It is probable, however, that it began early in the following century, in the famous and much-frequented watering place in England called Bath. It was in this resort that a young British fashion leader and gambler named Beau Nash appointed himself master of the ceremonies and served in that capacity until gambling was prohibited in 1740.

It was in this brilliant yet brittle society that the title approached the meaning that it has today. Beau Nash supervised the entertainment, the gambling, and all social functions at the spa. He controlled the kind of costume to be worn to the extent of banning the wearing of swords in Bath and was considered the leading wit in England. It is said that the only time he was ever bested in repartee was when he once met John Wesley on a narrow sidewalk. "I never make way for a fool," said Nash insolently. "I always make way for a fool," said Wesley, stepping into the gutter and bowing.

Nash retired on a pension from the city of Bath in 1745 but the tradition remained. A master of ceremonies was maintained for a long time and his duties developed more into keeping with what we know about them today. At the beginning of the nineteenth century Jane Austen writes of the master of the ceremonies at Bath. There is still one at this time in the royal court also. But by this date there are occasional references to other persons bearing the same title for lesser and more varied functions. The term had arrived at its present meaning. The last century and a half has seen little change in its sense.

The Original Functions of a Toastmaster

We consider the functions of a toastmaster to be closely allied to those of a master of ceremonies, yet their origins are very different. The origin of toasts actually goes back to some kind of prehistoric religious ritual. The ancient Norse drank the "minne" to their gods, Thor, Odin, and Freya, and they also drank to the memory of their dead. The ancient Greeks had customs so similar as to make it near certain that these customs must date from a time in prehistory when these two widely-separated cultures were united.

At some date during or before Roman times toasts were being drunk to the living as well as the dead. A couplet from Martial seems to indicate that the gallants of that empire drank as many bumpers to their mistresses as there were letters in the ladies' names:

Six cups to Naevia's health go quickly round,
And be with seven the fair Justina's crowned.

In the first Christian millennium our Anglo-Saxon forebearers drank their mead to each other's health with the cry "Waes hael!" (Be healthy.) This is the origin of our word wassail.

It was an early custom to float a piece of bread or other pastry called a sop, in the glass of wine both for nourishment and, according to some, to improve the flavor. Thus Chaucer, writing about 1390, describes a franklin:

Wel loved he by the morwe a sap in wyn.

It seems fairly certain, however, that the term "toast" for referring to such a preparation was not used until about 1600. It was still customary for the toast to be drunk to a member of the fairer sex, and a lady was frequently referred to as a toast, as in "the toast of the town." Sir Richard Steele, writing of the latter part of the 17th century, tells the following anecdote:

"It happened that on a publick day (speaking of Bath) a celebrated beauty of those times was in the cross bath, and one of the crowd of her admirers took a glass of the water in which the fair stood, and drank her health to the company. There was in the place a gay fellow, half fuddled, who offered to jump in, and swore, though he liked not the liquor, he would have the toast. He was opposed in his resolution, yet this whim gave foundation to the present honour which is done to the lady we mention in our liquor, who has ever since been called a toast."

The Drinking of the Toast

Many unusual customs have been known to attach themselves for varying lengths of time to the drinking of the toast. It is known that, in Charles II's reign, very serious toasts were often drunk on bended knee, although the purpose of this genuflection is not known. Likewise, the Scottish custom, which some say still survives, of toasting with one foot on the table and the other in a chair, has its origins lost in antiquity. Samuel Pepys, writing in his **Diary** for June 19, 1663:

> "To the Rhenish wine house, where Mr. Moore showed us the French manner when a health is drunk, to bow to him that drunk to you, and then apply yourself to him, whose lady's health is drunk, and then to the person that you drink to, which I never knew before; but it seems it is now the fashion."

We are more fortunate in understanding why. Until the beginning of the present century, finger bowls were never served at dinners feting members of the royal family of Great Britain. Following the Bloodless Revolution of 1688, James II sought exile in France but maintained a large body of secret followers in the British Isles. When one of these followers was called upon to toast a new monarch he would propose the toast while surreptitiously holding his glass over the finger bowl, thus, "Long live the King (over the water)," or, the one in exile.

Origin of the Term "Toastmaster"

Much scholarly ink has been spilt in arguments over when the term "toastmaster" was first used. One school of thought adheres to the following anecdote as indicating the origin of the worthy office. It is quoted from the London City Press, June 4, 1879.

> "I recently heard, when dining in the City, that the origin of the custom of having toastmasters at City banquets was something as follows. It is said that at one of these banquets of the old East Indian Company the Duke of Cambridge (father of the present Duke), who was always partial to dining in the City, had to speak. Mr. Toole, who was one of the officials of the company, and a man by no means wanting in confidence, said, 'Some of the gentlemen have some difficulty in hearing your Royal Highness; shall I give out

what the toast is?' The practice was so convenient that it was repeated on many future occasions, and Mr. Toole developed into the great City toastmaster."

Of slightly earlier origin is the tale that during the short-lived peace of Amiens in 1802 and 1803 "the chairman at a banquet proposed, 'The health of the three consuls.' The toastmaster announced the toast as 'The health of the three per cent consuls.' "

Perhaps the earliest reference to the office of toastmaster, however, comes from the autobiography of the Reverend Alexander Carlyle. He records a visit to the Duke of Argyle in Inverary, Scotland, in 1758. At that time, he explains, it was the practice for persons in affluent circumstances "to employ a regular toastmaster to regulate the after-dinner drinking, which was a serious and heavy occupation, too fatiguing to be performed by the aristocratic host."

Thus we may see that, although today the duties of the master of ceremonies are closely allied to those of the toastmaster, nevertheless, in origin, they are considerably different. Both are as traditional as a coronation itself and have equally as respectable histories. The master of ceremonies may ride to his banquet in the latest model automobile and may officiate in the air-conditioned banquet room of a sky-scraping hotel, but in performing his duties he is merely continuing a tradition that began centuries ago.

Despite attempts on the part of Sir John Finett to describe his duties and obligations as a seventeenth-century master of ceremonies, we cannot, in truth, describe this functionary's duty today except in the broadest, most general terms. The program moderator's job today is very wide in its scope. He has but one obligation — to see that the program moves smoothly and intelligently toward its conclusion. Any attempt to describe his duties in greater detail is to unnecessarily hamper him with restrictions and limitations. However, it is possible to make a few statements pertinent to the general principle mentioned above.

Primary Requirements of a Good Emcee

The primary requirement for any such program or banquet chairman is tact. He must be able to keep all guests satisfied and happy at the expense of no one. He must have, also, a certain amount of intuition to enable him to feel when the program is in need of some heavy, serious oratory and when a light, comic spirit should be injected. He must, therefore, keep his finger on the pulse of the audience, knowing what sort of pill to prescribe next.

The whole program is in the hands of the toastmaster. He has the right to do with it what he sees fit. Although usually, at banquets and meetings, the program has been laid out beforehand, the chairman may alter, revise, or rearrange it as he feels is best. If, at the last minute, it seems advisable to change the order of the program, he may do so. In general, it is considered poor taste to schedule two instructive lectures in succession, but here, also, a capable emcee may sometimes bring this off successfully. Again, however, he must be careful that his changes bring ill to no one, catch no speaker unaware or unprepared, or otherwise hamper the successful progression of the program.

It is a misconception that the master of ceremonies needs to be an eloquent speaker or a brilliant wit. In fact, it is probably better that he be neither of these. True, he must be sufficiently eloquent to be able to express his thoughts articulately and succinctly, and he must possess enough wit to organize and marshall his thoughts on his feet before a public. But if he is too adept at these things he is often tempted to superimpose his own personality on top of the program thus subordinating what should rightfully be its main interest — i. e., the speakers themselves.

Toasting in the United States is usually carried on in a most informal way. It is better for the toastmaster to keep the toasting only sufficiently formal to maintain order. At a stiffly formal or traditional ceremony, however, there are certain practices which the toastmaster should perhaps observe. He should call the table to order at the announcement of each toast, inviting the attention of the guests to the gentleman wishing to propose the toast. The person proposing the toast may either repeat it himself or hand it to the toastmaster to be read. Either is correct. The chairman should call upon a complimented person to respond to a toast, but if that person appears unprepared to speak, the toastmaster should be able to change the subject without embarrassing anyone.

Usually, however, no such formal regulation of actions are necessary. The best regulation is to see to the merriment or instruction of all present, but keep your own personality in the background. A fortunate analogy has been suggested by the author and speaker, Arthur Gray:

> "The toastmaster is like the flour in a plum pudding — he is necessary to hold the other good things together, but the moment he predominates and thrusts himself forward at the expense of the plums, the citron and the spices, he becomes a nuisance — and he spoils the pudding."

Spontaneity and Quick Thinking are Essential

It has been stated that the success of a program depends largely on the ability of the master of ceremonies to keep it going smoothly. We might refer to him as the skipper of a boat, for it is he who keeps the vessel from dashing on the rocks and reef. His inability to keep the craft in the safer channels can mar the whole course of this business or pleasure trip, and result in disappointment to the audience as well as the discomfiture, even embarrassment, of the speakers or entertainers.

Although the master of ceremonies may be blessed with the ability to be a wonderful skipper he cannot depend on spontaneity alone. He must always be prepared for every eventuality, considering well the nature and spirit of the occasion. There are no hard and fast rules to which he must adhere, but there are generalities that pertain to all phases of the emcee's contribution. He must promote the best of feeling among all, especially between speakers or between entertainers. If more than one speaker is on the program the emcee must be careful to show no partiality. If more than one entertainer is to appear, all should share equally in the emcee's pleasantries. He should make every effort to make the entertainer or speaker feel extremely welcome, and the audience to feel very glad they came.

When introducing the guest to the audience the emcee should sound sincere, and maintain the appearance of spontaneity. The audience should get the impression that his words of praise are impromptu, no matter how much care and thought has been given to it beforehand. It should not be given like a small boy reciting a poem from memory.

An experienced speaker never begins his talk with the meat of his message. He must start with an attention-catching phrase or joke in order that the audience may immediately get into focus with him. This is also true for the master of ceremonies who must snap his audience out of complacency with a quick pun or quip. If the program lags there is apt to be fidgeting and whisperings among the audience that can be disconcerting to those on the stage as well as others in the audience who wish to hear.

In some countries people are compelled to listen. In our country people are glad to listen if what is said to them is interesting or entertaining. There should be plenty of pleasantry, witty epigrams appropriate to the person or subject, and carefully selected anecdotes to preface introductions.

The emcee should acquaint himself thoroughly with the speaker and the speaker's subject or with the entertainer and the entertainer's act, and arrange his repartee accordingly. If he senses that the speaker or entertainer is of the emotional type, or is of a sensitive nature, he should proceed with much tact, and not rush in where angels fear to tread. The average length of a preface should not exceed two or three minutes. People holding very high office, or those very well known to the public require very simple introductions. They don't need a long one. The President, for instance, is introduced thus: "Ladies and gentlemen, the President of the United States."

Jokes and How to Use Them

Washington Irving once said, "Honest good humor is the oil and the wine of merry making. And there is no jovial companionship equal to that where the jokes are rather small and the laughter abundant." From this we learn that a very long drawn-out joke or story is not acceptable. Did you ever listen to a poor joke teller wander sideways and bring in so many unnecessary details that the point of the joke was entirely lost on the listener by the time he had finished? Keep jokes concise and to the point, and have the punch line at the very end of the story. Never explain a joke after it is told. If it doesn't explain itself, it is not worth the telling.

The master of ceremonies should pick his jokes to fit the occasion; he should keep them consistent with the subject at hand, and with the personality of the guest. A little browsing through the following pages will save the emcee much valuable time and provide him with material arranged in a professional manner. Just about every subject has been considered and the master of ceremonies will find here a veritable gold mine packed between the covers of this book.

If it is possible for the emcee to contact the guest before the program, it is well to review with him what he intends to say. In this way he will know that what he says in public is entirely acceptable to the guest.

For example, the guest may have just recently returned from Nationalist China. Knowing beforehand that the speaker will talk on the country visited, the emcee will thumb through the following pages of this book until he finds material relative to China. He might preface the guest's introduction by saying, "We are going to have an interesting talk this evening by a man who has just returned from that problematical country beyond the Pacific. I have never been to China, but I have visited Chinatown. One could hardly say there is a world of difference between the two places. Perhaps half a world would be more correct.

"Anyway, not too long ago I had a dinner in one of the

charming Oriental restaurants in Chinatown. The first dish I ordered was Fum Foo, Foo Fum, or something was a Fum. Whatever it was it was delicious. It seems they make it with several kinds of vegetables and meat. The dark meat they used hit my fancy. I wanted to find out what it was, so I called the waiter. He was a solemn-looking Chinaman, whose English I could not understand. I pointed to a morsel of the delicious dark meat, and, rubbing my tummy to give the impression I liked it, I asked, 'Quack, quack?' The waiter grinned, and said, 'No, sir. Bow-wow.'

"Whenever I think of the Chinese I recall the story about the one who was walking through a San Francisco alley. He saw a woman accidentally fall off the back porch of a house and land in the garbage can. He shook his head and remarked, 'Amelicans velly wasteful. That woman good for ten years yet.' "

These jokes are, to some extent, related, although the repartee has no continuity. A number of jokes may be told, one after the other, but they should be short, and like those above, should be related to the general subject of the evening. In this case they should deal in some way with China or its people.

In a sense, the emcee's repartee is a monologue, and a real monologue must have continuity. Sometimes it is best to tell the stories all about a single character. In this way he achieves continuity plus unity of character.

What to Use in an Introduction

Jokes are not the only material that may be used in prefacing an introduction. Appropriate epigrams are always effective. Short poems or limericks may be used, or humorously worded want ads from the newspapers. Again, the master of ceremonies may present his preface in a humorous letter which he claims he has just received. However, it must be stressed, the material should be compatible with the guest and his subject, or with the entertainer and/or his act. Much care should be exercised in selecting the jokes. This may take considerable time, but is well worth the effort. The wording of many jokes may be changed to make them more apropos. The punch line, too, may be re-worded, but care must be taken not to lose the point of the joke in the changing. For example, he may use the age-old joke about division but change it to fit a particular occasion: "If I divide an apple in four pieces, what do I have?" "Quarters." "And if I divide it into eight pieces?" "Eighths." "And if I divide it into eight thousand pieces?" "Applesauce." By substituting pork chops for apples we would have "sausage," or steak and we would have "hamburger."

The emcee, as he thumbs through these pages, may discover that he can take jokes from different parts of the book and form his own continuity. The variations of jokes and continuities which may be derived from and suggested by this book are limited only by his own imagination. Real comedy and good humor possess a tremendous power in holding the public's attention. A master of ceremonies must be a student of mass psychology, able to analyze and detect the mood of the audience at once, and proceed accordingly. If he discovers that the audience is a little "stiff," he should endeavor to break the ice by being exceptionally lively, full of pep, and raring to go. It happens so often that when you yawn, others will yawn. We are all, more or less, imitators. Joviality begets good feeling; good feeling begets friendliness; and friendliness soon leads to a good time by all.

Practice and Experience are Essential

How can one prepare himself if called upon to officiate as a master of ceremonies without having had the benefit of previous experience? Undoubtedly the simplest and most effective way would be to buy, rent or borrow a recorder. Try a bit on repartee on that. Play it back. Are you satisfied with that playback? Forget that it is your own voice you are listening to. Think of it as someone on the radio or television. Is he really a pleasing and enjoyable announcer and story-teller? If not, why not? How would you improve your performance? You will discover flaws, some perhaps minute to you but glaring to others. Much can be learned by watching professional emcees on television. One will find all kinds, some not so good, many indifferent, some very good. Pick the best and try to be as good. Emceeing may really be classified as an art, and one most worthy of cultivating. A good emcee, or master of ceremonies, is a valuable asset to any group and contributes a vital service in the broad field of entertainment.

A Good Personality and Clever Repartee are Helpful

Just a word about personality. Webster defines personality as "The totality of an individual's characteristics." Therefore, it might be well to analyze one's characteristics and study the total.

Robert Burns was quite correct when he said: "The best laid plans of mice and men gag aft astray," and sometimes much practiced repartee misfires. Usually the quick-witted emcee can cover this so it will pass unnoticed. A few instances that really occurred may be given here.

An emcee's tongue suddenly seemed to become thick, causing him to pull a tongue-twister unintentionally. He quickly said with a laugh, "Reminds me of the woman who entered the office of the probate judge, and said, 'If you're the reprobate judge, I want to tell you my husband died untested and left me four little infidels, and I want to be their executioner.' "

An emcee who received less response than he expected for his repartee, remarked, "I see our audience contains a number of members of the London Semi-Weekly Club. On Tuesday they meet to listen to American jokes. On Saturday they meet to enjoy a hearty laugh."

An emcee who, for a moment, was at a loss as to what to say, got back into the groove by saying, "I was told one time if I ever wanted for words, just to say anything. Reminds me of the man who entered a restaurant and said to the waiter, "Waiter, did I leave an umbrella here yesterday?" "What kind of an umbrella?" asked the waiter. "Oh, any kind," said the man. "I'm not fussy."

It might be well for the emcee to have a few of these life savers on hand just in case.

It is said that no person is indispensable, but in our eyes the master of ceremonies comes as near as anybody in deserving this honor.

He is a general without lieutenants on the field of prattle.

—Arthur L. Kaser.

Acknowledgement is made to David E. Kaser, University of Michigan, for the historical research.

Chapter Two

SUGGESTIONS FOR THE MASTER OF CEREMONIES

The Role of the Emcee

Perhaps you are a master of ceremonies for the first time. Perhaps you have already had considerable experience as an emcee. In either case one of your principal responsibilities will be to introduce certain personalities to audiences. Among these personalities will be included lecturers, comedians, musicians, acrobats, singers, magicians, etc. You may be called upon to preside at bachelor parties, wedding anniversaries, the awarding of testimonials, stag parties, club banquets, and greetings to returned war heroes. The list of those you may be called upon to present, or affairs in which you will be the guiding force is long and varied, containing representatives of most professions and occupations. While each event should be handled as an individual matter, basically the general rules for presentation apply to all of them.

In making an introduction your job is to smooth the path of the person you are about to introduce and make his task lighter by helping to create a receptive audience. In many years of appearing before the public in various capacities I have found the following suggestions to be quite helpful. I pass them along to you, in the hope that they will make your chores lighter and easier and pleasanter. If I seem to be an exponent of the obvious at times, it is because of a desire to express my ideas clearly and effectively.

Establish A Happy Relationship With Your Audience

The person you are going to introduce is, in most cases, one in whom the audience is interested. For various reasons they want to see and hear this person. As the master of ceremonies your principal function in making the introduction is to build up that mood of interest. If, as sometimes happens, that atmosphere doesn't exist, he must try to create it—which isn't as difficult as it sounds.

To make a really successful presentation of an entertainer an entente cordiale, a relationship of good will should be established between you and your audience. If your audience enjoys hearing you, they will like you. If they like you, your job will be much easier, and your entertainer's task will be easier. He will face a much more receptive audience than if he stepped out before them "cold."

Look upon your audience as being composed of friends, and they will usually reciprocate the feeling. While audiences may differ as to size and personalities, they all possess one basic characteristic—they all want to be interested and entertained. They are ready to believe that you have the ability and are capable of pleasing them in carrying out your assignment or you wouldn't be there facing them. Consequently, they are prepared to like you—but you must like them in turn. It is seldom difficult to like people who show an appreciation and liking for us.

Primary Aim Should Be to Create Audience Interest in the Entertainer

When that relationship is mutually established you will find it of exceptional value in carrying out your mission of building up interest in your entertainer. BUT don't let your ego get the better of you and lead you astray because you have a friendly audience and try to make yourself more important than your program. While I am not trying to minimize the importance of your job—which is really an important one—nevertheless your chief responsibility is to the person you are introducing. Your main objective, the sum and substance of your introduction, is to make or keep him the important one, the one they want to hear.

Being obtrusive is one sure way of defeating your purpose of building up an interest in the program.

Don't Embarrass the Talent

Never embarrass your speaker or entertainer. Any unkind or insinuating comments or reflections on the personality, character or integrity of the talent for the purpose of getting a possible laugh shows extremely bad taste, a lack of respect, and helps to tear down the atmosphere you are supposed to help create for the entertainers, and certainly doesn't help the emcee fulfill his obligations. No matter how big a laugh he might get from his derogatory remarks, any such comments from the emcee will generally arouse a feeling of resentment toward him from some members of his audience, if not all of them. Regardless of how well the comments seem to have been received, which naturally tends to destroy any pleasant relationship that might have previously existed between the emcee and the audience, to say nothing of the irritating effect it will have upon the entertainers. I have heard emcees whose whole introduction seemed to be based upon this destructive process. Don't misunderstand me. A little kidding, or ribbing, so long as it is understood that it is all in fun, is an excellent way of creating a little merriment and relaxation, but it should never be carried to such an extreme that it sounds insulting.

The emcee can also embarrass his talent by being too effusive, by the use of too many flattering adjectives. It will be better for all concerned if the emcee restrains himself and does not become overly enthusiastic in pointing out the entertainer's many good qualities, his talents and his achievements. These things may be mentioned, of course, but they should not be enlarged upon until the emcee's talk becomes very boring or tainted with the ridiculous. A few appropriate words of praise will carry more weight than a long tiresome review of the entertainer's virtues.

Complete Preparation is Essential

Now, obviously, a long-winded speaker can become a bore —but a long-winded emcee is worse. He not only misses his objective by causing a loss of interest in his own talk, but he creates an obstacle that might be difficult for the entertainer to overcome. Sometimes an emcee, even when making a comparatively short introduction, can appear to be long-winded. He is usually the type of genius who becomes just as tiresome in two minutes as he could in twenty. Because of a lack of proper preparation he can't interest his audience nor hold their attention, with the result that the audience becomes annoyed and restless. But he can conquer his failings by a little thought and a diligent application of observation, self-appraisal and common sense.

The reaction of an audience perceptibly reflects the attitude and delivery of the emcee. It goes without saying that he should have poise. Poise is based on self-confidence. If he is inclined to be nervous when first facing an audience he should tell a good story immediately. The resulting laugh should relax and calm his nerves and give him the self-confidence he needs, in addition to helping induce the good-will relationship between him and his audience. Another aid to self-confidence is the knowledge, as stated in the first few paragraphs, that his audience is prepared to like him and willing to give him credit for being capable. But he can disillusion the audience about his abilities very quickly and easily by being uncertain in his delivery, ill-at-ease and awkward appearing in his demeanor and attitude. If he knows his material thoroughly, if he is sure of what he is going to say and how he is going to say it, there is little reason for him to give the appearance of being unsure of himself. He has a number of potentially friendly, interested listeners before him. By following the suggestions offered above, he should be able to solidify that feeling of friendly interest and hold their attention. But he must know his material well enough for his talk to flow smoothly. If he doesn't know it well, his chances for making a good presentation will decrease in proportion to his lack of study and the emcee, entertainers and audience will suffer.

Of course some emcees, with a background of years of experience making presentations, can successfully ad lib their introductions, but the average emcee usually has a prepared speech. The wise emcee will provide himself with a number of such prepared speeches covering almost every occasion on which he might be called upon to make an introduction. He should read these speeches and study them, for he doesn't always know in advance when he might be called upon to introduce such varying personalities as a scientist, a saxophone player, a statesman, a trained animal act, a grand opera singer, a variety act, a businessman, etc. If he has read and studied the introductions, which are for the greater part written by and for emcees for these and other occasions, he should be able to quickly prepare himself.

Get Specific Information About the Talent

He should learn something about the speaker and his lecture, although he should not dwell too much upon the speaker's subject. Let the speaker do that. If he is introducing an entertainer he should know what the entertainer's specialty is, whether it's juggling, ballet dancing, singing torch songs or telling jokes. He should know whether the speaker's lecture or the speaker is the more important to the audience. As an example, suppose a minor city official, practically unknown outside of a small circle, is to deliver a talk on a proposed tax amendment. In that case the speaker's talk about the tax bill is the important thing, not the minor official, although, of course, the emcee will have to build up the official, so that the official's talk may be more impressive—which certainly does not mean that he must give the talk himself. When you introduce an entertainer, the entertainer is the one the audience wants to see and hear.

It will help the emcee if he knows something about his audience. I refer to a previous statement — "audiences may differ as to size and personalities." That is true, but it is almost always possible to judge the character and personality of audiences by knowing who or what they have come to hear or see. An audience that comes to enjoy the jokes and stories of a popular comedian will be quite different from one who comes to hear a lecture from a world-famed economist. Each will require different treatment. If the emcee will keep these thoughts in mind, he will find it to be of great help in arranging his introductions.

If he has had the foresight to provide himself with prepared introductions beforehand, he can easily select one fitted to the occasion and if necessary adapt it to the particular event. He can eliminate any parts of it that he doesn't want to use, and change any wording or phrasing that isn't suitable or doesn't conform to his particular style of delivery or personality. While it isn't necessary to use a prepared speech, word for word, as it is written, it is advisable to follow the pattern, as they were written for specific situations, and, in making changes be sure that the "meat" or essential qualities are not eliminated or rendered meaningless.

In general, introductions should not be any longer than is necessary to establish the entertainer's identity, with perhaps a few words about him personally, a mention of some outstanding achievement, with a few witticisms and an anecdote or two included to keep the audience in a pleasant frame of mind. Naturally, in preparing your introductions you will differentiate between personalities; a famed violin virtuoso or a supreme court justice will require a much more dignified type of introduction than would a fast-talking comedian or a champion prize-fighter. When you have your introduction arranged to your satisfaction it is advisable to copy them, a method used by many actors as an aid to their memories when studying their parts.

Last-minute emergencies, such as the entertainers being late, or a change of program, might make it necessary for you to alter or change an introduction. It is wise to allow for this and be ready if such contingencies should occur.

All this stresses the necessity of preparation. An emcee must be prepared and alert at all times. A speaker or entertainer who has to cope with a poorly-prepared or inept emcee is at a very great disadvantage. The bungling of an incapable emcee can place the entertainer in a much more unenviable position than if he had no introduction at all.

Select and Use Appropriate Stories

Now, if you use stories—and what emcee doesn't?—be sure your stories are appropriate for the occasion, that they are funny or witty, that they are not too lengthy, that you know them thoroughly from the beginning to the punch line—and that you know how to tell them. Many a program has been saddened by emcees not adhering to the use of the above rules.

Do not tell any story, no matter how good you may think it is, if the story does not apply to the situation—unless you can connect it to the occasion with a few well-chosen words. Even if it has been a knockout, if it doesn't fit in with the speaker or his subject, and you can't adapt it to the circumstances—don't use it. If you do, you will distract your audience by departing from the main theme of your talk.

There may be a place for the risque story—in a Pullman smoking compartment, or a men's stag, or some place where men congregate. But it is using very bad judgment to tell an off-color story to an audience — especially a mixed audience—when you are making an introduction. You might get laughs with them, but you are lowering your dignity and that of your audience. Don't tell them. There are plenty of clean stories that are very funny that will receive better results.

In the stories that you tell eliminate all useless words. Don't stretch them out — get to the punch line as quickly as possible. A few superfluous words can sometimes make a story seem interminable and kill the laugh you are expecting. That is one of the most disconcerting things that can happen to an emcee. When he tells a story, confidently expecting a laugh at the finish, and gets only dead silence, or at best a few polite and weak snickers, that is really embarrassing. If you should get a laugh at an unexpected spot in your story, humor it. Don't continue with your story until they have had their laugh. Remember the spot. If it has never happened before, it might be because of some slight incident. The line that got the laugh might recall something that has happened to some prominent person that the audience is familiar with. It might have happened because of a different inflection you have given a certain line. If that is the reason you can find out the next time you tell the story, and it would be well to remember it and repeat the inflection or action that caused it. Don't tell a story as though you think it's going to be tremendously funny. It might not be. When you have finished your story, if the expected laugh doesn't come immediately, give them a slight chance to laugh. Some audiences are unpredictable in that they don't get the point in a punch line for a moment or so. But don't wait too long for them to get it. When you get a laugh on your punch line, don't "step on it," as the comedians say—meaning don't start to talk again until the laugh has reached its peak and is starting to die away. It is better to continue with your talk before the laughter has entirely stopped, as it leaves your audience in an exhilerated state of mind. It is common knowledge that laughter has a tonic effect. One good story that brings a hearty laugh is much better than any number of bad or mediocre ones that bring little or no laughter; and it's part of the emcee's job to find out which is which.

"Ladies and gentlemen," "My friends" and "Folks" are probably the most common expressions used in addressing an audience. The emcee will have to decide himself whether to use one of these, or use his imagination and find some other form. In this he will be guided by the type of his audience. Here is one that I wouldn't advise using on many occasions. The emcee faces his audience and says:

"My friends, I think I may call you friends—I feel that I know you too well to say 'Ladies and gentlemen.' "

In this chapter, based on practical experience, I have tried to set forth my views and ideas. It is my sincere wish and hope that the reader will find something here that will be of benefit to him. —Earl Jay Gilbert

SECTION TWO

INTRODUCING TALENT

On the following pages there are assembled complete introductions for a wide assortment of talent, aimed for use by both professionals and amateur emcees. Many of these speeches have been contributed by professional emcees who have used them in actual situations. In all instances, the real names of the talent introduced have been eliminated for obvious reasons.

As is stated in the preface, it must be understood that these introductions are merely patterns to be adapted by the emcee to the situation. It would be stupid to adhere to the exact treatment as given here.

INTRODUCING AN ACTRESS

By Arthur L. Kaser

Ladies and gentlemen, we are honored, highly honored, I should say, by having as our guest this evening, someone you have heard a lot about, and, no doubt, have seen many times in the movies, or on your television screen. And if I am not mistaken she has appeared on the Broadway stage. My friends, as an actress, our guest is without a peer. When she was in England she could have had a peer or a count or a duke. She wants to stay single.

Many actresses are overly sensitive. Recently a well-known actress married an equally well-known actor. Two hours later she was in a lawyer's office discussing divorce. The lawyer was amazed. He asked, "What in the world could have happened in just that little time to cause such an irreparable breach?" The bride sobbed bitterly, "It was at the church. He signed his name in the register in bigger letters than mine."

An actress, applying for a job, was asked, "Are you married?" "Yes," she answered. "Have you been married before?" "Yes." "To whom?" "Say," she burst out, "what's the big idea? Humph! To whom have I been married? What is this, a memory test?" Then she showed the lawyer her necklace. "Take a look at this necklace. Made up entirely of my wedding rings." Not so with our guest. Ladies and gentlemen, Miss **(name.)**

INTRODUCING A SPEAKER ON DOGS

By Jeff Branen

Most people like dogs. It is the people who do not like dogs that care very little about dogs, and even more so you will invariably find it that way and vice versa. I have an uncle who never liked dogs and always will. He may be wrong, but he's not far from it.

We have with us this evening an expert on dogs. He has devoted his entire life to the study of dogs. His parents noted that at the tender age of three years he started going to the dogs. He is the proud owner of many blooded dogs. Some of them still have their blood. Recently he paid eight hundred dollars for a dog, part collie and part bull. The part about the eight hundred dollars is the bull.

He also has a beautiful dachshund. Dachshunds are all long on beauty. This particular dachshund—you don't find many dachshunds that are very particular—but this dachshund is three dogs long and half a dog high. Its legs are only three inches long, but this is because it was born under a refrigerator. A dachshund is an ideal pet for a large family of children. They can all pet it at the same time. Years ago I bought a dachshund, but I didn't have him very long. Many dogs are killed by automobiles, but my dachshund met its end going around a tree.

My brother Charlie bought a police dog. The man that sold him the dog said it was very friendly and would eat off his hand. Now they call my brother One Paw Charlie. Every one should have a watch dog in the house at night. If you hear a suspicious sound, all you have to do is to wake up the dog and he'll start barking. Before I introduce our speaker I would like to leave this thought for the day—be kind to dumb animals. Ladies and gentlemen, my friend, and a friend of all other dogs, Mr. **(name).**

INTRODUCING AN ACTOR

By Louis J. Huber

Without all the fuss and fanfare that is usually used by an emcee I am going to begin at the beginning and tell you quickly: Our next guest is an actor.

He is a great actor. This I did not need to tell you. Because many of you have seen him. And if I hadn't told you, he would have done it himself. But it sounds better coming from other people so I did this small chore for him.

Speaking of chores reminds me of some of the various roles that our guest has played in the theatre. He started at the very top. The very first day in the theatre he was there at the top of the ladder — helping the stage hands hang a new curtain.

On the second day he also had a leading part. In costume, no less. In a scene from Ben Hur he led one of the horses across the stage. He was destined to be great and they knew it. He has always been a hero. One time he saved an entire audience from slow torture. That was the day he didn't show up at the theatre.

If you think I'm fabricating these things, you're right. All the stories that I could tell would disappear from your mind the moment you see and hear him. So why not now? Yes, why not now? Right now! I present to you that well-known actor, a thespian who is a credit to his profession both on and off the stage, Mr. ————.

INTRODUCING AN OPERA STAR

By Louis J. Huber

At this time, ladies and gentlemen, it is my privilege to bring to you one of the most talented performers of the operatic stage. Actually, I should just tell you his (her) name and then sit down and let him keep you enthralled with his presentation.

It can't be that way, ladies and gentlemen. Because I have heard some deep and sinister things about this man and his voice. There have been stories that his voice was cultivated the hard way. They did it without using a plow.

There was also a very dark rumor that he did not always know as much about opera as he does this day. He was given a ticket to see the opera, Carmen. He tried using it to get a ride on a street car. Those car men were the only ones he knew about at that stage.

This isn't really true, ladies and gentlemen. I've told you these things because I'm jealous of his voice. I would like to have one just like it and then he could introduce me. But it is my pleasure now to do this for him and so I give you **(Name)** singing **(Title.)**

INTRODUCING A VOCAL SOLOIST

By Louis J. Huber

At this time, ladies and gentlemen, it is my great privilege to introduce a gentleman (or lady) who needs no introduction. So why should I give one? Because it is my assignment and I'm the type of individual who carries out all assignments. I also carry out the ashes and the wishes of my wife. Or I wouldn't be here right now and that might be a good thing. You would have an emcee who gets to the point much faster.

The soloist will sing for you **(Name of song.)** He had several other selections in mind but turned them down because they did not fit his vice. I mean, they did not fit his voice. One of the numbers which he is not going to sing is entitled "She was an innkeeper's daughter but her father threw him out." The second choice was also voted down. It was entitled "Take back your heart, I ordered roundsteak."

Without any more nonsense I would like to present a man with a voice that will make you remember for a long time. Mr. ———— singing **(Name of song again.)**

INTRODUCING AN ACROBAT - CLOWN ACT

By Richard Drummond

Ladies and gentlemen, we are not having a three-ring circus here tonight, but we do have one act that's a ringer, and I'll wager you will have a circus watching them. It is an acrobatic-clown act.

How I did love circuses when I was a kid! A small circus came to our town when I was a mite too small to go galavantin' off to it all by myself. So I just sort of sneaked off in the evening and walked to the other side of town. I came to a large tent. I didn't have any money, so I crawled under the tent. It must have been the wrong tent. There was a revival meeting going on inside.

A number of years later I attended a real circus. I met the India rubber man. I had heard much in those days about the India rubber man who could twist himself into every shape imagineable. I said to him, "How do you like this kind of work?" The India rubber man said, "Just fine except for one thing. Every time the strong man writes a letter he uses me to erase the mistakes." The last I ever heard of the India rubber man, he was sent up for a stretch for writing checks that bounced.

But I am meandering down the wrong road. As I said, we have just one ring in which you'll see the acrobats.

One of our acrobats went to a baseball game not long ago. There was a very spectacular play made on the diamond. He and a lot of others leaped to their feet in their excitement. Those sitting behind yelled, "Sit down in front!" Our acrobat was the only one that could sit down in front. The others couldn't bend that way.

Ladies and gentlemen, our one-ring circus.

INTRODUCING A JUDGE

(Or a member of the legal profession.)

By George A. Posner

Well, here I am, up before the judge! I'm not going to tell you just how familiar this is to me. But, really, it's a novelty in one way. Since when does a fellow like that—a judge—let a mere man like me do the talking? Isn't the gimmick usually: "Speak up! Guilty or not guilty? **SHUT UP!**"

I'll bet that's where my wife gets her ideas. (I hope she isn't listening.) If she **is** listening, it's the first time. No, no, I'm only kidding, darling. Honey-kins! Snookums! Please believe me!

What a profession, anyway—the legal profession! If one of us ordinary people should give another an orange he would simply say: "I give you this orange."

But when the transaction is entrusted to a judge, or a lawyer, to put in writing he adopts this form: "I hereby give and convey to you, all, and singular, my estate and interests, right, title, claim and advantages of and in said orange, together with all its rind, juice, pulp and pips, and all rights and advantages therein, with full power to bite, cut, suck, or otherwise eat the same or give the same away with or without the rind, skin, juice, pulp or pips, anything hereinbefore or hereinafter or in any other deed or deeds, instrument or instruments of whatever nature or kind whatsoever to the contrary in any wise notwithstanding."

And then another lawyer comes along and takes it from you.

You judges. You lawyers. What a soft job you have! What a racket! The judge? He just looks at the prisoner and says to himself: "Well, if he isn't guilty, what's he doing here?" And GUILTY it is. Simple, isn't it?

I was in court the other day—just slumming. Yes, I was! There was one fellow brought up before the judge, and the judge said to him: "You're drunk."

"I am **not** drunk, Your Honor," said the prisoner.

"There you are, that proves it," said the judge. "If you

were sober you'd **know** you were drunk!" That ended that. You just don't have a chance!

Reminds me—did you ever hear of the three drunks who were brought up before a cross-eyed judge?

There they stood in a row before him. He turned to the first one, and said: "What's your name?" And the second answered: "Thomas Jones."

So the judge said to the second one: "I wasn't talking to you." And the third one answered, "I didn't say anything."

But that's neither here nor there, of course. It just illustrates one judge's way of looking at things from different angles.

The case was nothing unusual. You can't guess **what** the judge is thinking by looking at his face. In fact, you **hope** not —because from the looks of his face—! B-r-r-r!

There was the judge who had one eye made of glass. And do you know what those who came up before him were told to look for? Find the glass eye. The advice was: "Study his eyes until you finally notice that there is one which looks more human and warm. That's the glass one!"

So now, how is one to greet a judge? Some of them are absent-minded, too, you know. I once met a friend of mine, a judge, —on the street—of course! —and I said to him: "Good morning, Judge. How are you?"

And he answered: "Fine, twenty-five dollars."

And you may know what happened to the former governor of California, Earl Warren, who is now a Supreme Court Justice? Well, if you do or you don't, you're going to hear it anyway.

He appeared before the assembled convicts in Sing Sing to make a speech. Forgetting his audience he began in his usual manner: "Fellow citizens"—A murmur of laughter sounded through the room.

The Governor became confused. "Fellow convicts," he changed. There was louder laughter.

"Oh, you know what I mean," he stammered. "I mean I'm so glad to see so many of you here."

They led him out into the air.

Seriously, it is time to present our distinguished visitor, Judge ———. I am very happy to have been selected for the honor of presenting his Honor. Ladies and Gentlemen, Judge ———.

ADDITIONAL MATERIAL

The law is a strange thing. And it, and its servants, move in wondrous ways its marvels to perform. It surely does.

Art Baker, the noted news commentator and philosopher, once told me of a story he claimed was true, though it does sound a bit fishy to me. He claims he got it from the court files of a Massachusetts town.

It seems there was a man who owned a tobacco store. And one day he laid in a supply of expensive cigars. Then he got a bright idea.

He loved cigars himself. Smoked a great many of them.

So what does he decide to do but get fire insurance on the stock of cigars. And when they were all gone—he had smoked most of them up himself—he went to the fire insurance company, presented the cigar ashes as evidence, and claimed the insurance!

"These cigars were insured by you against fire. And they most certainly were consumed by fire. And you owe me the insurance," this man insisted. "If you don't pay my claim, I'll take it to court."

The officials of the insurance company at first thought he was joking, then that he was mad. Then they raged that he was a crook, and would never get away with it.

But when the case came to court, the judge awarded the judgment to the storekeeper. Said the judge: "I'm convinced, of course, that you're a fraud, but I'm unable to do anything about it—with that agreement, you are inside the law."

The infuriated fire insurance officials took the case to a higher court, and hired a new legal counsel.

And at this trial the decision was reached that the tobacconist, when he had smoked those cigars, had set fire to property which he knew was insured and with the knowledge and purpose of collecting the insurance on the same; and that therefore he was guilty of arson, and of intent to defraud, and God knows what not—and they put him in jail for five years and fined him five thousand dollars!

INTRODUCING AN IMPERSONATOR

By Sidney Steele

Do you like impersonations? Good! So do I. We have someone with us this evening who can certainly impersonate.

Impersonating is an art, and if it so happens that you are blessed with this talent do not hesitate to develop it. It comes in handy so often when the party or gathering begins to lag. There is one string attached. Don't try to impersonate somebody bigger than you unless you do a good job of the imitating.

If you decide to practice impersonating, don't do what an acquaintance of mine did. He went nuts. Every day for six months he would stand in front of a large mirror trying to impersonate himself. Every evening he would shake his head, and bemoan, "I'm not myself today."

One time a would-be mimic stopped a very distinguished actor, and said, "Pardon me, but I have been practicing impersonating you. Could I have your attention for just a minute?" He thereupon went through some facial grimaces and gestures. "There," he said. "What do you think of my ability as shown by my impersonations of you?" "Well," said the actor, "one of us is awful."

A number of years ago a certain actor played the part of Lincoln for so long that he actually thought he was Lincoln. He walked and talked and even dressed like Lincoln all the time. One day he was walking down the street, clothed in the cape and high hat of Lincoln's period. Someone pointed him out, and remarked, "That man will never be satisfied until he's assassinated."

Now, ladies and gentlemen, Mr. **(name)**, our impersonating guest.

INTRODUCING A MAGICIAN

By Arthur L. Kaser

Know what we had for dinner last evening? Chicken? Nope. Duck? Nope. You'd never guess. We had a magician for dinner, and could he make food disappear! Now I know how they can make things on the stage disappear. They swallow the things. They're hollow. Then my wife set some stewed rabbit on the table. The magician took one taste and immediately left the table. I believe it is the first time on record that a rabbit made a magician disappear.

We have a magician right in the family, though. My wife. Lay down some money—Poof! That's all—just poof! Great people, magicians. They all start out with the same routine. Tap my right hand—nothing there. Tap my left hand—nothing there. Tap my forehead—I won't admit it.

Ladies and gentlemen, allow me to introduce our magician, **(name.)**

INTRODUCING A NOVELTY ACT

By Louis J. Huber

Ladies and gentlemen, we are about to be entertained by an act that is billed as a novelty act. To tell you about it would be detracting from its value.

So what can I say? I'd better find something. An emcee without something to say would be in a bad way. I'd just like to tell you about what to expect in anything that has the word "novelty" in it. Take hash, that's a novelty. And do you know what to expect in it? If you did know, it wouldn't be hash.

Take a blind date. Now I am not trying to compare this with hash but it has the same ingredients and it is a novelty. My wife met me on a blind date. She was told that she would meet a very nice boy and she did. But she didn't get to go out with him; she got stuck with me.

Did you ever play in the fish pond at the county fair? You

pay a dime and you put the pole over the enclosure. Out comes your package. My brother got caught that way. They ran out of prizes and put him on the end of the line. The lady who won him took him home and we haven't seen him since. He was some novelty.

Novelty? Oh, yes, that's what brought me here — a novelty act. What is it? I can't tell you. But I can tell you that you will be delighted when you see it. I give you a great act that will please and entertain you, the ————.

INTRODUCING AN ANIMAL TRAINER

By Louis J. Huber

At this time, ladies and gentlemen, we come to the highlight of the evening's entertainment. We bring to you a type of entertainment that always brings out the beast in me — I mean the best in me.

The error I just made gives you an idea of the kind of act that you are about to witness. You are to be thrilled by an animal act. There are animal acts and there are animal acts but this one has novelties and innovations never seen before.

At the very beginning of the act you will see the animal trainer order the lion to open his mouth. You will expect that the trainer will put his head into the mouth. I'll let you in on a small secret. This won't be true. He does this because he is reminded of his mother-in-law and he likes her very much.

We have many strange twists to this act. You will see one hundred and ten horses on the stage. What's that? (Speaking off stage.) Oh, they're not horses. I'm sorry, folks, they are not going to be horses. They are going to be horse flies. We couldn't get the horses so we settled for the animal that settles on them.

Not one word of this is true, folks, and you know it. And I know it. But this is true: You are going to witness an animal act that will make you wish you were a cat even if you had to lead a dog's life. I give you that master of animals, Mr. ———.

INTRODUCING A TUMBLING ACT

By Louis J. Huber

Ladies and gentlemen, the feature attraction of the evening is an act that will make you wonder why you can sit still. It is an act that finds the performers booming and bouncing and bounding all over the place. This is our main attraction and features the **(Name)** Tumblers.

Allow me to tell you a little about tumbling. I know this field quite well because I've tumbled many times myself. There was the time a man came up to me and asked me for a dime for a cup of coffee. I gave it to him. It happened the next day and also the next. I asked him if he was a coffee lover. He stated that he hated the stuff. He also explained that it was the one sure way he could get a dime off a man like me. He explained that he was really using the dime to buy a box of snuff. He wanted something he could get his nose into. I tumbled immediately and he got no more money.

There was the time my wife asked me to buy her a set of tumblers for Christmas. A set of tumblers seemed like an unusual gift but I was ready to do my best and grant her wishes. I had quite a time and finally had to admit that there were no tumblers available. I was told that I didn't look very hard. Then they explained to me that a set of tumblers was nothing more than a set of small stemless glasses. When I heard that I almost tumbled right out of the room.

But enough of that type of tumbling. At this time you are going to witness an act that will astonish you. As you watch the agility of these performers you will marvel and wonder how a human body can be trained in this manner. I'm sure you will enjoy the **(Name)** Tumblers and here they are, ladies and gentlemen.

INTRODUCING A VENTRILOQUIST

By Vance Clifford

We have an act just a little out of the ordinary this evening —a ventriloquist act.

I always envy a ventriloquist who can talk without opening his mouth. It ought to work just dandy for those who just had all their teeth pulled out.

I met an old friend recently who remarked, "I wish I was a ventriloquist." I said, "So you could throw your voice?" He said, "No. So I could throw my wife's voice—out the window."

When I was just a lad Dick Turner and I were asked to contribute an act on an amateur show. We decided to put on a ventriloquist act, I to be the ventriloquist. We were going to fake it, of course, because I couldn't throw my voice any farther than I could throw the U. S. deficit. I came out on the stage and Dick stayed in the wings. I said, "Ladies and gentlemen, I will now throw my voice to the right." So I called off right, "Hello-o-o!" Dick answered from off right, "Hello-o-o!" Then I said, "I will now throw my voice to the left." I turned left and called, "Hello-o-o!" Dick ran backstage and answered from left stage, "Hello-o-o!" Everything was going fine. Then I announced, "Now, ladies and gentlemen, the most difficult part. I will throw my voice up." Throwing back my head, I called, "Hello-o-o!" No answer. I called again, "Hello-o-o!" Again no answer. I was getting fidgety. I called once more, much louder, "Hello-o-o!" There was a pause. Then Dick, in a half whisper that was audible all over the auditorium, "I can't find the stepladder!"

Ladies and gentlemen, our ventriloquist, **(name).**

INTRODUCING A HYPNOTIST

By Louis J. Huber

Our next entertainer, ladies and gentlemen, is a man whose feats have won him the acclaim of many lands. Just as my feet, because of their size, have won me a name in many places. It would not be easy for me to tell you some of these names but they would come in very handy if you ever wanted to frighten anyone.

All of this, quite naturally, has nothing to do with the act you are going to see. It does make a good topic for me to start on. Just as my feet make a good topic for me to stand on and that is what I am doing right now. I am not very clever today, or at any time, or I would be off my feet and let the real entertainers take their rightful place.

However, I have a few sentences that must be spoken or I would burst at the seams. And a master of ceremonies who has burst at the seams would be a sorry sight indeed. It might also be dangerous. Just think how serious it could be if you picked up your newspaper tomorrow and read this headline: Man Injured by Flying Master of Ceremonies.

The man you are going to see, as soon as I get these extra syllables off my chest, is a hypnotist. Many of you men are going to shrug your shoulders and say "so what?" We married men know what it means to be hypnotized. It has happened to all of us or we would still be bachelors. If you ladies are listening, please remember that I don't mean it.

I have also had my moments when I practiced the art of hypnotism. I can well remember when I used it on my landlord. He came to collect the rent that was due. I realized it was time for me to act and to do it quickly.

Most of the time my landlord is a very nice man. The only time I don't like him is when the rent is due. That happens to be most of the time. Then the day came when I gave him a sample of my hypnotic powers.

Little did he suspect what was going to happen to him. He came into my parlor, just like the fly into the domain of the spider, and he asked the usual question: How about paying your rent?

It was then that I did my most diabolical deed. I looked him straight in the eye and I knew he was in my clutches. I asked him if he was sure that I owed him one hundred dollars for one month's rent. He said he wasn't sure. And the plot began to thicken.

Then I asked him if he knew that I had paid him the month before. He replied that he wasn't sure. He told me he wasn't sure of anything but the fact that he had just raised my rent and that I now owed him one hundred and fifty dollars. I paid the amount immediately. Only later did I learn that my landlord was a hypnotist and that he did that to all his tenants.

But enough of my personal troubles and experiences with hypnotism. I would like to present the feature attraction of the evening. A man whose eyes will remind you of your mother-in-law because they can see right through you. A man whose hands move with a dexterity that will make you grab for your hip to feel if your pocketbook is still there or if it has been taken by a pickpocket. I give you "The Great Gabbo" and he will give you a show that will make you forget my weak introduction. Let's have a nice hand for him, "The Great Gabbo."

INTRODUCING AN INSTRUMENTALIST

By Richard Drummond

We live in a neighborhood of musical instrumentalists. Everybody plays something, including croquet to canasta. Some are strings, some are brass, some are woodwinds, some are awful. The lady just east of us used to thump the piano nine hours a day, but since they have small children she doesn't have the time to play. Children are such a comfort, aren't they? Now she thumps the children. We still have some music from that quarter. Her husband plays second fiddle.

A neighborhood saxophone player died and a friend of his asked me to donate five dollars to a fund to bury the saxophone player. I gave him thirty dollars and told him to bury six of 'em.

The young man living west of us drove us crazy with his violin. It was awful. The strings on his violin must have come from howling cats. He didn't have a bridge on his violin so he couldn't get the music across. We stood it as long as possible, then I confronted him with a proposition. I offered him one hundred dollars a string if he'd quit. He accepted, and then turned right around and bought a harp. He said he bought it, thinking of the future. Well, if he goes where I think he should go, he'll not need a harp.

There are a number of tiny kids in the neighborhood, but they're not so loud with their music. They play on the linoleum. There is a shoe salesman living half a block away, but we don't kick about him. He plays a shoe horn, but concentrates on foot notes.

So now, ladies and gentlemen, without further etude, we will hear from our well-known instrumentalist, **(name.)**

INTRODUCING A COMEDIAN

By Earl Jay Gilbert

Folks, I've just heard a little story and I'm going to pass it on to you. It seems a fellow was attending a political meeting and he suddenly discovered his wallet was missing. He jumped up on a chair and shouted: "I've just lost my pocketbook with five hundred dollars in it. To anyone who finds it and brings it to me I'll give fifty dollars!" Someone in the rear shouted: "Bring it to me and I'll make it seventy-five!"

There's nothing like a laugh to chase the blues. If you want to enjoy life you've got to be abie to laugh. Laughter is healthy, it's stimulating, it aids the digestion, it helps the circulation. We like to be around people who can make us laugh.

We've all encountered sourpusses who couldn't even smile. What a miserable time they give themselves and other people. What a treat it is to get away from people like that. Laughter and joy go together. When you're down in the dumps, when everything seems to go wrong, there's nothing like a good laugh to snap yourself out of it. There's no tonic to equal it.

Well, you're going to meet and hear a man here whose principal purpose in life is to make others laugh. That's what he was born for and that's what he's here for. He brings joy and laughter into people's lives.

He told me a few minutes ago that he had some friends over to his place last night and they had a wonderful time diving into his new swimming pool. I said: "You must have had lots of fun." He said: "Oh, we did, but we're going to have more fun tonight. We're going to put some water in the pool." I said: "Sissies!" "No, we're not," he said, "we're going to do it just for laughs."

Well, anyway, I want to dedicate a little poem to him:

> This world would be a gloomy place —
> We couldn't stand this modern pace,
> With all the problems that we face
> If we had no joy or laughter.
>
> So that is why we made this plan
> To have you meet this funny man
> Who always does the best he can
> To bring folks joy and laughter.
>
> So let's relax — forget our woes —
> And hail this man of wit who shows
> That we can dismiss Life's hard blows
> When he brings us joy and laughter.

And now, folks, I'm really happy to present to you that well-known dispenser of laughs, Mr. ———— !

INTRODUCING A QUARTETTE

By Earl Jay Gilbert

My friends, we're all familiar with some things in life that seem to belong to each other, to fit each other — like certain food combinations — ham and eggs, spareribs and sauerkraut, bread and butter. All those things blend together.

Well, we've got another kind of a blend for you. It isn't food, but you'll like it. It's a quartette whose voices blend together perfectly. They really harmonize.

Someone once said that a quartette consisted of four people who harmonize and each of them thinks that the other three can't sing. That doesn't apply to the group you're going to hear. As a matter of fact each member of this quartette thinks that the other three sing so much better than he does that they all sing better than they know how — and it's real music.

You've all heard that old saying: "Music hath charms to soothe the savage breast." Well, I thought of that last night when I was in a restaurant trying to eat some breast of lamb. That lamb was really a hard baby. It was so tough that when I tried to cut it it turned the edge of the knife. Whenever I tried to tackle it it got away from me. I chased it all over the plate and when I finally caught up to it, it fought with me. I tried to stab it and broke two tines off my fork. That breast of lamb was so savage no music in the world could have soothed it. Finally I was worn out trying to wrestle with it and called the waiter. I said: "You tell the chef or whoever cooked this chunk of rhinoceros hide that I'd like to stuff it down his throat." The waiter said: "I'm sorry, sir, but you'll have to wait your turn. There's a steak, two orders of pork chops and a veal cutlet ahead of you."

Anyhow, to get back to music I almost became a singer myself. When I was a boy I took voice lessons — at five bucks a lesson. Every time I paid my teacher the five-spot he'd pat me on the back and say: "My boy, I'm going to make a second Caruso out of you." He was wrong. I will say though, that the only thing that stopped me was my voice. I could sing louder than Caruso, but we had different tonal qualities.

Why, at a little gathering one night I sang "My Old Kentucky Home." When I finished my song an old man sitting over in the corner started to cry very bitterly. He was overcome with emotion. I said: "Pardon me, but are you from Kentucky?" He shook his head and sobbed, "No." I said: "Then why are you crying?" He said: "I'm a musician." I used to get many compliments like that.

Well, one night when I was practising my scales some of the neighbors gathered in front of the house. They were carrying a rope and some tar and feathers. They offered me a number of suggestions about my voice. I adopted the suggestions and quit practising.

So the world lost a glorious voice and I had to go to work for a living. And now, my friends, you're going to enjoy listening to the really glorious voices of this group of harmony makers. Here they are. Let's give them a nice greeting to start them off. The ———— Quartette!

INTRODUCING A DANCING TEAM

By Arthur L. Kaser

Dancing is as old as human feet. And people all over the world have feet. So, no matter what country you might visit you will find dancing. In some countries dancing just seems to come as a natural part of growing up. In this country what is missed naturally is taken care of by dancing schools. I took a quickie course in dancing. I upset a beehive.

I've been told a number of times I'd be a wonderful dancer except for two things—my feet. But I think it's just my nervousness. Whenever I try fancy toe steps I have a feeling there are a couple of heels right behind. How I wish I could dance like the team you are about to see.

Ladies and gentlemen, **(name of dancing team.)**

INTRODUCING AN ANIMAL TRAINER

By Franklin Phelps

Did you ever realize how many wonderful stories come out of the jungle? Most of them are rather tall stories, but they are amusing and interesting. How I have longed to go back to those jungles. Of course, I've never been there, but I'd love to go back there, anyway.

Some years ago my Uncle Toby Johnson was hunting in the wild jungles of Africa. He had many close shaves and they weren't from electric razors, either. One day Uncle Toby came across a big elephant that was limping badly. Uncle Toby followed the animal for some distance. Finally the elephant sank exhausted to the ground. My uncle ran forward and examined the feet of the elephant. In one foot was an enormous thorn. He very carefully removed the thorn and went on his way.

A number of years later Uncle Toby returned to this country and attended a circus in St. Louis. He was sitting in one of the cheapest seats in the tent. There was a procession of trained elephants on the bill. They marched very near to where Uncle Toby was sitting. One elephant limped slightly. When this elephant came near Uncle Toby he stretched out his trunk, encircled Uncle's waist, lifted him from his seat and set him down in a comfortable chair in a private box.

Some of the most ferocious wild animals can be trained with patience and fortitude, and in many instances are smarter than our domestic dogs. Uncle Toby had brought home a young lion cub from Africa. He trained him for several years, and that lion grew up and could do about everything except talk. One night Uncle Toby's house caught on fire. Everything was confusion.

Finally all living things were out of the house. Then, to the surprise of everybody, that lion dashed madly back into that burning inferno. Now here is the part that is hard to believe. A few minutes later that lion came dashing out of the house, and in its mouth was the fire insurance policy wrapped in a wet towel. That is what I would call **some lyin'**, which brings me to the introduction of our guest, who I know, will stick closer to the truth than I did. Ladies and gentlemen, **(name)** the world-famous animal trainer.

INTRODUCING A COLLEGE GRADUATE

By Louis J. Huber

Ladies and gentlemen, it is my great privilege to present to this great gathering a man who comes to us with every recommendation that it is possible to obtain. Some of these are poorly written, others (those he wrote for himself) are cleverly contrived.

It had to be this way, ladies and gentlemen. Our man, even though he may not look brilliant, had a great career in college. It is this time of his life that I would like to highlight. Because it is this time that he would like to forget.

Our speaker was quite a wit in college. He started at the bottom to get there. First he was a quarter-wit and then a one-third wit and then—what comes next? Oh, yes, he was a half-wit. You'll pardon my poor arithmetic; I was never very good at fractions.

Speaking of arithmetic—and I was doing that—this study was also our speaker's best subject. He was given one certain problem in which he showed his keen mind. If a man sells a car for one thousand dollars after he had bought it for nine hundred, what does he have? Our speaker dove deep for an answer. He reasoned that the man would have the down payment on another car.

It was this kind of thinking that got him an E for effort. Only one thing was wrong: Grade E was not the passing mark. But he has passed with us and so I present him to you, Mr. ——————.

INTRODUCING A COMEDIAN

By Arthur L. Kaser

Sometimes the funniest people are those who try to be, or are naturally, very serious. Like the man who was on a speeding train. He was lonely and downhearted, so he took a rather big nip from the bottle he pulled from his suitcase. Everything went suddenly black. He yelled for the conductor. "I've gone blind!" he screamed. "I can't see a thing!" "Brace up, old man," said the conductor. "We're going through a tunnel."

An unfortunate prisoner was sentenced to be hung. He called for the warden and said, "I need exercise, Warden. I need exercise." "Okay," said the warden, "what kind of exercise would you prefer?" "I would like to skip the rope."

See what I mean? They weren't supposed to be funny, but they were. Or were they?

A man in Missouri was driving a mule on a country road when the mule suddenly decided to balk. It stopped short and refused to budge. The driver tried all the tricks he knew but the mule stood as still as a statue. The doctor from the nearby village drove up and stopped. "Having trouble, Lem?" he asked. "Yep, plenty trouble," replied Lem. "Can't git the danged crittur moving. Just won't budge." "Maybe I can help you," said the doctor, as he took a couple of large pills from his kit. "Here, Lem, try and get them down the mule's throat." After some difficulty the mule was made to swallow the pills. A moment later the mule gave a snort, and dashed ahead like something possessed, leaving Lem standing in the road gaping. He turned to the doctor. "How much?" he asked. "About fifteen cents," said the doctor. "Fifteen cents? Quick! Gimme a dollar's worth for me. I gotta ketch that mule!"

Folks, those shorties were just a forerunner to something a whole lot better, and much more professional. Ladies and gentlemen, I take great pleasure in introducing one of the country's leading comedians, **(name.)**

INTRODUCING A P.T.A. ENTERTAINMENT

By Sidney Steele

Tonight some of the children's parents and the teachers are going to do the entertaining. The parents have the children and the teachers have class.

Schools to the right of us, schools to the left of us, schools all around us, and not enough schools for anybody. There are so many children in every room that the teacher doesn't call the roll. She says, "Will all children present hold up their hands? Now all children not present hold up your hands." That's the reason the first thing a child learns is to run around with a burpy gun yelling "Hands up!"

But what would we do without schools? Think of the children. If it wasn't for the schools the children wouldn't have any holidays. There have been a lot of changes in the teaching of children, but we still have the three R's—Rah! Rah! Rah!

A teacher said to one of her pupils, "Richard, seven cows are coming up the lane single file. Now which cow can turn around and say, 'I see six pairs of horns'?" Richard didn't know. "Why, Richard," explained the teacher, "it would be the first cow that could say it." "No, teacher," said Richard, "cows can't talk."

A mother—she may be here this evening—was quite upset the other day because her little boy got such a poor mark in his history exam. She told her neighbor, "And it wasn't his fault he got such a poor mark in history. Why, do you know, his teacher asked him things that happened before he was even born."

A teacher said to Wilbur, "I have went. Now that is wrong, isn't it?" "Yes, ma'am," answered Wilbur. "Why is it wrong?" asked the teacher. "Because," said Wilbur, "you ain't went yet."

So, parents, there you are. And, teachers, where are you?

INTRODUCING A COMEDIAN

By Arthur L. Kaser

Ladies and gentlemen, we're shooting high tonight. We have as a guest one of the country's outstanding comedians. In fact, he is rated so high we had to go up into the stratosphere to capture him. We brought him back alive. He is quite a sober character. Hardly ever laughs, especially at his own jokes.

Not so long ago this man was at the theatre. A man fell out of the balcony. Everybody laughed except our guest. He was the man who fell out. He said it was quite a come-down for him. Don't get the idea that he doesn't like a good joke on himself. He does.

Not long ago he rushed into a drugstore, and shouted, "Quick, gimme something for hiccups!" The clerk very obligingly banged him a dinger on the side of the head. Our friend was so surprised, he gasped, "What'd you do that for?" The clerk said, "Well, you haven't got hiccups now, have you?" "It's not me," said the customer. "It's my friend outside in the car."

He tells me that when he was young the biggest joke ever pulled on him was his own fault. He was trying to sell vacuum cleaners. At one house he did exactly what the sales manager had instructed him to do. After finishing his preliminary sales patter he took a large bag from his kit and emptied it all over the lady's lovely living room. There were stones, dust, bits of paper, crushed egg shells and sand. "Madam," he said, "I'll eat every bit of this stuff that my vacuum cleaner doesn't pick up." "Just a moment," said the lady. "I'll get some salt and pepper. We don't have electricity."

Ladies and gentlemen, allow me. The one and only **(name of the guest.)**

INTRODUCING AN OLD - TIME ENTERTAINER

By Jeff Branen

Tonight, my friends, we are going to bring you an entertainer out of the past. Don't misunderstand me. This person is still very much alive. In his heyday he was known from coast to coast, and believe me, to scale the heights in those days wasn't as easy as it is today. It meant long jumps from one tank town to the next. And if the tickets didn't sell the actors didn't eat. There was no such thing as jumping into a taxi and a few minutes later appearing on radio or television. It was easier on the audience. They didn't have to listen to commercials. Staging facilities were meager, lighting was poor, and in some sections the audience was a hard nut to crack.

Our friend of the evening told me about the time he wired to the proprietor of a small theatre in a small town where his company was due to appear: "Would like to hold rehearsal next Monday afternoon at three. Have stage manager, carpenter, property man, electrician present at that hour." Four or five hours later he received the following reply: "All right. He'll be there."

There was very little money in theatricals in those days. Another old-timer told me of the time he was playing the lead in a company touring one night stands. They were billed to play "Romeo and Juliet." As soon as the troupe arrived in the small town the leading man approached the manager and asked for a dime. "A dime," shouted the manager. "Do you think I'm made of money? How can you use a dime in this town?" The actor explained that he needed a shave. He could hardly expect to play Romeo with a three-days' growth of beard. The manager thought for some time. "You won't need a dime. We'll change the bill to 'Othello.' "

Ladies and gentlemen, meet our old-timer, the famous footlight idol of years gone by, **(name.)**

INTRODUCING A DANCER OR DANCING ACT

By Earle Jay Gilbert

And now, folks, you are going to be entertained by a dancing act that you'll really enjoy. Everybody likes good dancing. I know I do. A few weeks ago a friend told me about a wonderful girl dancer. He said: "Boy—she's wonderful—she's great—she's got everything!"

So I went to this night club and got a seat at a table down front and watched a lot of good acts of various kinds until finally this dancer was announced. The music started and she came out. She was wearing a kind of a thing that started here, then stopped, then started again down here and then stopped till it got down to her feet. She didn't wear anything on her feet. Well, the music started to get hot. I kept on watching her feet, and watching her feet. Oh, I must have watched her feet for ten minutes. The music got hotter and hotter and finally it ended in a big clash of cymbals.

Everybody applauded and cheered and the girl walked off the stage. Then she came back and bowed half a dozen times until everybody stopped clapping. Well, naturally I was annoyed. I was waiting to see her dance and nothing had happened.

So I called the waiter over and said, "Say, when does this girl start to dance?" He said: "She's all through." I said, "Quit clowning. I watched her feet for ten minutes and I didn't see her dance." He said: "You were looking at her feet?" I said: "Naturally." He said: "That explains it. You were looking at the wrong place."

Well, anyway, I know you'll like this dance you're going to see now. Oh, by the way, about this dancing act. I have just been informed that the laundry neglected to send back the leading lady's tights. I understand there will be several other novelties. Folks, it gives me a great deal of pleasure to introduce ————.

INTRODUCING A MAGICIAN

By Earl Jay Gilbert

Folks, get ready for some enjoyable entertainment. We are presenting next a past master of legerdemain whose art and adroitness will amaze, amuse and mystify you. To make it clear, he's a magician and a good one. Like the hill-billy says, "He makes things seem like they ain't."

Of course there are many kinds of magicians. Some of them don't call themselves magicians, like some politicians I know who get eleven hundred votes out of three hundred voters. That's really magic.

Then there are the female magicians. I know girls and women who can turn a bright man into a jackass in five minutes — and make him like it. Then there are the kind of magicians who work in certain eating places. They'll take an old piece of stewed veal and a couple slices of stale bread and make you a delicious chicken sandwich.

Speaking of eating places reminds me of the fellow who went into a high-priced restaurant. After eating the most expensive meal on the menu he sent for the manager, who said, "I trust everything was satisfactory, sir?" "Oh, yes," said the customer. "Everything was fine, except the pheasant under glass was perhaps a trifle overdone, but that wasn't what I wanted to see you about. You may not recall the incident, but several months ago I had dinner in here and when I got through eating I discovered I didn't have enough money to pay for my meal — and you had several of your waiters throw me out on the sidewalk — bodily!" "I'm sorry, sir," said the manager nervously, "but we can't always recognize the kind of person we're serving. I'm terribly sorry it happened." "That's perfectly all right," said the customer, "don't apologize. I sent for you to tell you I'm afraid I'll have to trouble you again." That's one way of saving the price of a meal.

But to get back to magicians. There's an old saying that people like to be fooled. I enjoy seeing a magician put an egg in a hat and pull out a rabbit, which makes me think of the fellow on his first trip to Paris. He went into a little restaurant and ordered rabbit stew. He took a couple of bites, then said to the waiter: "Is there anything else in this stew besides rabbit?" "Well," said the waiter, "there's some horse meat in there, too." "How much horse meat?" asked the diner. "It's fifty-fifty," replied the waiter. "One horse to one rabbit." That's mathematical magic.

While I like to see magicians do their tricks I saw one do something once that I didn't like. This magician put a beautiful girl in a wooden box, then nailed a cover on it. When the box was opened, it was empty. The girl had vanished. Now, I don't approve of disposing of pretty girls that way, so I yelled: "Hey, if you've got so many of them you don't know what to do with them all, give 'em to me!" Just then the same girl appeared on the other side of the stage. He didn't give her to me, though.

Speaking of making things disappear makes me think of the magician doing his stuff on shipboard. In addition to the crowd of tourists, the ship's parrot was also watching intently. The magician put a napkin over a small dish, said a few magic words, lifted the napkin, and the dish had disappeared. He next placed a table cloth over a chair, said his magic words, and the chair disappeared. Then he put a large cloth over the piano — and the piano disappeared. Just then there was a terrific explosion and the ship suddenly sank. The magician was thrown in the water. He swam to a piece of driftwood — and there was the parrot clinging to it. The parrot looked all around at the empty ocean, turned to the magician and said: "Don't you think you went a little too far that time?"

But some magicians can do wonderful things. For centuries they've been puzzling and pleasing people with their skillful tricks and manipulations. In ancient times religious rites were based on the practice of magic.

Even today certain tribes have their medicine men and witch doctors, which recalls the story of the press correspondent who went to a British Army Camp in Africa to interview the commanding general. To his great surprise he found the general to be a very small man, about three feet tall. He said to the general's aid: "I thought the general was a big six-footer." The aid said: "Sh! He used to be, but he called an African witch doctor a faker!"

My, I always think it's better to be polite to those guys. There's no sense in making them sore. Some people can work magic without realizing it — like the young couple on their honeymoon. They were standing on the beach, looking out over the water, when the young husband suddenly became poetic. He waved his hands dramatically towards the water and sang out in a deep voice: "Roll on, wild waves — roll on!" A moment later his young bride delightedly exclaimed: "Oh, George — **look!** They're **doing** it!" Love is wonderful.

Well, my friends, it's time for our man of magic to start doing things also. He's a good trickster and a nice guy and a master of his art. So let's all give him a hearty welcome — and watch him make our troubles disappear! Our talented magician, ———— !

INTRODUCING A VOCAL SOLOIST

By Vance Clifford

There is a gigantic contrast between the singer I am to introduce shortly and the one who took vocal lessons from Professor Von Hoopzig. It was during her tenth or eleventh lesson that the professor threw up his hands in despair. "Ach! Id is no use. Such a voice never have I heard. I blay on der vhite keys, und I play on der black keys, und all you do is sing in der cracks!"

It sometimes pays to encourage singing in your family. Uncle Ben had a daughter who dreamed of being a great singer, so Uncle Ben spent a few hundred dollars for her vocal education. But he made some good money on the investment. The people living next door sold their house to Uncle Ben for less than half price.

And now, ladies and gentlemen, our soloist, **(name.)**

INTRODUCING A DIRECTOR OF AN AMATEUR PLAY

By Forbes Milliken

As regards the benefit to be given (date) we have asked **(name)** to come here and explain the procedure employed in organizing a group of entertainers for the event. There will be the customary tryouts. **(name)** will advise us in detail about these tryouts. If you have any type of talent don't hesitate. It's fun.

A number of years ago I attended a show celebrating vaudeville's one hundredth birthday. Many of the original jokes and hundreds of their children and grandchildren attended the celebration.

When I was a lad I used to miss so much of a play. I'd go in and see the first act and then leave because the program said that act two was the same as act one. And then, too, I didn't have time to wait for the second act in some shows because the programs would say, "Second act two years later."

The first time I ever did anything on the stage I was very much embarrassed. My act followed a monkey act, and when I came on everybody applauded. They thought it was an encore. Later on I got up a trained rabbit act. I trained these rabbits for a long time, but I couldn't get a booking. I waited and waited and waited. Finally I got a telegram: "Can use your rabbit act. Report at once." I wired back: "Too late. I've eaten my act."

I made up another act, a monologue, but nobody would laugh at my jokes. I couldn't understand it, because when I finally threw them in the furnace the fire roared. Perhaps I'd better stop talking before I have a repeat performance of what happened several years ago. I was emceeing a program. Someone said, "I heard someone call that Master of Ceremonies a monkey." Somebody else said, "Who called that monkey a Master of Ceremonies?" Friends, let me present **(name.)**

INTRODUCING A MIND READER

By Arthur L. Kaser

We have tonight, a rather rare and out-of-the-ordinary act for you. It is a mind-reading act wherein the performer can actually look right into your mind. So, friends, if you are entertaining any questionable thoughts you'd better take them back to the exchange desk at once.

I'm in the boat with a lot of other people. I don't know how it is done. Even so, I know it will be entertaining. I went to one of these cranium-peering persons one time, and asked, "What town will I die in?" She said, "What good will that do you?" I said if I knew what town I would die in I'd never go there. A buddy tried once to teach me how to do it, but it didn't go so good. Only once did I come anywhere near success. I saw a man enter a pool room once and sit on the pool table and right away I knew he was a sailor. Easy. He was wearing a sailor uniform.

One time in Chicago I went to a mind reader. She looked at me, and said, "I'm tired out. I've been reading minds all day. I'm glad you came. You'll be sort of a vacation." I said, "Aw, come on, I'm serious. What do you charge for reading one's mind?" She said, "For a great mind, I charge fifty dollars. For average minds, twenty-five dollars. Sit down. It'll cost you fifty cents." She did warn me, however. She said, "Beware of a tall, stately woman who will constantly be in your path. She's bad luck." I said, "If she's in my path, it'll be her bad luck. I drive a truck."

The mind is a funny thing. A friend of mine stopped me on the street just yesterday, and said, "I'm afraid my wife's mind is about gone." I asked, "What makes you think so?" He said, "She's been giving me a piece of it ever since we were married."

Prepare yourself, friends, for the great mind-reader, ——.

INTRODUCING A KISSING BOOTH

By Louis J. Huber

Hear ye, hear ye, ladies and gentlemen. Now is the time for all good men to come to the front and be kissed. We are about to open the kissing booth at this bazaar.

Come, come, boys, let us not be bashful. When this booth opens we will have a variety of kisses all to be sold for charity. Now don't get me wrong. The money you spend will go for charity.

There will be kisses for the boys and kisses for the girls. Just in case that there are a few folks who do not know anything about the gentle art of osculation allow me to demonstrate. You form your lips into a pucker. What's that, young man? You do not know how to pucker. Permit me to show you how.

There are different methods of puckering. There is the wide method which is used when you are kissing a girl with a wide mouth. Great care must be taken that this method is not overdone. I can recall, some years ago, when a boy used this type of kiss thinking that he was going to kiss a wide-mouthed girl. It was a horrible mistake. When he actually kissed her he missed and bit her on both ears at the same time.

In order to use this type of kiss a boy must practice a bit first. You take a watermelon and hook one side of your mouth over one end. Then you take the other side of your mouth and hook it over the other end. Do this for three nights and you will be able to kiss any girl in the neighborhood. In fact, you will be able to kiss several of them at one time.

Come closer, folks, and get a liberal education in the art of kissing. I have just told you how to kiss a wide-mouthed girl and now I am going to go into the next phase. What's that, young man? You only have five cents to spend for a kiss? Yes, sir, we have them at any price. Here you are, sir, for five cents you are entitled to one candy kiss. (Hands him the candy and takes the money. This is done best by planting someone in the audience.)

Now to show you how to kiss a girl with a small mouth. Yes, sir, we do have those kind in the kissing booth which is about to be opened. In order to kiss this type a man must learn to say the word tomato. Just pucker up and say tomato. That's right. Like this: Tomato, tomato, tomato.

You will note how perfect your pucker will become after you do this for a little while. Do it for an hour and you will have all the girls demanding that you spend some time with them. Do it while walking down the street. Just keep saying tomato, tomato, tomato. Of course, if someone mistakes you for a vegetable vendor it would be wise to know the price of tomatoes.

You, sir, how would you like to be the first customer? You would? Fine. What kind of a girl would you like to kiss for a dollar? One who kisses and looks exactly like your wife? That's good, we have such a girl. Bring her out, folks, and let this man spend the first dollar. What's that? It is your wife and you can kiss her for free? Not here, sir, not here. Here, in the name of charity, all kisses are sold and you must pay. (This is also accomplished by having a man and his wife ready for the bit. Unless it can be arranged to have her behind the booth without the husband's knowledge.)

All right, all right, there goes the first sale. We have them for you, gentlemen. Kisses by the dozen. Are there any ladies who would like to buy a kiss? If so, please form a line at the right and I shall accommodate them right now. Open the booth and shout to the world that we are in business!

INTRODUCING CLOWNS

By Louis J. Huber

At this time, folks, we are going to be entertained by entertainers whose origin is rooted back at the beginning of time. There have always been court jesters, there have always been clowns.

I'm reminded of the often-heard expression, "Laugh,

Clown, Laugh." Why am I reminded of it? Because it involves a time when I was an entertainer in the world of funny faces and funny make-up.

Not many of you know that I was a circus clown at one time. I can recall when our show was in an eastern city. I was in my tent putting on my costume when I started laughing and I just couldn't stop.

One of the other performers came to me and wanted to know what was funny. I just couldn't answer him. I laughed harder and harder. It was getting to the point where my laughter was annoying. They told me it was all right to work that laugh-clown-laugh routine but I was overdoing it.

They tried to stop me by telling me sad stories. About the girl who was caught in a snow storm and perished. Very sad. But I still laughed. Finally, someone got the idea that I might be able to do something with pencil and paper. They handed them to me. I wrote down the source of all the trouble. I had heard a funny story three days before and I just then had got the point. From that time on no one ever again told me a humorous story.

You will enjoy tonight's act because they are genuinely funny, because they have mastered their art to perfection. Without any more syllables I stand aside and make room for those gentlemen of comedy, The **(Name)** Clowns.

INTRODUCING AN INSTRUMENTAL TRIO

By Louis J. Huber

Ladies and gentlemen, the next act on our program is an instrumental trio. That should suffice as an introduction but I can't stop there because instrumental music is one of my favorite forms of entertainment.

You will see, when this musical organization is brought on, that they have no fife in the group. You will find that there is a violin, a cello, a piano. (Name the instruments.) There is a deep and sinister story behind the fact that there is no fife.

There was a time when they had a fife although it is not considered part of an organization of this type. Let me repeat: They had a fife. It was always played by the musician at the left side of the group. One day he was asked the old wheeze that you've all heard. It went like this: Who was the lady I saw you out with last night? The musician answered: That was no lady, that was my fife.

You can see why the fife was eliminated. And you'll be glad that they put another instrument in its place because you would have missed the treat that you are to get. I give you, ladies and gentlemen, the **(Name of trio.)**

INTRODUCING A HARPIST

By Franklin Phelps

There are too few really good harpists in the world. Perhaps There is a reason. Every time I watch a musician play a harp I wonder if he will be able to finish his program with any of his fingers left. However, it might be that playing the harp is easy picking for some people. Anyway, on our program this evening is a harpist, and a good one, too.

Once upon a time there was a sort of moron walking down the street carrying a tangled mess of wires. An acquaintance stopped him and asked, "Pete, what are you doing with all those wires?" The moron grinned and said, "These wires are off of my harp. I'm taking them down to the music store to have 'em tuned." He said, according to law, he should be allowed to play his harp with no strings attached.

There is one disadvantage about being a harpist. Can you imagine serenading your best girl while riding in a canoe? Perhaps some players can do it. Can-oe?

A man died and went to heaven. As he passed through the gates St. Peter handed him a big harp. "I can't play this. I never practiced while on earth." "Of course, you didn't," said St. Peter. That's the reason you are up here."

Ladies and gentlemen, **(name of the harpist,)** who will play **(name of the number.)**

INTRODUCING A MAGICIAN

By George A. Posner

The gentleman I'm going to introduce to you is a magician. You know that a magician makes things disappear—your watch, your money, your best girl—say, why didn't I bring my mother-in-law? I mean, she would have enjoyed this, of course.

So he can make money disappear? So what! My wife's been doing that for years—and **mighty** expertly, let me tell you. Card Tricks Maggie, I call her. How that girl can make the **jack** disappear! The government doesn't do so bad, either.

But this fellow's good. We were helping him move into his new apartment, and he gave us a few samples—how he could make himself disappear, and so on. You'll know he's good when I tell you that his landlady demanded her rent in advance!

You know, my dad was in this magician business. His stunt was sawing a woman in half. I remember well that when he met another member of the magician fraternity, they always had that standard salutation: "Say, who was that lady I sawed with you last night?" Ooh!

I used to help my dad occasionally with those old saws and gals. But with my usual luck I'd always get the half that eats!

There used to be a bar on State Street in Chicago that was a favorite hangout for these magical boys. And the things that would come up there—or disappear there, whichever way you happened to look at it! There was many a layman, who walked into that place unsuspectingly, who came out later to sign a pledge of teetotaling abstinence—but for life!

I was in there one day, looking for my dad, when I saw a fellow come in, walk up to the bar and order a Martini. He drank it, ate the olive, and then began taking bite after bite out of the glass, with evident relish. Soon he had chewed up everything but the stem, which he threw over his shoulder.

Then he ordered another drink. And went through the same process all over again. Drank the drink, ate the olive, then chewed up and swallowed everything but the stem of the glass, which he threw over his shoulder. This went on for about six drinks while gents, evidently of the non-magical fraternity, standing by, looked on goggle-eyed.

Then this drinker, producing a silk hankie from mid-air, dabbed his lips with it and then paid for his drinks with money pulled out of his ear. After which he walked across the room, up the wall at that end, and on across the ceiling, down the other wall, and then floated gently out of the door.

One green-gilled customer turned to the bartender and said huskily: "Well, I declare! Did you ever see anyone so outlandish?"

"He's odd, all right," agreed the bartender. "Never says 'Goodnight.'—And besides, you know," he added, "the stems are the best part."

My dad's favorite tale was about something which happened at sea, when a number of magicians were featured in a show given in the ship salon one evening. You know how on theater programs the actors are billed: "Cast in the Order of Their Appearance?" Well, these magicians were billed: "Cast in the Order of Their **Disappearance."** Oh, it was better than the wildest Murder Mystery novel, the way those characters disappeared.

It seems that in a cage nearby was a parrot belonging to one of the passengers, and this parrot was an interested observer. When a stack of cards disappeared, he scratched his head. Then a chair disappeared, and the bird uttered little squawks as he shifted about on his perch and stared in amazement. When next a woman disappeared the parrot was getting really excited, hopping up and down, and uttering little shrieks of excitement.

Then suddenly the ship struck an iceberg and split in two. There was complete darkness as the lights were extinguished, screams and cries, and shortly afterward nothing on the black sea, but a few heads bobbing on the water. There, says my father, was that parrot, clinging to a piece of driftwood, looking about at the emptiness of it all, and squawking: "Marvelous trick! Marvelous! Marvelous!"

Yeah, that was my father's favorite story. But Dad was no slouch at making things disappear. It seems he was able to make **whole audiences** disappear. Anyway, that man looked at more empty seats than a—than a tailor!

But let's get along. We have a handsome, a talented, a most charming young performer here this evening so let's forget about me. There will now appear before you that talented rabbit destroyer, that now-you-see-it, now-you-don't expert, Mr. ——————. Give him a hand!

INTRODUCING THE FATHER OF A NEW BABY

By Louis J. Huber

Ladies and gentlemen, our speaker of the evening has many attributes to his name. You know most of them. But it was when he became the father of a new baby that he gained his most enviable—question mark—reputation.

It was when the new arrival did more than his share of crying that our man came through with his cutest remark. In his house he makes the cute sayings, not the babies. At that time he admitted that he didn't mind the baby's crying. He would cry too if he were the baby and he got a good look at the man who was his father.

When the baby was born he rushed into the hospital room. He wanted to be the first to tell his wife. But you know how it is—women always seem to get that kind of news before the men. A short time later our speaker had a sprained ankle and was taken to the hospital. He was quite exasperated when they discharged him without giving him a baby to take home.

He had another odd experience with his child. For three days he didn't know whether it was a boy or a girl. He waited until they dressed it. As soon as he saw the trousers he knew it was a girl. That's who wears them at his house. When he arrived home he was told that it was one o'clock. One o'clock and one baby, the nurse told him. He was sure happy that he missed the five o'clock train.

So here he is, the proud father of ( ) wonderful children. Mr. ——————.

INTRODUCING AN IRISH COMEDIAN

By Arthur L. Kaser

One cannot deny it—the Irish are a fun-loving people, and when we have a well-known Irish comedian in our midst we can forget our troubles and woes.

Our guest said he lived in the noisiest neighborhood imaginable. The only time it was quiet was when the trucks drowned the noise. This man calls himself a linguist. He says he can understand any language in the world if it is spoken in Irish. He says it is unbelievable how he got on the stage. He was working for a construction company and he dropped a load of dynamite when the noon whistle blew. When he came down three days later he crashed through a theatre roof and found himself on the stage. Where the footlights, the rest of him lit. That same day his old boss looked him up to notify him that, because of his carelessness, he could consider himself fired. Our guest, bringing his Irish temper into use, blew a fuse. He shook his fist at the boss, and blurted: "The sooner I never see your face again, the better it will be for the both of us when we meet!" He said that the boss was one of those people that pat you on your back before your face, and hit you in the eye behind your back.

We tried to get this comedian to come here some months ago, but he had to refuse because he had just had his appendix taken from him. He said it was his own fault; he should have had it in his wife's name.

Ladies and gentlemen, our Irish comedian, **(name.)**

INTRODUCING A CHALK TALK ARTIST

By Richard Drummond

Ladies and gentlemen, tonight we have an unusual act, because it is an act not often witnessed. We have a chalk talk artist. He talks while he chalks. I have been told that he is very good.

Personally, I have always longed to be an artist, but I have been hindered by a certain deficiency: I can't draw. I can't even draw my breath without breathing.

There are some artists very good at one kind of drawing only. They may draw beautiful flowers, but could never draw a cow. It reminds me of a New York artist who was stranded in Rio de Janeiro. He decided to try his hand at murals. He needed money badly. He approached the proprietor of a large restaurant and suggested that a pair of North American buffaloes be painted on one of the bare walls. "No," said the owner, "no buffaloes. I used to be a seafaring man. If you can paint me a couple of full-rigged schooners, I'll hire you." "You're sure," persisted the artist, "you don't want a couple of buffaloes painted there?" "Of course, I'm sure," snapped the proprietor. "Ships or nothing." "All right," replied the artist, "I'll paint your ships, but any resemblance to a pair of buffaloes will be purely coincidental."

I've watched artists at work. Many of them shut one eye while drawing. Some of their finished work looks like they shut both eyes.

My brother was a portrait painter. He was good, too. When he was only twelve he painted a picture of Santa Claus. It was so natural we had to take it off the wall twice a year to give it a haircut. He once painted a life-size picture of the Grand Canyon. I never saw anyone who could draw a picture that could look so natural.

He drew a picture of a beggar in India. When you looked

at that beggar you were transported to India. You'd swear you could see that beggar breathe. You could see his eyes blinking. The picture was just about finished when my brother was called from the room to answer the phone. When he returned his lunch had been eaten.

Ladies and gentlemen, **(name of artist)**, the chalk talk artist.

INTRODUCING A BACKWOODS PIANIST

By A. Guy Visk

Ladies and gentlemen, I am very happy to introduce the next act. The gentleman you are about to meet is a concert pianist who was **reared** in the backwoods. To this day, he plays the piano standing up. In the words of the poet laureate, "There's no stool for an old fool."

Actually, all the southern states are putting their claim in for this famous artist. Georgia claims he comes from Florida. Florida claims he comes from Alabama. Alabama isn't taking any chances. Down there they claim he comes from Perth Amboy, New Jersey.

He's a true son of the South. His childhood was spent along the shores of the beautiful Suwannee river. Last night I heard him play for the first time. It's a pity he never went wading.

It may interest you to know that he refused a position with the Boston Pops just to be here tonight. Boston Pops . . . that's a married men's softball team.

I know you're all anxious to hear this famous musician, and I won't keep you from him, I mean I won't keep you waiting any longer. Unlike other pianists, this gentleman does not use a candelabra. He owes all his success to Eveready Flashlight Batteries.

INTRODUCING A SWEDISH COMEDIAN

By Arthur L. Kaser

Some people have the mistaken idea that the Swedish people on the whole are rather a slow-moving type. This is far from the truth, especially when it comes to verbal comebacks. I am reminded of the Swede who fell into a manhole, and began yelling for help. A passerby, looking down into the hole, remarked: "How did you come to fall in?" The Swede said: "Ay not come to fall in. Ay come to cross the street." "Then," said the other, "you **did** fall in the hole?" "Nah," said the Swede. "Ay yust happen down hare and somebody they build pavement all 'round me."

This is just a little preface to the introduction of a well-known Swedish comedian we will have the pleasure of meeting shortly.

As a young fellow this man was very shy and bashful. He met a very charming and beautiful girl. He wasn't too bashful to fall in love with her, but he was too bashful to propose marriage. He tried very hard to get up enough courage to pop the question. One evening he called on her. There was a long silence after they were seated. Finally he hit upon a plan of strategy. He stuttered some, and then burst out, "How—how would you like to be buried with my folks?"

When he first arrived in this country he decided to see a lot of his new homeland, so he boarded a bus for the west coast. When the bus entered the farming country and was passing a watermelon patch our guest remarked to the bus driver: "Dem bane nice watermelons." The driver jokingly said: "They're small cantaloupe, but they're still green." Farther on the passenger saw a field of six-foot corn growing some distance away, and asked: "Dat bane corn?" The driver said: "Green onions." It wasn't long before they reached the Mississippi River. By this time the tourist had caught on.

"By yimminy!" he exclaimed, "somebody's radiator bane leaking."

When he reached California he found that two could live as cheaply as one, only it cost twice as much. So he sent for his wife.

Ladies and gentlemen, **(name of comedian)** will now take over.

INTRODUCING A VARIETY REVUE

By Arthur L. Kaser

Tonight we are to be blessed with a variety revue, which, by the way, is a pleasant afterglow of the once very popular vaudeville show.

Joe E. Brown, as every mirth-loving person knows, has been pulling funny ones for a long time. At one time he played St. Louis for a one-week stand. He picked a restaurant near the theatre and ate there every day he was in town. On the first day when he ordered his meal he instructed the waitress to bring him whole-wheat bread. Somehow or other she brought him white bread instead. The next day he ordered whole-wheat bread again. Again he was served white bread. This same thing happened Wednesday, Thursday and Friday. Joe gave up. On Saturday he said to the waitress, "Just for a change, I'll have white bread today." The waitress looked at him a moment and then said, "That's funny. Aren't you the customer who always orders whole-wheat?"

Here is one from a TV actor who, a long time ago, was in vaudeville. It was about time for the show to start in a rather small midwest town. The stage manager motioned to the substitute stagehand, and said, "Okay, Mac, run up the curtain." "Not me," loudly answered the green stagehand. "I ain't no bloomin' squirrel."

Whether it's vaudeville or variety revue, the whole world is its stage, and the people like it.

INTRODUCING A RETIRING TEACHER
(Lower Grades)

By Richard Drummond

When a teacher, who has been in the system for many years, steps out of the scene, there is a gap that detracts from the picture for a long time. And now, when our beloved Miss **(name)** leaves us, we feel there is something gone from the school family that can never be replaced. It is like losing a diamond from a jeweled cluster.

During her teaching of the younger fry for many years Miss **(name)** has experienced many dreary incidents which, however, have been overshadowed by more humorous and pleasant ones. For instance, there was the time Miss **(name)** was trying to impress upon her young pupils the importance of doing right at all times, and to bring out the answer, "Bad habits," she inquired, "What is it that we find so easy to get into, and so hard to get out of?" One little fellow piped up with, "Bed!"

Miss **(name)** also recalls the time she received a note from a mother on the opening day of school: "Dear Miss **(name)**, our dear little Bertrand is a delicate, nervous child, and if he is naughty at times, just punish the boy next to him. That will frighten Bertrand so he will be good."

Our retiring teacher says she has had more difficulty teaching the parents than the pupils. There is only one really brilliant child in the world and every mother has it. Too much coddling at home makes a child self-centered and selfish. Miss **(name)** says this was illustrated recently when she asked one of her pupils: "Herbert, if you had six apples and I asked you for three, how many would you have?" The pupil said, "Three."

One of the most amusing answers she ever received was when she noted that little Elsie had forgotten to dot the "i" when she was writing the word "nice." She asked the pupil, "Where is the dot over the i?" "Oh," said Elsie, "it's still in the pencil."

Friends, let's have a big hand for Miss **(name)**.

INTRODUCING A CONTRALTO

By Sidney Steele

With Miss **(name of singer)**, our contralto, on the program we can look forward to a very enjoyable evening.

Many singers are called but few are chosen. Yes, many singers are called, but, my, oh, my, what they are called. I have a girl cousin that I could easily invent some names for. What a voice that girl has. It's a cross between a train whistle and a blowup in a can factory. And the worst part of it is, she thinks she can sing. She doesn't speak to me any more. She's mad on me. She was butchering "Il Trovatore," and then had the nerve to ask, "What do you think of my voice?" I said, "It makes me think of the poor sailors." "Of sailors? Why?" she asked. "Yes," I explained, "Sailors. Your singing has a tendency to die at high C's."

Her father is quite deaf, but he is postponing buying a hearing aid until his daughter is married and gone. She sang at a banquet just once. When she had finished a portly gentleman said, "Fine! Fine!" He was a municipal judge. She was paid five dollars for singing at that banquet. But I think she broke the law. She accepted money under falsetto pretense.

A good case of embarrassment is worse than rheumatism combined with the seven-year itch. Not long ago I was so embarrassed I could have crawled through a keyhole with my shoes on. I was at a recital. As one woman finished singing I turned to the man sitting next to me, and said, "What a terrible voice. Who is she?" He said, "That's my wife." Then I stuttered, "Oh, I beg your pardon. Of course, it isn't her voice, really. It's the stuff she has to sing. I wonder who wrote it." He looked sharply at me and said, "I did." I crawled under the seat and they swept me out the next morning.

But now, my friends, a real singer, the well-known contralto, Miss **(name)**.

INTRODUCING A GERMAN COMEDIAN

By Arthur L. Kaser

I've often wished that vaudeville would come back and bring with it such German comedians as Weber and Fields. They were great. However, we do have a few good German comedians scattered around today, and one of them is with us this evening.

This comedian likes to tell of some of the funny things that has befallen some of his relatives across the Atlantic. During the war his Uncle Herman worked in a large factory there that made just about everything. His wife, Lena, wanted a baby buggy very badly, so Uncle Herman promised her he would purloin a few pieces at a time from the factory until he had sufficient parts to construct a perambulator. Every day he would bring home a few parts, and finally the day arrived when he could assemble the parts. He worked for hours in their back yard. After about five hours Lena went out to see how the project was proceeding. She found a tired and sad Herman. "What is wrong mit, Herman?" asked Lena. "Och," exclaimed Herman, "no use it is. No matter how I do it. It always comes out a machine gun."

And then, too, there was Uncle Heinie who was a shoemaker. One night when Uncle Heinie closed his shop he forgot to turn off the gas light, and during the night a gust of wind blew out the flame. When Uncle Heinie arrived the next morning he struck a match to light the gas. There was a terrific explosion. Uncle Heinie was blown through the front door and almost across the street. A policeman rushed up and helped Heinie to his feet. "You was hurt?" asked the officer. "Nein, I'm not hurt," said Uncle Heinie. "I got out shust in time."

I think our guest of the evening has some that are much better than these. Ladies and gentlemen, I feel honored to present **(name of the guest.)**

INTRODUCING A PIANIST

By Sidney Steele

When I first heard that the great pianist, **(name of pianist),** was to appear on this program I recalled the experience of a neighbor of ours. She said to me: "I'll never forget the time I accompanied my husband on the piano." I interrupted: "Your husband sings?" "Well, not exactly," she explained. "You see it was like this. It was during the hurricane flood along the east coast a number of years ago. He and I were sitting at home when suddenly the hurricane struck. Before we knew what was happening our rooms were flooded, the furniture was floating about the room. My husband leaped upon the dining room table. I climbed upon the piano. A savage wave struck the house and the table and my husband were carried out of the house." "Awful," I said to her. "You were left alone in the house?" "Oh, no," she said with a smile. "I accompanied him on the piano." Humph! I should tell something like that at my age.

Our guest pianist of this evening tells a rather amusing thing that happened one time at one of his concerts. He had just finished playing "Melody in F," and had acknowledged the thunder of applause when a lady hurried to him, and said: "Will you please play 'Melody in F'?" "But I just played that piece," protested our guest. The lady looked a little sad. "What a pity," she exclaimed. "I wish I had known it. It's my favorite composition."

At another time he was playing when he noticed a lady acquaintance of his, who, though she was in her forties, had never married. With her was her young nephew. When our pianist had finished playing Mendelssohn's "Wedding March," the boy said to his aunt, "What is that piece he played?" She said gravely, "That is 'The Maiden's Prayer'."

Now, ladies and gentlemen, I feel greatly honored to be permitted to present **(name).**

INTRODUCING A JUGGLER

By Earl Jay Gilbert

My friends, for your edification, pleasure and amusement, as the old-timers used to say, we've secured the services of a marvelous manipulator. He nonchalantly tosses various objects into the air and skillfully catches them with the greatest of ease. In other words, we've got a clever juggler coming up next and, friends, he's really good.

I looked up "juggler" the other day, and it covers a lot of territory—trickster, conjurer, necromancer, magician, medicine man, witch doctor—and a lot of other things.

I don't know everything our juggler tonight is going to do, but if he lives up to half those definitions he'll be more than good—he'll be a wizard. Of course there are all kinds of jugglers. There are the kind that will juggle a luncheon check all around the table until it lands next to your plate. There are the political bosses who'll take a candidate who has been defeated for office and juggle him into a job that's better than the one the voters refused to give him.

One of the best jugglers I ever knew worked in the accounting department of a bank. He juggled those books like nobody's business. At least, he thought it was nobody's business until the bank examiners stepped in and made it their business. They arranged a nice promotion for him. They handed him what was practically a ten-year contract working for the state. All he had to do was juggle a big sledge hammer, making little ones out of big ones.

I was almost a juggler myself once. I tried to juggle an antique vase belonging to my mother. They called it an antique because it had been in the family for years. My mother's sister-in-law bought it originally at a bargain auction sale. She gave it to my aunt for a Christmas present. My aunt gave it to another aunt the following Christmas. That aunt gave it to a cousin the next Christmas. It travelled for years, until my mother got it back for the fourth time and couldn't get rid of it. I overcame that obstacle when I tried to juggle it with the new saxophone my young sister was learning to play. The family sure missed it. So did I. My father called me aside and slipped me two dollars. He said: "Son, see what you can do with that floor lamp your mother gave me my last birthday."

Some jugglers make wonderful money. I know the jail-houses are filled with people who made money, but got caught, but I mean regular, legitimate money—the kind you catch a glimpse of once in awhile as it flies through your hands on its way to the income tax department.

When you watch our juggler tonight, as he nonchalantly tosses things in the air and casually catches them, think of how easy it is to make a good living without working. All you need to start with are a few dishes, a couple of chairs, some rubber balls—just a few odds and ends. You can pick up the dishes in anybody's china closets or dining rooms. The rubber balls can always be found at the top of the stairs in any home where there are small children. The kids put them there in case anybody wants to go downstairs in a hurry.

I explained this to a friend who wanted to be a high-class juggler. He took my advice and he's on top of the world today. He started out by going to parties and raiding the premises until he had his equipment. Then he'd begin to juggle. Friends, it was terrific! You could hear the sound of falling dishes and broken crockery for blocks away. It used to take the hostesses hours to clean up after him. But after his third party he was in business. Whenever he'd hear of a party he'd invite himself. People would give him good money to stay away. He did all right for himself financially just by not going to parties.

Now here's a tip I'll pass out to storekeepers who carry dishes or ceramics of any kind. The next time a juggler appears in a local theatre, give all the kids in the neighborhood free tickets to the show. You'll more than make up for it. In the next few days every mother in the vicinity will have to replenish her supply of dishes and crockery. You can see, there's a lot more to juggling than most people might think.

Oh, yes, I almost forgot something very important. In addition to the dishes and other things a juggler needs, he's got to have a pretty girl in a short dress, just to stand around and hand him his props. That's very essential. I'd go in the juggling business myself if I could find a pretty girl in a short dress—or just a pretty girl.

Now, I don't know everything our friend is going to juggle tonight, but I did notice he brought a couple of baskets with him. One was filled with eggs that have long since passed their first youth. The other one was filled with senile tomatoes. But don't worry, folks, I understand he rents out umbrellas in case he misses any tricks.

I hope he doesn't mind my kidding him a little. Seriously, my friends, he's an excellent juggler—one of the best. I know you'll all agree that it's a treat and a pleasure to watch him. So let's sit back and relax and enjoy his skill—and here he is—that clever entertainer, ——————!

INTRODUCING A MINSTREL SHOW

By Richard Drummond

What type of entertainment can we pull out of the past that is more colorful, more hepped up with vim, vigor and what have you, than the minstrel show? The minstrel show was a show that had everything—lively music, fine singing, dancing, snappy dialogue—Yes, folks, when they buried the minstrel show they buried the goose that laid the golden egg of entertainment.

But here is a top secret: That goose is beginning to poke its head out of the ground and may again strut the cakewalk and the hi-jinks across the boards. (Imitates an interlocutor.) "Gentlemen, be seated. How are you, Mr. Bones?" "I's fine. Yes, sah, I's finer den pulverized red pepper—an' jest as hot."

Ladies and gentlemen, the **Minstrel Show!**

INTRODUCING A GAY NINETIES REVUE OR ACT

By Arthur L. Kaser

Tonight we are going back to the good old days, the Gay Nineties. In those days everything was modern—for those days. Today those same things are old-fashioned. We call it old-fashioned simplicity. A shining example of old-fashioned simplicity is an unpowdered nose. And today when grandmother tells little Susan to act like a lady, she means an old-fashioned lady, of course.

It would be almost impossible for us moderns to go back to that way of living. For example, recently an old-fashioned merchant in the East wanted people to return to wearing red flannel underwear. It didn't work. It couldn't work. People are too restless now as it is. Where are the bustles the ladies wore in those days? Like lots of other things, they were left behind. Come to think of it, they were always left behind.

In those good old days if a fellow wanted to make a date with a girl he would get on his bicycle and ride across town to her house. But now we have the modern convenience of the telephone. Now if he wants to make a date with a girl he patiently waits three days until everyone else is off the party line.

Back then if you wanted to make a trip you'd get on the train and six or seven days later you would arrive at your destination. Today you board a jet liner and arrive at your destination day before yesterday. It is getting so complicated you unpack your luggage before you leave and pack it when you arrive.

Fifty or sixty years ago everybody had their tonsils and appendixes. Today nobody has them except the doctors.

Ladies and gentlemen, if you will all climb aboard the hayrack we will drive back and enjoy a Gay Nineties Revue.

INTRODUCING A PSYCHIATRIST

By George A. Posner

We have as our guest this evening a gentleman known as a psychiatrist. I presume you all know what a psychiatrist is? Well, he's a sort of a doctor—or is it detective?—on the mental side. You **pay** him to do what your wife does for nothing.

Oh, you know what I mean—I mean that third degree stuff, of course.

That reminds me. There were a couple of psychiatrists who met, and one said: "I'm not feeling so good these days, Bill. Could you give me a going over?"

And the other answered: "Well, you know the business. Why don't you give yourself the works?"

So the first said: "At **my** prices? I couldn't afford it!"

Psychiatrists! Someone has said: "A psychiatrist is a man to whom you go when you're slightly cracked, and come back completely broke." Another definition: A talent scout for Bellevue.

And still another that comes to mind at the moment: "A psychiatrist is a guy who goes to a burlesque show, and watches the **audience.**"

Anyway they're an odd bunch of characters. But aren't we all? Most of us aren't much different than that fellow Andrew MacDougal. He said to his crony: "It seems everybody is queer in some manner or other, my friend, except thee and me—and you know, sometimes I'm not so sure of thee!"

So what? Someone has also said, in the present-day world you've got to be crazy, or you'll go nuts!

It's a complicated affair, when you get right down to it, this present-day world. Who knows all the diverse motives, the hidden causes which are driving people.

A used car dealer—the Smiling Swede, or something—told me of an incident which happened to him the other day.

It seems a woman drove into his lot in a swank car. It was a beauty. Looked almost a block long; with a motor purring like a politician; a coat shining like a bride's eyes at the altar.

Or putting it another way, shining like the seat of last year's blue serge pants.

And what accessories! That tony kind of horn that, instead of honking, it sneers at you. So high class it back-fired with a British accent. In short—a wow—W.O.W.—and by W.O.W. I don't mean Worn-Out Wreck, but wow!

The woman driver asks the Smiling Swede: "Would you buy this car?"

"Oh, lady," answers the Smiling Swede, beginning to hesitate and to think, wondering where he was going to get all the money. "I'll have to look this over thoroughly first, and see—"

"Would you give $100 for it?"

"$100?" gasps the Smiling Swede. "Say, lady, this isn't a 'hot' car, is it? What's wrong?"

"Nothing's wrong," answers she. "It runs like a million, doesn't it? You can see that!"

Then the Smiling Swede gets anxious, rushes into the office, and feverishly hunts for a bill of sale, meanwhile glancing at the newspaper sidewise to see if maybe an escaped lunatic is at large. He then rushes the papers to her to sign before she might change her mind.

Then when the transfer had been made, he asks: "Tell me, madam, how come you sell a swank car like that for only $100?"

So she answers: "It's very simple. My husband just died, and among the terms of his will it says that the proceeds from the sale of his automobile is to go to his blonde secretary."

Oh, the things you can dig up when you begin to hunt for hidden causes! . . . .

There was the case of a fellow named Jimmy Jones who was drafted into the army. And immediately it seemed to do something to his mind, when all the time the army doctors, and army sergeants and army physical directors were doing different things to his body.

It seems he would be found prowling around the camp, always looking for something. He'd pick up every bit of paper he could see, unfold it and read it. Then he would shake his head and say, "That ain't it." This went on and on. "This ain't it;" "that ain't it."

After a few days the sergeant noticed his behavior, and reported it to the captain. The captain thought that was indeed a strange behavior for a man, and went into consultation with the camp psychiatrists and doctors. And it was finally decided that poor Jimmy Jones was off his rocker, with those mysterious "this ain't its" and "that ain't its."

So one day they called him up into the captain's office, and presented him with his army discharge papers. As they handed the paper to him, he unfolded it, read it, and said: "This is it!"

Oh, psychiatry is nothing new. We had something like that, but under a different name, that was the rage a little after the turn of the century. It was called phrenology. I remember those charts that fascinated me as a boy—the human head divided up into different sections, showing where the different traits of character were housed. Acquisitiveness in this section; memory in that; cautiousness here; firmness there; love way down there; and that you could tell by the sizes and shapes of the different bumps on the cranium just what quantity of each characteristic you had. So went this science, and it was pretty generally accepted, you know—still has quite a following today.

There was some controversy, too. My father used to say, "How are you going to tell, from the size of the smokehouse, how many hams there are hanging inside?" And he liked to tell the story of the Irishmen who went on strike for better pay.

"How did you manage to win the strike so soon, Pat?" one of the Irishmen was asked.

"Oh, indade it was aisy," he answered. "We found out where the bumps of generosity were located on the bosses; and thin went at them with clubs and made thim larger!"

Well, this is all in fun, of course; and by no means is meant to disparage any of the army of fine men and women who have come into this new science; and who have been devoting themselves unselfishly to what is undoubtedly a vital branch of therapeutics. We can hardly do other than to let them know we appreciate them and wish them every success in their work.

And now I have the honor and pleasure of introducing to you, ——————.

INTRODUCING AN ACTOR

By Arthur L. Kaser

Thou goest where, Lothario, me boy?
To bless the world, thine audience, with joy?
Or just to tromp the boards in gleaming light,
To bring the light of day on blackened night?
Keep up the laughter, lad, with ne'er a frown
'Til time runs out and brings the curtain down.

Which, in everyday jargon, means we have as a guest this evening, an actor.

I scanned the dictionary to find an authentic definition of actor. It said, "An actor is a man who can walk to the side of the stage, peer into the wings filled with theatrical props, dirt and dust, other actors, stage hands, barrels, boxes, old clothes, junk and more junk, and say, 'Ah, what a lovely view there is from this window'."

An actor fell in love with a girl in his home town. He called one evening at the girl's home and boldly told her father he wanted to marry his daughter. "And," thundered her father, "what do you do for a living, young man?" "I'm an actor," proudly replied the young man. "Then," said the father, "hurry up and get out before the footlights."

It was then the young man decided to get into the movie business, so he got a job with a transfer company. Where he used to be in the center of the spotlight, he is now half way between the headlight and the tail light.

It is quite different with our guest this evening. He is still in the spotlight and that light is getting brighter all the time. Ladies and gentlemen, **(name.)**

INTRODUCING AN ANIMAL TRAINER OR AN ANIMAL ACT

By George A. Posner

You may have heard of the little boy who asked his mother: "Mummy, am I descended from monkeys?" And his mother answered: "I don't know, sonny; I never met any of your father's folks."

Man has slowly developed from the lower beasts. The scientists proudly tell us he is the most perfect of the animal kingdom. So what does that make us? **Perfect beasts?** Hm!

I sometimes question that alleged superior intelligence of man as compared to the animals. You don't find animals working themselves to death to remain alive, or saving their money, so when they are old they can afford the things which only a youngster can enjoy!

That reminds me of a speech I once heard a lecturer make on this subject. He had waxed eloquent and expounded at great length on the superiority of man to the beast. And he finally wound up in this manner:

"Man, as we have seen, is a progressive being, but other creatures, in the main, are stationary. Take the ass, for example. You never have seen, and never will see, a more perfect ass than you see at the present moment!"

It's all the way you look at it.

Well, we have an animal trainer, and an animal act coming up. And that brings on a nostalgia for me.

I had an uncle who was a wild animal trainer, you know. Ah, what a magnificent lion tamer he was, to listen to him. Oh, the tales he could tell of his exploits in capturing or shooting wild animals on the Dark Continent. What a lion tamer! I remember, my old mammy — our cook — saying to him, after listening to an especially exciting evening's recital of his: "You ain't a lion **tamer** — you is a lyin' **louse!**" But she was just jealous, I guess. I loved to listen to his exploits by the hour, when I was a kid.

"Why do they call Africa "The Dark Continent?" I asked him once.

"It's very lucky that it's the Dark Continent," was his answer, "the way the natives run around without any clothes on."

You couldn't phase him on anything. I remember once he was really spreading himself on his experiences in shooting a lot of tigers in Africa. Oh, the tigers he shot in that tale! When finally one of the men listening—a college professor—stopped him, and remarked: "But, sir, there are no tigers in Africa, didn't you know?"

Without batting an eyelash, my uncle answered: "Of course I know there aren't any tigers in Africa. Didn't I kill them all?"

When he was asked: "Didn't you have a lot of narrow escapes?" he answered, "Narrow escapes? Listen, if there were any narrow escapes, those animals had them!" Oh, he was magnificent.

Once someone asked him if he found any elephants in Africa. He answered: "Find any elephants? Those things are so big, how could they ever get lost?"

"But where's there any glory in overcoming elephants?" he would add. "When those beasts are so dumb the ivory is busting out all over them! Tusks and such, you know."

But he admitted to going on a number of elephant shoots. That was his alibi, one time when he went out duck hunting with a number of cronies.

When a flock of ducks arose and he banged away, and didn't get a single one, do you think he was embarrassed? Not at all. He looked very nonchalant, then calmly said: "Used to elephant hunting, you know. Can't see these bally little things!" The gnus were the most vicious, said he. "Haven't you heard the saying, 'No gnus is good gnus?'"

Another time I was with him when a favored lady friend of his was along, and it was evident unc wanted to make a good impression. He had just finished telling her what a dead-shot he was, when suddenly a duck arose from a covert and winged leisurely by. Unc took careful aim, then fired.

The duck sailed on with scarcely a feather flurried. Uncle turned calmly to his lady friend and said: "There, Emilie, you see a miracle. A dead duck, and he's still flying!"

Uncle admits he went to Africa on a cattle boat.

"But that was just so as to get acclimated, used to animals," he alibied.

Asked how the meals were, he said they were very good — he got tired of all that milk, though. But the service was fast; and snacks any time you felt like it.

Along with them, uncle relates, were a bunch of hunters with a Frank Buck "Bring 'Em Back Alive" expedition. Unc says he could well believe it, since one of the things they were going to collect was a Flea Circus.

The way they kept scratching, he also opined they had already collected a portion of the cargo.

One incident which uncle relates as happening over there in Africa, which I thought exciting but which unc sneered at for some reason, was the time he came running full tilt for camp with a ten-foot tiger in hot pursuit. He had no gun — I suspect he had thrown it away to make faster progress — but did he admit to defeat of any kind? Oh, no. He was shouting: "Hey! Everybody! I'm bringing him back alive!"

Then unc saw the bushes parting ahead of him, and inwardly he evidently was exulting: "Ah, here's my rescue at last!" When what does this guy do, but poke out a camera and shout at unc: "Can't you slow down a little? I can't get you both into the picture!"

Oh, unc was a card. But he didn't feel like the Joker at that time.

I guess unc figured he would rather be a live coward than a dead hero. Huh?

He joined an animal act later, too. But that was natural for an old alibi-er like him. When a critic says your act "smells" — and it's an **animal** act — you have your alibi! Blame it on the animals!

But, seriously, let's get on with the show. It is my pleasure to present to you ————.

ADDITIONAL MATERIAL

A tourist stopped his car at the roadside and said to the farmer: "I say, that's the worst-looking horse I ever saw. Why don't you fatten him up?"

"Fatten him up, indeed!" said the farmer. "Why, it's all he can do to carry what little flesh he has on him now!"

At an army auction, a Negro hack driver had purchased an old cavalry horse.

"Remember," they cautioned him as he led his purchase away, "this is an old army horse and he can only respond to military commands. When you want him to go, you must say, 'Forward' and when you want him to stop you must say 'Halt'."

All went well until one day his fares were a dignified old Southern colonel and his buxom wife, whom the Negro had picked up at the railroad depot. The destination was a downtown hotel. They proceeded at a good pace, but as the hotel was reached the hack continued on by without any visible slackening of its speed.

"Stop," shouted the colonel. "Stop! This is the place, I say."

The darky spoke up: "Kunnel, if yo' desires to stop, Ah reckon yo'll have tu jump, 'cuz I done fo'got de word whut makes dis yeah hawss stop."

We hunted deer—it was too cold to hunt bare.

My little daughter said to her mother, the other day: "Our new cat is a lady cat. So some day it'll be a mamma cat, won't it?"

"Not this cat," said my wife. "We're not going to let it out of the house."

So the little tyke looked at her mother with a puzzled look for a minute or so, and then said: "Why, Mummy, does it need fresh air to become a mother?"

"Circumstances!" exclaimed the man from the city. "That certainly is a queer name for a mule."

"Not very," returned the farmer. "Hain't you ever heard of circumstances over which a man ain't got no control?"

Speaking of cats, you know one day the wife told me to take our cat away out in the country and lose it. I put it into a basket and walked way out in the country for about six or seven miles—to make sure it wouldn't find its way back. And, boy, was I embarrassed! . . . When I got home, the wife asked me: "Well, did you lose the cat, all right?"

"Lose it?" I said. "If I hadn't followed it, I never could have found my way home!"

You've heard of "shaggy dog" stories, undoubtedly. But the one I am about to relate to you, probably ought to be called a "shaggy lion" tale. It concerns a couple of hunters who went to Africa on a big game hunting expedition. Mo Lyon and Les Action were the gentlemen's names.

For months they hoofed it through the jungle—safari here, trek there—until one of them, Action, began to get quite fed up with the whole matter.

One day he said to Lyon: "A mighty hunter you are, but so far you've bagged nothing but your pants. If you're so good, why don't we have less lyin' and more action?"

And Lyon answered: "Last night I was studying the tracks on this trek, and boy, I'm not lyin', this time the lions are practically in the bag. I'll bet you I get a lion before nightfall."

Action answers: "Put your money where your big mouth is! It's a dollar, I'm saying, that you're wrong, as usual."

So Lyon says: "O.K., you got yourself a bet. But let me go up ahead for a while by myself. Good?"

He does, and hours and hours go by, without a sign of him.

Suddenly there is a fierce roar of a lion—right in camp! Action, scared out of his wits, and out of reach of his gun, unfortunately, ducks under his cot, as a lion sticks his head inside the tent and roars: "Is Les Action here?"

"Y-y-yes," answers Action tremblingly.

"Well," says the lion, "your partner owes you a dollar."

Shaggy dog stories. Here's one which maybe we should call a Shaggy Turtle story.

Anyway, it seems there were three turtles—two big ones and a little one—who were awfully thirsty, and went into a bar to slake their thirst.

They ordered three big mugs of root beer, and these had just been placed before them by the barkeep, when a big rain storm suddenly came up.

"Oh, my gosh!" said one. "We forgot our umbrellas, too!"

So immediately there followed a discussion as to who would go for the umbrellas, since there was no sense in all of them going, and getting wet.

It was finally decided the little one should go.

"Oh," protested he, "when I'm away, I'll bet the rest of you will drink up my root beer!"

But they promised him solemnly, on their word, that they wouldn't touch a drop of his root beer. When they finally convinced him, he started on his way.

Hour after hour went by; then day after day; and then weeks. And finally, three weeks later, one of the big turtles said to the other: "Know what I'm going to do? I'm going to drink that guy's root beer."

"That's just what I've been thinking," answered the other turtle, "so let's."

When just then the little turtle's voice piped up from a place near the door:

"If you do, I swear, this minute I'll quit going after those umbrellas!"

While we're at it, I guess I might as well give you this fish story.

There was one fellow who had an idea he would like to have a fish as a pet, and train it to follow him around like a little dog. It would be unusual and different.

He thought that if he would keep it out of water for just a minute or so the first day, and then just a mite longer each succeeding day, he could gradually wean it of the necessity for the moist habitat it had been accustomed to.

So patiently hc worked with it, daily extending each time the length of the fishy's stay out in the dry air. Finally, sure enough, he had this little beggar following him about faithfully along the village streets. Until one day—do you know?—sniff! sniff!—while he was crossing a bridge, this beautiful fishy friend slipped off, fell into the water—sniff! sniff!—and was **drowned! . . .**

Well? . . . I said it was a fish story, didn't I?

A young woman came into a police station and said: "I want this dog shot at once."

"But we can't shoot him here in the residence section," the cops told her. "The bullet might go through him and hit somebody."

So she said: "But couldn't you shoot him lengthwise?"

You know, my girl hasn't spoken to me since I took her horse-back riding. Perhaps she's sore about something.

INTRODUCING A QUARTETTE

By Arthur L. Kaser

Barbershop quartettes have surely come back into their own in the past few years, and I believe they are better than they were in their semi-demise. It was back in the gay nineties when the barbershop singers were in their heyday, but at that time there was as much competition over the handle bar mustache as there was over musical bar melodies.

The gay nineties was a little before my time, but when I was young I did belong to a singing quartette. There were five of us in the quartette. Yes, five. You see we always carried a spare in case one of us went flat. We sang "Sweet Adeline," but after we sang it a few times we were advised to change the title to "Sour Adeline." We could not find a bass singer so they made me stand out in the rain till I caught cold. Then I'd sing bass. We just sang to kill time, and what a weapon we had. The last time we sang before an audience a man came up and asked, "Do you know 'the Road to Mandalay'?" I said, "Yes, do you want us to sing it?" He said, "No, take it." But, folks, don't judge other quartettes by ours. For instance, let me present a quartette that is a quartette. Ladies and gentlemen, **(name of quartette.)**

INTRODUCING A HOUSEWIFE

By Louis J. Huber

Ladies and gentlemen, seldom is any master of ceremonies given a finer opportunity than has been awarded to me tonight. The lady I am about to present is known in many fields but I want to introduce her in the field that she prizes most highly. She is a housewife; she is a homemaker.

A homemaker? What is that? It is a title given any woman who makes it home in time to get her husband's dinner. A homemaker is a definition of the lady of the house who has the ability of getting her man to do the dishes while she stands there and tells him how hard she works.

Now I did not say that our speaker is guilty of this. I am merely talking about homemakers. She does have a very admirable trait that is not always found in a housewife. She, like a Boy Scout, is always prepared. Her husband called one night and told her he was bringing a friend home to dinner. Was she excited? Was she flustered? No, she was ready. She had her bag packed and she left and went home to her mother.

But we can forget all that and come to the high point of the evening. I give her to you under the title she loves best. May I present a homemaker, Mrs. ——————?

INTRODUCING AN ENTERTAINER

By Jeff Branen

Our next entertainer is a young man who has appeared before some of the crowned heads of Europe and others who should have been crowned. He appeared in Washington before our own dear president ————— was elected. He is a versatile actor capable of carrying many parts. He acquired some of this in a crockery store where he carried many parts —mostly broken ones. As is the case with many successful actors he started out as an awful ham. He was such a ham he felt at home between two slices of bread. Then he branched out some and did an Oriental act accompanied by burning incense. It was a punk act. However, he began to be recognized. One thing that brought him popularity was the time he stood too near the footlights and his corns began to pop. It was a hot act. From then on he was a success. He had good lines and most of his jokes got across—on the Mayflower. He had altogether some eight hundred jokes—all told. He never pulled all his good jokes in one performance. Some of them he had in his head for years. You know, sort of aged in the wood. And now allow me to present (**name.** Entertainer should be of a moderate moronic type.)

INTRODUCING A SPEAKER ON FIRE PREVENTION

By Arthur L. Kaser

And now, ladies and gentlemen, before I introduce Fireman Smith (real name) who will speak to you on fire prevention, I would like to offer a few preventive measures myself. And I hope you will take notes. What good is a speech without notes? What good is a song without notes? What good is a bank without notes? A musical staff holds the notes. The bank staff holds notes. If you hold a musical note a long time, there usually comes a rest. If the bank holds your note too long there comes arrest.

But back to the fire, and I repeat, I hope you take notes. As this has to do with fire, you will kindly use a fire proof pen and an asbestos pad. All ready? Okay. First, do not spread your fire insurance policy on the floor in front of the fireplace to keep the sparks from getting on the rug. It might ruin everything in the policy except the fine print. Remember, the big print giveth, and the fine print taketh away.

Fire cannot get very far without oxygen, so if a blaze starts, do not hesitate. Push the oxygen back as far as possible. Always keep an easily trained cat in the house. Then if you accidentally burn a hole in the living room rug, just teach the cat to sit on it so it won't show. If you must smoke in bed, be sure to dunk your sheets in the bathtub before you retire. It might prevent sheets of flame enveloping you. You might be surprised to find yourself in Hot Springs.

Don't let the small fry play with matches. They might go on a strike and make it hot for you. And last, but not least, inspect your chimney occasionally. A flaw in a flue might make you flee. And now, Fireman Smith.

INTRODUCING AN IMPERSONATOR

By Richard Drummond

I believe everybody enjoys good impersonations, and I also believe that the impersonator we have as guest this evening is one of the best. Impersonation is an art. I had an uncle who was an impersonator. In fact, he made his living by doing impersonations. He would imitate worms. It took him a long time to learn it, but now he is an expert in making holes in antique furniture.

While in the family, I had a cousin that got the bright idea that he was a good imitator, but he soon got cured. He called on a new girl one evening. It was getting late, and he began boasting about his ability to imitate people and things. He told her he could imitate any bird that she could name. She said, "How about a homing pigeon?"

After introducing our guest I am going to impersonate an Arab and silently steal away. Friends, our impersonating guest, **(name.)**

INTRODUCING A MINSTREL SHOW

By Louis J. Huber

Ladies and gentlemen, please stand and I will present to you our next piece of entertainment. (They do this.) And now, ladies and gentlemen, be seated!

Aha, I've done it! If, by this time, you haven't become aware that we are to be entertained by members of a minstrel show, then I've wasted all my talent. And, ladies and gentlemen, I have so little of it that I can't afford to waste it. So please forgive me.

Do I hear you saying, to yourselves, what is a minstrel show? I do? Well, I've got good ears. I've also got a tongue and I'd better get on with the business at hand. The art of minstrelsy, ladies and gentlemen, goes back to the middle ages.

The word takes us back to the early days of the Mississippi River when show boats brought this type of entertainment to its banks.

I had an uncle who was in a show boat minstrel. He got into the business in a strange way. He was watching a show one day when they took him along. They thought he was part of the company. Poor Uncle Herman! If he had only washed when he came home from the mines that day, he might never have got into show business.

The time is here, folks, so hold your hats. I give you the minstrels with their dancing feet and clapping hands to beat out the rhythm of the South, with their voices blending in song and their singing to bring you forward in your seat as you strain to catch every single beautiful note. And here they are!

INTRODUCING AN OPERA STAR

By Forbes Milliken

Never before have we been honored to have with us such a prominent member of the opera stage.

When I was much younger and would vocalize in the bathtub I had dreams of someday doing the same thing on the opera stage—that is, without the bathtub. And, I might say, dressed differently. I remember one time I was singing something from "Ill Trovatore." I was absolutely bubbling over with harmony—I'd swallowed the soap. I always sang by ear, but unfortunately, that was the way the neighbors listened.

I finally got so I could sing "Faust" pretty good. I could either sing faust or slow. But my singing career began and ended in the bathtub. When I finally tried something from Carmen the neighbors called the fire department. They didn't know whether I was singing or scalding to death.

Ladies and gentlemen, it is my great privilege to present one of the greatest, if not the greatest, singers of today, **(name.)**

INTRODUCING A SCOTCH COMEDIAN

By Arthur L. Kaser

We haven't seen or heard many Scotch comedians since the famous Harry Lauder. However, we have a treat in store for us this evening. We have as our guest no other than the well-known **(name.)**

It isn't often that a Scotchman comes across with anything, but recently our guest's Uncle Jock came across—from Glasgow. He hadn't been here a week when he sued a baseball organization for injuries received while watching a ball game. He fell out of a tree. He couldn't see the game very well, anyway. He has only one eye. Later he went to a movie and demanded a half-price ticket because he had only one eye. The ticket seller said he should pay double price because it would take him twice as long to see the picture. But there are times when he can see pretty good with that one eye. He found a box of corn plasters on the street the other day and right away borrowed a pair of tight shoes. When he came to this country everybody on the boat got seasick except him. He didn't dare get seasick. He was holding a quarter between his teeth.

Our guest tells this one on himself. Some time ago he went to the races and bet a quarter on a ten to one shot, and won. The bookmaker paid him in quarters. Our friend picked up the quarters one at a time and bit them. "Just why are you biting them?" asked the bookmaker. "Do you think we are counterfeiters?" "No," said our guest. "I'm just making sure I'm not getting the one I gave you."

Now, ladies and gentlemen, the man who always takes his fountain pen to the bank for a transfusion, our Scotch comedian, **(name.)**

INTRODUCING A HUMORIST

By Louis J. Huber

Ladies and gentlemen, are there any of you with cracked lips? Are there any of you who have been ordered, by your doctor, not to laugh? If there are any in this gathering who will injure themselves by laughing, let them heed this warning: Get out.

The reason for this notice of danger is that our next form of entertainment will be a serious threat to anyone who is not allowed to laugh. We have with us, as your feature entertainer, a man who is known as a humorist. He is a man with a million funny stories. He is, as the French would say, a raconteur.

Ladies and gentlemen, there is a vast difference between a comedian and our kind of entertainer. A comedian can employ mannerisms and gestures and facial expressions and props to make his material funny. A story teller has only his material and his ability to put it over to you.

Our man stands at the top of his profession. But that does not deter me from telling a story about him. To bring it down to plain words: I have a story about our story teller.

This happened to him just the other day when he took his small son to the pet store. The object was to buy a dog. Our humorist, who is never one to pass up a chance for a pun, wanted a low-priced dog. The man at the store told him he had none at a small price but he did have some high-priced dogs at a bargain. Our man bought immediately and do you know why? He reasoned that a bargain dog never bites.

This, folks, gives you an idea of the kind of stories he does not tell. So you may hear the kind he does tell I ask him to take over immediately. Here he is, Mr. ————.

INTRODUCING A CELEBRITY

By Louis J. Huber

We now come to the moment, ladies and gentlemen, when I step forward to perform the most pleasant task of the evening. It is time for me to introduce our guest, a celebrity of whom you have all heard, one whom many of you have seen.

You would think that a person of his fame would need no introduction. You are wrong. Without introductions there would be no need for an emcee and without an emcee, where would you all be? Don't answer that question.

Being famous is not all fun, ladies and gentlemen, and I would like to prove this by telling a story that happened to our guest. He came home one night and found his wife with about twenty pictures of himself cut out of a newspaper. He was pleased that his spouse would think so highly of him. He explained that she didn't need to do this because he could furnish her with real pictures. Only then did he discover that she was not cutting out his picture, she was using the reverse side of the paper. It happened to be a free coupon for a can of scouring cleanser; she was saving them for her next trip to the store.

So, if he looks cleaner than other folks, you will know that he used some of the cleanser on himself. I proudly present to you that well-known celebrity, Mr. ———.

INTRODUCING AN AUTHORITY ON DIET

By Arthur L. Kaser

On our program this evening, ladies and gentlemen, is a man a good many of you already know. He hardly needs an introduction. Also, I think he is going to speak on a subject that you are more or less familiar with. It is the importance of correct diet.

Better health and longer life may be traced to correct dieting. Many people think they are dieting right when they are not. This kind of dieting does a lot for the will power but so little for the waistline.

It used to be that for the proper food it was "Back to the Farm" movement. Now it is "Back to the Form" movement. Nature, in a good many ways, is wonderful, but she did slip up on one thing — she put most of the beneficial vitamins into things we don't like.

However, our guest speaker will straighten you out on these points. So, listen closely, you people who are broad-shouldered all the way down. Ladies and gentlemen, Doctor **(name).**

INTRODUCING A JUGGLER

By Louis J. Huber

Our next act, ladies and gentlemen, comes from a section of the entertainment field that has always been a source of envy for me. Of all the different acts in show business this is the type that I would like to be doing.

I know a bit about juggling. There was the time I did it with some figures. When the auditors came around and checked the books they soon told me that it would take a sentence to put me on the right track. I heard that sentence. A certain judge said: You're guilty.

Juggling is one profession that differs from others in many ways. It is the one piece of business in which you must let your right hand know what your left hand is doing. Say, that's it! That's what I never did. I think I'll just try a small amount of juggling right now and use that system. No, I can't do it. My right hand is mad at my left hand and they don't get along well together.

So why don't I get on with the introduction? That's a good question and it deserves a good answer. I will get on with it. So I give you that juggling sensation who keeps a lot of things in the air and who is more than happy when they come down at the right place. Mr. ————.

INTRODUCING AN ENGLISH COMEDIAN

By Arthur L. Kaser

Our English comedian, whom we have the honor of introducing soon, tells me that comedy films dare not be shown in England on Saturday nights. They cause too much laughter in church on Sundays.

In some ways, our guest explains, it is more gratifying to play before an English audience than an American audience. An Englishman first laughs out of courtesy. Then when the rest of the audience gets the joke, and third, when he gets it himself. An American seldom laughs at all—he's heard it before.

Our guest is somewhat puzzled that there are so many Smiths in this country. He saw the Smithsonian Institute, and remarked: "Think of a building like that just to educate the Smiths." He was also amazed to see the construction of a mammoth electric sign in New York. He spoke to a policeman about it, and was informed that it was to contain 20,000 red lights, 17,000 blue lights, 10,000 white lights, and a central sunburst of orange and purple. "Most extraordinary," said our guest. "But won't it be a bit conspicuous?"

The English are a wonderful people but rather phlegmatic. My cousin tells about the time he was with the U. S. Army in England. He was invited to spend the weekend with an English family. By accident he opened the wrong door and happened in on the Mrs. taking a bath. Making a hurried retreat he sought out the host, who was reading in his room, and proffered his apologies. The host brought his head up out of the book, and remarked: "Skinny old thing, isn't she?"

Ladies and gentlemen, I am happy to have the privilege of presenting our English comedian, **(name.)**

INTRODUCING AN ACROBATIC GROUP

By Earl Jay Gilbert

Now, folks, we're going to see some wonderful acrobats. You know, those fellows who fly through the air with the greatest of ease. Naturally, to become a good acrobat a man has to work hard and practice to acquire skill and strength. Of course there are all kinds of acrobats. Some of them do their practicing in peculiar ways, like the golf acrobat. That's the fellow who gets so much exercise trying to get into a proper stance to hit the ball that he winds up all tied up in knots like a Polish pretzel. It takes two other players and the caddy master to untie him.

This reminds me of the fellow who had never played golf before. He made a hole in one the first time he hit the ball. He teed the ball up again and drove for the second hole. The ball landed on the edge of the green, slowly rolled toward the hole, hesitated on the rim of the cup for a moment, then dropped in. The fellow mopped his brow and said: "Whew! I was afraid for a moment that I'd missed it this time!"

The wives of these golf acrobats are known as golf widows. One of them said to her husband: "You spend so much of your time playing golf that you don't even remember the date of our wedding anniversary." "I'll never forget it," he said. "That's the day I won twenty-two dollars for sinking a forty-foot putt."

That guy will cover more mileage marching around that cow pasture than a Marine recruit will drilling in boot camp. But if his wife asks him to go out and mail a letter—brother, is he hurt! "What? You want me to walk clear down to the corner? You know the doctor told me to take it easy!"

Then there's the tennis acrobat. Is he a pip! He'll get out on a tennis court on the hottest day of the year with a pair of cutie-pie short pants on and practically knock himself out jumping and leaping and twisting and turning and smashing at the ball with a boy's size snow-shoe and consider that he's having a nice little workout.

But let his wife ask him to go out and mow the lawn—boy, does he yell murder! "What? You expect me to go out in this weather and cut grass? Why, in this heat I'd collapse with a sunstroke in two minutes!" The thought of doing any actual work runs his blood pressure up so high his wife has to put cold cloths on his head and feed him cooling drinks. He might have the right idea at that.

And take the dining table acrobat. He gets all his exercise when he eats. He sits down, spreads his elbows on the table and starts his calisthenics. He'll reach clear over to the other side of the table and spear a chunk of bread. He'll lay it on his palm (Illustrate with the palm up.) and smear about a quarter of a pound of butter on it. Then he doubles his hand up (Illustrate.), gets a firm grip on it and he has a nice squashy bread and butter sandwich which he demolishes in two bites.

Then he bends his head down close to his plate and really starts to work. He gets a strangle hold on his knife and starts shoveling food into his mouth as if he were stoking coal into a factory furnace. He eats with his mouth open. You can hear him champing and chewing a block away. To the clicking of his teeth he adds a little obligato of gurgles and grunts and groans of satisfaction. You see food flying through the air and disappearing into that capacious cavern. He never misses! He's a wizard with the knife!

By the way, I understand the Knife Swallowers Association has a new racket. They dip their peas in honey. They say it tastes kind of funny, but no peas can roll off the knife.

This reminds me of a certain political leader from Buffalo (or any rival city) who was invited to a banquet here in our fair city. He was industriously using his knife when one of his dinner companions called his attention to the fact that most of the other diners were using their forks to convey their food to their mouths. He looked around, watched for a few moments, then picked up his fork awkwardly and tried it himself. He said with a pleased smile: "Say, that ain't bad. I'm goin' to start this gag back in Buffalo!" (Or a rival city.)

Now, while it is generally understood that the natives of Buffalo (or a rival city) are not inclined to accept any startling, new-fashioned innovations—although I have heard that some of them have secretly installed telephones in their tepees—I have been told that since this politician returned home, the use of the fork in eating has become quite a fad among certain of the upper classes there. Which could be true. Almost anything can happen in Buffalo. (Or a rival city.)

However, there are many other kinds of acrobats in addition to those I've mentioned—including the real acrobats, like those who are going to entertain us tonight, which makes me think of the acrobat who told a theatrical agent: "I have a wonderful act. I dive head first from a hundred-foot tower into three inches of sawdust." The agent went to look at the act. Sure enough the acrobat dived one hundred feet from a platform and landed on his head in a small pile of sawdust. The agent was highly enthusiastic. He offered the acrobat five thousand a week, but the guy said: "I've kinda changed my mind about doing this act. You see, that's the first time I ever tried it."

Now, I don't know whether the group you're going to see now has ever tried that stunt or not, but at any rate they have some really skillful and dangerous tricks to show you which I know you'll like and appreciate. While their stunts are original, they have very generously given their permission for you to try any of them in your parlor sometime. So let's show them we're glad to see them. Here they are, the ——————!

INTRODUCING AN AMATEUR THEATRICAL

By Richard Drummond

Tonight we have the opportunity of seeing local talent upon our stage.

Ah, the good old amateur show. There is nothing that is more fun—mixed with a lot of hard work—than getting up an amateur show. When I was younger I tried to push myself into every amateur entertainment that came along. Once or twice I was let in.

I'll never forget the night we put on "Uncle Tom's Cabin." I was Uncle Tom. I rehearsed the part of that old man so long I had rheumatism for six weeks after. We couldn't find any bloodhounds so we had to use a couple of pointers. All they did was point at the audience. We tried to teach them that to point was impolite, but you know dogs. Anyway, the play moved along rather sluggishly, most of us forgot our lines and had to be prompted.

Some of those in the audience decided they had more important business elsewhere and left. Finally groups left. Then everybody rose to go. Little Eva ran out on the stage, and yelled, "Remember, women and children first!" The curtain went down with Liza sitting on a cake of ice. She was the only one that made an impression.

I know you all are anxious to see our young people in action, so up with the curtain, and **(name of production.)**

INTRODUCING A FIRE PREVENTION SPEAKER

By Arthur L. Kaser

This being Fire Prevention Week we have invited one of our city firemen to give us some advice on how to prevent fires. It is said that fire can be man's best friend or his worst enemy.

A lady here in town—you might know her—called the fire station, and said: "I've just had some landscaping done on my place—" The man at the fire station interrupted her. "This is the fire station."

Ignoring him, the lady continued: "There are some expensive shrubs and new plants—" Again she was interrupted. "Where is the fire?" She couldn't be stopped. "The way it is now, the yard is beautiful, and—"

"Lady," said the man, "what you want is the flower shop." "I do not want the flower shop," snapped the lady. "I just want to tell you I don't want your men to trample over everything I've had planted. Now, please hurry. My house is on fire!"

INTRODUCING A GARDENER

By Louis J. Huber

Folks, our speaker this day is a man who has many accomplishments to his credit. But he has a hobby about which I would like to tell you before I present him to you. He is an amateur gardener.

What is an amateur gardener? No one has been able to supply that answer up to this time. We would like to try it. He is a man who can keep warm by looking at a seed catalog in the middle of winter.

Our speaker, despite the fact that we sound as though we are trying to minimize his hobby, has had great success with his gardening. There was the time he crossed an ear of corn with a pod of peas and completed this by adding a stalk of tomatoes. He waited for it to grow and develop. It did. Are you wondering what grew? You guessed it—succotash.

At another time our speaker planted a small seed which he did not recognize. It was a great disappointment to him when he had to uncover them again. It turned out that they were a small headache pill that the doctor had prescribed for his wife. Another time he planted a seed and can you guess what came up? The sparrows and they ate every one of them.

That, folks, is the hobby our speaker has developed so be happy you came to hear him. Mr. ————.

INTRODUCING A JUGGLER

By A. Guy Visk

(The emcee enters, carrying binoculars. He is looking up at the sky. Suddenly, he closes one eye and pretends to wipe something from his eye.)

It came from outer space, from the picture of the same name. (Laughs.) It must be the mating season at Capistrano. How do you do, ladies and gentlemen? My name is ———, I'm an official Flying Saucer Observer. Here's my badge. (Opens his coat and reveals a saucer dangling from a string attached to the inside of his coat.) That's one that missed me.

Three years ago I was appointed by the government to watch the skies. I was to notify Washington as soon as I saw any strange goings-on in the sky. Of course, I never did tell them about the time a friend of mine took his girl up for an airplane ride. Well, if you kept your head in the sky for three years your mind would be cloudy, too.

Tonight I have come prepared to bring you the truth about flying saucers . . . what they look like . . . where they come from . . . and how they get here. I have proof! I swear this on a stack of Johnnie Walker Black Labels.

A flying saucer is an object hurled through space by some great force. I know this for a fact . . . that's just the way I feel when some bartender tosses me out of his joint.

The majority of flying saucers are spotted in the month of August, and right around Labor Day. Just when the tourist trade is the strongest. The saucers are piloted by people from other planets who have two weeks' vacation and just want to get away from it all. These people are over nine feet tall and have a low I.Q. And if that isn't the height of stupidity, I don't know what is.

They would look exactly like us except for one small detail. Their eyeballs curve outward! This is definite proof that they are pioneers in 3-D movies.

The people from outer space do not wear clothes. They go about wearing radio-active fig leaves. Up there, a man wouldn't be safe with a girl unless he was carrying a Geiger counter. Of course, the girls down here are quite active, too. I was out with a girl last night and believe me, I had to have a Geiger counter for my Geiger counter.

And now, ladies and gentlemen, (Drum rolls) a few days ago I sent an official report to the Pentagon in Washington, D. C., stating that I have captured the world's first flying saucer. In a few hours, they are going to send a man out to pick me up, I mean pick it up. (Laughs) Before that man arrives, I want to show you what a flying saucer looks like. If the ushers will kindly guard all the exits, I will uncrate the only flying saucer in captivity.

(The emcee moves over to a large box previously placed on the stage. The following sayings are conspicuously painted on the box: "TOP SECRET" — "THIS END UP" — "FLYING SAUCER—DO NOT DROP." The emcee reaches into the box and slowly pulls out the "flying saucer." The saucer is a toilet seat complete with a lid. The lid is painted silver with black lettering, "EARTH OR BUST." The emcee shows this to the audience. He lifts the lid to reveal the multi-colored seat. The seat is painted red and white in target fashion.)

Contrary to popular belief, this is a one-man flying saucer. You won't believe this, but where this thing comes from, they have space ships in the bathrooms. The fascinating thing about this gadget is the safety device. It cannot operate with the lid pushed forward . . . repercussions, you know. The pilot sits here and controls the ship by thought waves. In fact, that's how I happened to capture this saucer. The pilot let his mind wander!

I'm sorry, but it's getting late and I have to hurry home and drop my brother a line. Every time I do this act, he falls through!

However, it now gives me great pleasure to present a most amazing fellow who really knows a lot about saucers. He doesn't spot them, he juggles them. Here he is, ——————.

INTRODUCING A RETIRING TEACHER
(Upper Grades)

By Arthur L. Kaser

Our hero—Yes, I mean just that. Any teacher, man or woman, who can teach hundreds and hundreds of upper grade students through so many years, and can come through with body intact and still in his right mind, must be a hero. Such a person, in my estimation, is the hero we are honoring today.

When I was a senior in high school we had an instructor in science that had weathered the storm for many years. We liked him. For one thing, he knew how and when to ease the tension in the class when the subject became too involved and intricate. I remember one morning he realized that the students were beginning to show the strain of constant concentration, and decided to ease the situation with a rather pointless question. He said: "If a chair has five legs and is painted purple, and is rigged with sails, how old am I?" We sat amazed at such a question. After a pause the most backward student in the class said meekly: "Forty-four." It was the instructor's turn to be dumbfounded. "Why, that is correct," he said. "How did you ever arrive at that figure?" "Easy," said the youth. "My brother is twenty-two, and he's only half crazy."

Another time, our instructor announced: "This afternoon we are going to experiment on a frog. We are going to find out what makes it croak." It was the same backward student I spoke of that interrupted the instructor. "My uncle croaked and we found out why he croaked. He had a bad heart." The instructor tried to overlook the interruption, and continued: "In other words, we are going to dissect a frog. I have a frog in my pocket." He reached into his pocket and drew out a paper bag which he emptied on the table. Out rolled a badly squashed sandwich. The instructor paled. "My, oh, my! Oh, my!" he stammered. "I distinctly remember eating my lunch!"

It was nearing the end of the school year. Our instructor was delivering the final lecture of the term. He dwelt with much emphasis on the fact that each student should devote all the intervening time preparing for the final exam. "The examination papers are now in the hands of the printer," he said. "Are there any questions?" A voice from the rear inquired: "Who's the printer?"

Now, my friends, we all owe this retiring teacher much. Let us demonstrate just how much with a big hand of applause.

INTRODUCING A CHORUS

By Vance Clifford

There are a couple of boys here this evening who are pretty nervous. They were held up by stage robbers. Yes, sir, stage robbers. They took a couple of chorus girls to dinner.

A college girl gets her education by degrees. The chorus girl by stages.

A chorus girl is one who never worries about getting ahead because she doesn't need one.

Pity the poor chorus girl who got nine bouquets at the last performance, and she had paid for ten.

The only thing they have in some towns in the way of a good show is a censor.

"So you want a job in the chorus?"

"Yes, my mother says I sing beautifully."

"Bring a recommendation from your neighbors and I'll give you a tryout."

A chorus girl fell one time while rehearsing a new routine, and broke her leg. Her doctor put it in a cast, and warned her not to walk up or down any stairs for three months. At the end of that time the chorine went back to the doctor. He took off the cast, and she asked, "Now can I climb up and down the stairs?" "Yes, you can now," said the doctor. "Oh, I'm sure glad," the girl said. "It was sure tough, me going outside and shinnying up and down that drainpipe all the time."

And now, on with the show.

INTRODUCING A COMEDIAN

By A. Guy Visk

And that, ladies and gentlemen, was television's answer to 3-D movies. TV was looking for a new illusion so they hired him. He has his own show. He comes on every morning just before the test pattern.

Back home the folks used to go for him in a big way. In fact, five hundred of them escorted him across the state line. Of course, he managed to keep a little ahead of them all the way. The home-town folks really loved that chap. In fact, he was their pride and joy. It's the truth. Before 3-D movies came into their own, he was the only eye-sore they had.

Folks always said he was a natural for 3-D. They claimed he had an added dimension. He was an idiot!

Not so long ago, Hollywood filmed his life story. Perhaps you were among the lucky three who saw it. It was called, "Creature From the Black Lagoon." His part in the film was portrayed by another actor. Of course, they only used the actor's first and second dimensions. His third dimension was dubbed in. The picture was so successful, they made a sequel to it and included his entire family. You might have seen this one, too. It was called, "Them." That was the picture that put an end to his movie career. His relatives stole the picture from him. They could crawl faster.

INTRODUCING A CHOIR OR CHORUS

By Louis J. Huber

Ladies and gentlemen, you are about to hear one of the finest musical organizations of its kind. In my humble opinion there has never been any instrument that can produce the sweet music of the instrument that they use: the human voice.

If you take a quick glance into your past musical delights you might immediately think of a violin and you would be perfectly right in saying that it is beautiful music. But the violin was put in the hand of the musician by another human being, the violin maker.

A choir and a chorus does not rely on human ingenuity, on human mechanisms. They give to the world their beautiful music with an instrument put there by the hand of the Creator.

It is not as simple as it sounds. After it was put there the recipient of the gift had to work to refine it. Many hours of practice are needed to put this gift of God into its finished stage. We all have voices, but only a few of us can use them in such work.

I bring to you such a group. The blending of voices that will make you wish you could do likewise, the **(Name of the chorus or choir.)**

INTRODUCING A DANCING ACT

By Louis J. Huber

Ladies and gentlemen, we come to the part of our program that will stay with you for a long time. We come to an act that follows in the footsteps of Terpsichore. This word, just to refresh your memory, was one of the Muses in mythology, the originator and patroness of the art of dancing.

Which is just a long way of saying that our next act is a dance team. (Or solo act.) It is the kind of an act that makes you feel younger if you are old and if you are young—you just want to get into it yourself.

I have been asked to get into the act, ladies and gentlemen, and I would have done it except for one small fact. It so happens that I was born with two left feet and I would prove that if someone gives me permission to take off my shoes.

Please don't insist on it. You can see the same thing in a circus sideshow. Let us get back to the act, you'll be more pleased with it. The act that will make you wish that you could do likewise, the dance team that will make you feel the rhythm of their dance in your own bones. I give you **(Name of team or soloist)**.

INTRODUCING A VENTRILOQUIST

By Louis J. Huber

Ladies and gentlemen, we are about to hear a form of entertainment that goes back many years. Not that this particular entertainer goes back that far but the type of amusement that he brings to us carries with it the astonishment of many generations.

Our next act features a ventriloquist. Now that I've come right to the point there wouldn't be much use in just saying "here he is" unless I would also give you a brief thought on his act.

Ventriloquism, as many of you know, is the art of speaking and making the listeners believe that the sound comes from another person or from another place. I'll let you in on a small secret. I know how to do this even better than the man you are about to hear.

The secret of ventriloquism is breathing properly and then exercising the larynx and palate. It's such a simple matter that anyone can do it. First, we must all learn how to breathe. Like this. (Deep breath.) That's all there is to the first part of the trick.

Since we all have a voice it is also easy to use that. Try this sentence: Lend me five dollars, lend me five dollars, lend me five dollars. Just like that. If you find anyone who is willing to lend you that much money you are on your way to success. If you can find ten thousand people who are going to do it, you will have fifty thousand dollars and—what am I saying? Oh, yes, to get away from finances and back to ventriloquism.

I shall now give you a practical demonstration of how a good master of the art plies his trade. This is the type of thing that drives an ordinary craftsman to learning the plumbing business.

Let me explain just a bit further before I show you what I mean. Most men who make a dummy do the talking hold him on their knee. Very simple. I do it in a much harder manner. My dummy is stationed offstage as you will hear. Now for the act. Listen to this and be astounded.

Ready! (Calls offstage.) Is there anyone in the house who would like to buy my dinner? (From offstage a voice answers.) What would you like for dinner? (Calls again.) I'll have some baked beans. (From offstage comes the next sentence.) Coming up as soon as I can find the can opener.

Sounds a lot like that might be my wife answering but it gives you a rough idea of how simple the whole thing is and how easily it can be done. There were times when I was working at this game when I was stopped. Those were the times when I asked questions to which I didn't know the answer. They were mighty embarrassing times. Let me show you how a thing like that can happen. This time I shall again throw my voice offstage.

Here we go! (Calls off.) Hello, out there, answer me. (Voice off.) I am ready to supply all the answers. (Calls again.) Do you have a pitcher out there? (Answer.) Yes, I do. (Calls.) Does it have a handle? (Answer.) Yes, it does. (Calls.) On which side is the handle? (Returns.) On the outside, you dope.

Someone is asking for trouble, ladies and gentlemen, so I'll give them a chance to get into it. Watch this now. (Calls off.) Is the next act ready for presentation? (From off.) Yes, it is. (Calls.) The next act is one of the best in the game of throwing a voice. This man is known as **(Name of the act.)** and he is now on this show. Ladies and gentlemen, here he is! (The ventriloquist appears.)

INTRODUCING A MIND READER

By Louis J. Huber

So step right up close, ladies and gentlemen, and permit me to act as your emcee for the next act that is to be presented for your enjoyment and entertainment. You are about to be introduced to Madam Zaza, the most famous mind reader in the world.

(Softly) Step in close, please, as I want to tell you something about this act, something that Madam Zaza must not hear. Even if you do not have a mind you won't be wasting your money. Because she can read a mind even where there is no mind. I know because she read mine.

(Louder) What am I saying? I am saying that behind this curtain you will be mystified by the mind-reading sensation of the nation. Permit her to gaze into your eyes and from their depths she will transfer what she sees into her crystal ball.

Then allow her to gaze into that same crystal ball and she will bring forth the readings that will amaze you. Permit me to give a small demonstration of the things you will hear behind this curtain. Madam Zaza has taught me several of her mind-reading secrets and I have her permission to use them. You, young man, will you permit me to try them on you? Thank you, sir.

Now then, think of a number between one and ten. You have it, sir. Now don't tell me what it is. Let me read your mind? Is it odd or even? Odd? Odd, let me see. One? Three? Five? Seven? Nine? Aha, that's it. Nine is the number. You see, folks, how easy it is to read a mind. But there is more.

Let me tell you the mysterious ways in which Madam Zaza operates. Just yesterday we had a young man go into her realm. Madam took his hand and held it tightly. He asked a question. He wanted to know what had become of his long lost brother.

What did Madam do? What did she tell him? She had to admit that she didn't know but she did tell him something. She assured him that he had eggs for breakfast because some of it was still on his upper lip. A man with a moustache should never eat eggs.

As a palmist Madam Zaza has also had a fair share of success. She can take the hand of an average human being and tell you exactly what you are thinking. One day she took the hand of a man and she quickly said one dollar. She knew the man was wondering what it was going to cost him to have his palm read by the great Madam Zaza.

Madam won't need to tell you the price because I will do it for you. For one dollar, for one millionth of a million dollars, you can have the thrill and pleasure of gazing into the future. And if you are not satisfied with the future you may pay another dollar and Madam Zaza will permit you to gaze into your past. And if your past has been like mine you will be glad to pay another dollar to forget the whole thing.

It is quite a money-making scheme but it all goes to charity and, as most of you know, charity begins at home. Since I am at home right here you might think that I have a deep interest in the money. I do have. I am interested in making it and turning it over to a worthy cause.

I am also interested in seeing you good people go behind this curtain and have Madam Zaza predict your future. You can't go wrong; you must go right. So step right up and be mystified, be thrilled, be chilled. And if you are chilled, Madam Zaza will be glad to tell you where you can buy a blanket at half-price. Provided, of course, she gets her ten per cent commission. Which is also turned over to charity. So step up and open your mind and your wallet as the great Madam Zaza goes into action!

INTRODUCING SHARPSHOOTERS

By Louis J. Huber

Ladies and gentlemen, we come to the choice part of the evening's entertainment. I made this announcement in exactly thirteen words and this is all that would be needed to further the program.

But I also made a claim and it is up to me to prove what I have just said. I told you that it was the choice part of the evening's program. How am I going to prove it? By letting some of you folks get into the act.

The act which we are about to show you, folks, is sometimes forbidden in many parts of the country. It consists of a demonstration of sharpshooting. A firearm in the hands of an incapable person can be a dangerous thing. Tonight the gun is at the shoulder of a master of his craft. This man has been fully shot and he has been half-shot—what am I saying? I'd better get back to a previous line.

I told you that this type of act is sometimes forbidden. This is done because it is a dangerous bit of business. When a man with a rifle is aiming at the cigarette you hold in your teeth there can be many tragic consequences. Let's put it this way: Suppose the sharpshooter is aiming at the cigarette and then he notices that it is not the right brand. What could happen? Well, he might ask you to change brands and he might go on with the act and miss the target and there would be your little nose and—oh, it could be hardly any nose at all if he aimed too close.

I mention these things, ladies and gentlemen, to gladden the hearts of some lucky person within the hearing of my voice. As I hinted previously, one of you very fortunate listeners is going to get into this act. I shall shortly call for a volunteer.

Before I do this I want to make clear the part that will be

yours when you raise your hand. First, you will be asked to hold a tooth brush between your pretty white teeth. This brush will be covered with toothpaste. Our sharpshooter will aim his gun, knock the brush out of your mouth. In doing this he will also put a crease in your lip—no, I mean that he will also clean your teeth. So you can see that nothing is being wasted.

There is still another part of the act in which some lucky individual will participate. You've all heard of William Tell? This is a feature entitled, William Don't Tell. It is an odd title because it carries with it a certain request. The participant will be asked to put an apple on his head just as William asked his son to do those many years ago in Switzerland. Our sharpshooter will then take aim and fire. If he hits the apple there will be a small amount of apple juice wasted but that can't be helped. If he doesn't hit the apple the act will be called William Don't Tell. It's as simple as that. We know that William won't tell because William won't be able to tell. He'll be busy running away from the sheriff and the lucky holder of the apple won't tell either because he'll be . . .

Now let me have a show of hands to find out which one of you lucky folks will be a part of this act. Remember that you won't need to do any work. All you need to do is to put this apple on your head, close your eyes and hope. If you are able to open those eyes again, you'll know that the session was a success. If you aren't able to open them again you will know that—now who among you would like to take part in this show? (He keeps asking. If anyone should volunteer they are asked to go back home and bring their own apple. In some shows the expert's assistant can be planted in the audience.) And now, since we have an assistant, a brave and fearless person, let me introduce Mr. Rifleman, who will give you a demonstration of nerve and skill and ability to handle a gun. Mr. ——————.

INTRODUCING A SWIMMING-DIVING ACT

By Louis J. Huber

As we stand at the edge of this beautiful pool of water, ladies and gentlemen, I am reminded of something. Would one of the ushers please come over here? (An usher responds and the emcee whispers in his ear. The usher nods and leaves.) As I was saying, folks, I was reminded of something and I just now took care of that matter. I asked that usher to call my home and remind them that I forgot to turn off the faucet in the bathroom. Which, in itself is not a bad deed, but I forgot whether or not I took the plug out of the bottom.

Please permit me to start over, folks. As your master of ceremonies I come to you with clean hands. I washed them in this pool just before the show was ready to open. I also come with clean hands because we have for you one of the most astonishing acts in the entertainment field. We have a swimming and diving team that has no equals.

There is something about this type of entertainment, ladies and gentlemen, that makes you feel that you'd like to trade places with the performers. The grace of their movements, the rhythm of their styles, the smoothness of their actions. All this brings into a focus a part of the entertainment world that has no competitors because it is in a class by itself. (Looks at his hands.) I told you that I come with clean hands but I am mistaken. I must have dirtied them when I washed my face.

But, be that as it may, the show must go on. So I come to you with dirty hands but I still carry with me a grand entertainment. This is an act that is the envy of all the fish.

Did I say fish? I did. Now there is the place for me to digress for a moment and talk about fish. I do this because the folks in this act learned their trade by watching the finny fellows in action. This is not generally known and I am divulging it at a great risk.

Do you know what a fish really is? A fish is a cold-blooded, chordate or vertebrate animal, adapted for life in the water, breathing by means of gill slits all its life, having its limbs, if present, developed as fins. Now, there!

The next time you have fish for dinner remember all those things and you will be glad to go back to bacon and eggs or even stewed cabbage. Now we go back to fish. There are a lot of different kinds of fish but we shall take time to discuss only a few of them.

First I would like to discuss a wide-mouthed Bess. This is not to be confused with wide-mouthed bass; there is a great difference. Wide-mouthed bass is the same as small-mouthed bass except that one has a slightly larger opening for taking on a load of food. We now come to wide-mouthed Bess. Wide-mouthed Bess is a girl I dated one time. I never knew where she got her name until I tried to kiss her and then the trouble started. She puckered and I puckered. I was amazed. Her pucker started at one ear and went right around her face to the other ear. I never did get to kiss her because I learned, right then and there, why they called her wide-mouthed Bess.

Enough of this talking about fish. Rather, let us meet some humans who have all the facilities that are attributed to the finny tribe. I give you those wizards of the water, those sons of the spring board who will make you forget me and my dirty hands as soon as they hit the first drop and make the first splash. Folks, greet and meet the **(Name of act.)**

INTRODUCING A MUSICAL ACT

By George A. Posner

Have **we** got a show tonight! Have **we** got a show tonight!! (Looks back of the curtain.) Hey, answer me, you fellows! Have we got a show tonight? . . . We have a show, I **guess.**

Oh, I see, this is a program they gave me. I thought it was a menu, or something. Got it from a guy in a full dress suit and thought he was a waiter.

It says that the first thing we have is an instrumentalist. Well! I used to be an instrumentalist as a kid. At least, that's what my father said. I thought I was a singer, but my father always introduced me as an **instrumental** musician. When they'd call him on that, and say: "Mister, if your son sings, that isn't instrumental music," my father would answer: "Yes, it is; it was instrumental in making half the neighborhood move!"

Oh, he was sharp! By the way, isn't it funny how they'll say a person is talking **sharply** when he's blunt? And that he's **blunt** when he comes quickly to the point?

It was my mother, really, who had the ambition to make a musician out of me. She even wanted to send me to Europe to complete my musical education. And there was something the neighbors—what was left of them—highly favored. Do you know, they soon had a big collection made—for a one-way ticket. "Deportation," I think they termed it.

Along with the singing, Mother even thought I ought to take speaking lessons. Voice culture. "We're cultivating his voice," she'd proudly tell the neighbors. "Cultivating?" I remember one neighbor saying. "Sounded like it was **harrowing** to me!"

Well, my teachers seemed to agree at least that I was talented. My speaking teacher thought I would make a great **singer,** while my singing teacher thought I would make a great **speaker.**

I remember a neighbor asking my mother one day: "How's

your son coming along with his speaking lessons?" And she answered: "Fine! Just fine! All he now needs is a short course in electrocution—to sort of finish him up!" Of course she had it a little mixed up—I **think**!

Yes, our family was a family of musicians from away back. The farther back we were, the better people liked it. I might say I could claim a musical background of a sort—my father used to spank me with his mandolin. He really picked on me. I shouldn't have stood for it. But I did. Even for my meals, I stood.

I don't know why Dad was so critical, really. Judging from the way **he** was doing. He played in a string quartet. I remember a musical review which came out in a paper one morning after he played a concert. It read: "An amateur string quartet played Brahms last night. Brahms lost."

I remember the first show in which I appeared, as a vocalist. The emcee announced: "A boy soprano who will do a solo." And some so-called wag out in the audience shouted: "If he's a soprano, mister, how can he sing 'so—low'."

Gosh, I never saw so many vegetables as I did that night. I finally figured it out. It was this: The act ahead of me was so bad, and the fellow got away so fast, those vegetables were still coming when I got on the stage. That must have been it. It couldn't have been my voice, of course.

Didn't a musical critic once tell me: Caruso had some voice, but mine is better still?

Anyway, that was the night the family decided to turn vegetarian. We were in clover—and cabbages—for a long time after that.

I was very sensitive about that night. Whenever it came up, and anyone asked me about it, I always said: "Oh, I stopped the show." That was true; it was the last performance.

But they didn't stop me. Ambition egged me on, even if sometimes the audience egged me off. The show must go on! The theater was my living. And soon I was bringing home the bacon—sometimes with tomatoes, cabbages, and what not. People differ—you can't please everyone.

I'll never forget the night a big shoe was thrown and landed within just an inch of me there on the stage. It scared me so, I started for the wings. But my father grabbed me, and shoved me back on the stage while he hissed: "Keep on until you get the other one!"

After a while I added tap dancing to my act, or "repertoire," as we called it in Boston. You know—tap dancing around the stage? It makes a much harder target! I even added cartwheels, hand springs, flip flops. Everything! Some of it was spur-of-the-moment, I'll confess. But none of your static, or stately dances, like the Mombo or the Rhumba. Where you're practically standing still—with only your backfield in motion. (As the football people would say). Or, as someone else aptly put it, "where the front of you glides along smooth like a Cadillac, while the back part of you makes like a Jeep"—no, sir, none of that! One would practically be a sitting duck. How can you duck when you're a duck?

Anyway, that's why I'm still here. I gave the audiences plenty of action for their money—that is, I always presented a moving target. I might say I got ahead by leaps and bounds.

And so our musical family toured about the country for a long time—another healthy habit, when they were laying for us in the cities. We got along. Oh, we had our quarrels. But Dad quickly patched things up again—my nose, my lips, my jaw!

All we wanted was the chance to express ourselves. And we did, although often it was on the brake beams of the trains. And by request!

But enough of me and my family—let's get on with the show. Ladies and gentlemen, it is my extreme good pleasure to present to you the first act on our program, some young, good-looking, and truly talented musicians—and here they are!

INTRODUCING A HIGH SCHOOL SYMPHONY ORCHESTRA

By Sidney Steele

With us this evening is the (name of high school) Sympathy—Pardon me—Symphony Orchestra. We should feel very proud of this organization, proud of the students who participate, and proud of their very capable conductor, Mr. (name of conductor.)

I remember my high school days, and the high school orchestra in particular. That orchestra brings back one high spot that I will never forget. The orchestra was giving a concert for the parents of the high school students. The musicians were treading very carefully through a delicate passage when the drummer gave out with a terrific bang on his drum. The conductor stopped the music and glared at the embarrassed drummer. The poor boy leaned forward and looked closely at the music. Then everyone in the auditorium heard him mutter: "Darn those flies!"

I think it was during the same concert when the orchestra was thunderously loud. Suddenly there fell an abrupt and complete silence, beginning a brief but absolute rest in the music. Out of the stillness there came a high-pitched feminine voice. "But," it said, "I always fry mine in lard."

If I am not mistaken it was, also, the same evening the orchestra was on the stage playing Beethoven's "Leonore" overture, the two climaxes of which are each followed by a trumpet passage offstage. The first climax came, but not a sound emanated from the trumpet player in the wings. The conductor, annoyed, went on to the second. Again there was silence in the wings. The overture, being finished, the conductor rushed backstage. There he found the trumpet player still arguing with the janitor. "I tell you," the janitor was saying, "you can't toot that horn back here. There's a concert going on!"

Ladies and gentlemen, the (name of school) Orchestra, playing **(name of piece.)**

INTRODUCING AN AMATEUR SHOW

By Louis J. Huber

My friends: Unaccustomed as I am to public speaking, nevertheless it behooves me at this time to say a few words in behalf of my candidate. My candidate happens to be me—what am I saying? I'm sorry, people, I was carried away by the thought of addressing such a grand and glorious assemblage.

Actually, it was just a sneaky way of opening my mouth and having something to say without touching the topic of the evening with my very first sentence. But I must do that sometime so I had better do it now.

I've been chosen to act as your master of ceremonies for the amateur show that is to be presented this evening. I know that some of you will think that they made a wise choice in choosing an amateur emcee to introduce an amateur show. If any of you had that thought I want you to hang your heads and repeat after me: I am sorry that I was wrong. I should have stood in bed and let my left leg on the front doorstep near the waterplug.

Now that we've gone over a few things that do not make sense let us get to the part that will. The folks that you are about to see on the stage are those who have a deep desire to be in show business or they would not be here. They are just like you and me and this night they are going to achieve a burning ambition—the ability to display their wares and to have you, by your applause, tell them that they have done a good job.

Before I go into the actual introductions it might be well to tell you a few things that will be done here this evening. It isn't always that the master of ceremonies let's the audience in on the details of the show.

Many of you have seen the various types of performers that can be expected at this type of show. You have seen, for example, the man who imitates animals. Tonight we are going to be different. We are going to have animals that will imitate human beings.

What's that? (Speaking offstage.) I didn't hear you. (Pretends to listen again.) Oh, that is too bad. Ladies and gentlemen, I've made an error and I apologize for it. I announced that there would be animals who would imitate a human being. It seems that this is not to be. It seems that the animals refuse to do this. And in return they want all humans to promise that they will not try to imitate animals.

I'm afraid that there is one person here present who cannot make and keep this promise. This person has consented to imitate an animal and he must go through with it. The name of this individual happens to be (His own name.) and it is part of his contract. Oh, that's me.

Yes, I've consented to do an animal imitation for you good folks here this evening. All this and the rest of the entertainment too. Now let me see, which animal shall I imitate? Will you people help me out? Which animal would you have me imitate? Oh, a dog? That's great, it's one of my best acts. I will now imitate a dog. (He scratches himself.) Yes, I am doing two animals. A dog and his flea. It's quite an accomplishment.

Enough of this fiddle-faddle. We move on to the people who are really going to entertain you, the amateurs who are a part of this show. I know you will find that many of them deserve professional billing and that some of them, given the right opportunity, will get it in due time. Until then they are amateurs. Like the pros, they like applause. The more you warm your hands the more you warm their hearts. Don't be stingy with the noise. Here is the first act of your amateur show, **(Name.)**

INTRODUCING A STRONG MAN

By Louis J. Huber

It is my purpose at this time, ladies and gentlemen, to bring you the feature act of the evening. I'll get right down to the point and tell you of what it consists. It is an act commonly known as a strong-man show in the entertainment field.

Since this is a case of the weak introducing the strong I would like to remind you that I have not always been a weakling. There was a time when my feats of power caused many sighs of astonishment. At one time I was able to resist the combined efforts of many people and then—ah, yes, then I got married.

Allow me to tell you of some of my great performances before I weakened. My greatest strength was in my jaws. If some of you think that I still have a certain amount of this left, you are correct. My wife tells me that I have the strongest jaws she has ever seen especially when someone else is trying to get a word in edgewise. Now there is one of my attainments. I have such great power that not even a woman can get in a word, not even a woman with a very sharp tongue.

However, that is not the incident that I wish to relate. I'd like to tell you about the time I kept my jaws closed so tightly that it seemed no one could open them. I held them that way for four days. Then I got hungry and the dentist, who had been waiting with his drill, got the chance against which I had been fighting for these four days.

But it is in mental strength where I actually excel. Almost anyone can attain physical power by exercising and developing his muscles. I did this with my mental muscles and I shall show you what I mean. Take this example.

I want all of you people to see if you can keep up with me in this terrific test of mental agility. Here we go. A bus left the garage with no passengers aboard; only the driver and he is not counted as a passenger. At the first stop they took on ten passengers, at the next stop two of them left the bus. At the following stop two more entered the bus (I happened to be one of them) and at the very next corner there were three who got aboard. The driver turned the corner and stopped to allow one more to enter. At the same time there were two who got off the bus by the rear door. Coming down the main street the driver stopped once more and this time two passengers left by the front exit. He stopped long enough for a man, who was running down the street, to come aboard.

As I looked at my watch I saw that it was three-fifteen and that I would be late for that appointment with the dentist so I decided to get off the bus. The driver stopped. Do you know how many people were on the bus before I made my exit? You do? Just shows how good your subtraction and addition happens to be. But that is not the test of mental agility. I am not going to ask how many passengers are left. I want to know how many times the bus stopped to take on or to discharge passengers. How many? Do I know? Of course, I do not know. I can't count that high.

Now permit me to give you the final test of my strength. This is strength of mind or, as it is better known, will-power. There are many masters of ceremony who would keep right on talking. Not I. I have nothing more to say so I have the will-power to stop talking. This small matter I will accomplish as soon as I have finished introducing a mighty man of muscle whose feats of strength will amaze you. I give you a man whose strength is in his deeds and not in his words. Ladies and gentlemen, Mr. ——————.

INTRODUCING A BASSO

By Vance Clifford

I love singing. The fact is, I like singing so much I tried it once myself. I was in the bathtub. After two verses and one chorus somebody turned in the fire alarm. I put so much fire into my singing the smoke went out the window.

I was asked to join a barber shop quartette to sing bass. I couldn't sing the very low notes so the boys made me stand out in the rain until I caught cold. It was cheaper than taking singing lessons. But I've been all wet ever since. My singing career didn't last very long. I tried singing a solo. I got a big hand, but the hand was in the form of fist. I was called Digit-Eyed Dick for a month. Even so, the audience applauded when I had finished my solo. They called for me to come back. When I didn't come back they dared me to.

When I spoke to a friend the next day about it, he quickly said, "Please don't apologize. You're still alive." I said, "But it was a difficult number." He said, "You mean impossible." So now, instead of singing, I just listen. You will listen, too, when you hear the basso I am going to introduce. He can sing so low that his assistant has to bring the lowest notes up from the basement.

Ladies and gentlemen, **(name)**.

INTRODUCING A BALLET

By Arthur L. Kaser

Like ballet? Who doesn't? We are going to have some ballet this evening.

Ballet dancing is so expressive, so artistic, so pantomimic. I've often wondered why so many of the fair sex take up ballet. Not a word is spoken during the dance and that is so unlike a woman. I'll be shot for that.

I used to go with a toe dancer, but she couldn't dance on her toes. She always danced on mine. Fifty years ago the girls didn't dance like they do now. They couldn't. They were bustle-bound.

I took an old uncle of mine to see some modern dancing. We watched for awhile, and then I asked him, "Uncle, I'll bet you never saw dancing like this when you were young." He said, "Just once, my boy, but the place was raided." I'm guessing that since my uncle's time, dancing has developed in leaps and bounds. Every time a dance instructor wants to invent new dance steps he knocks over a hornet's nest.

Ladies and gentlemen, the ballet.

INTRODUCING AN INSTRUMENTALIST

By Louis J. Huber

Ladies and gentlemen, at this time it is my great pleasure to bring to you a man (or woman) who is the master of an instrument. I say this, in making a distinction between an instrumentalist and an ordinary musician, as one who plays in a band.

This type of musician, ladies and gentlemen, has no one to cover up his errors. There is no loud brass section, no blaring and booming bass horn to gloss over any mistake.

This artist comes to us tonight through the courtesy of the local bus company. This is true, folks. Actually, he had no bus fare when he got on and they brought him here for free. If any of you, after hearing him play, get thoughts about sueing the bus company let me tell you that you're too late. I thought of it first.

There was a time when our next entertainer tried his hand at composing music. He announced that he had written a little piece. The neighbors were delighted. A little peace is what they had desired for a long time.

But away with all this nonsense. You will know that I've been joking when you hear the calibre of his music. An artist with a deep understanding of the meaning of music. I present to you, Mr. ————.

INTRODUCING A MUSICIAN

By Arthur L. Kaser

Miss Blank (real name) will now play some of the old tunes that our parents and grandparents enjoyed so much. Ah, those old familiar melodies! "In the Shade of the Old Apple Tree," "Annie Laurie,"—oh, so many others that thrilled the country, and still does. However, Miss Blank refuses to play "In the Shade of the Old Apple Tree." She says the last time she played there an apple dropped on her head. Did you know that my grandfather wrote "Annie Laurie?" Yes, sir, but she never answered his letter. "Old Man River" is not so very old, but "Old Lady River" is. "Old Lady River" was written about Mrs. Ippi. I believe one of the best of the old songs is "The Return of the Swallow," by Belch. Perhaps some of you recall the old-time waltz ballad, "After the Bawl is Over."

> The baby is happy and gay,
> His face is red, but he's smiling
> As Mom scrapes his tears all away.

Silly, isn't it?

"Carry Me Back to Ol' Virginny" must have been written by a hitch-hiker. Nobody would be foolish enough to carry him there piggy-back. Yes, I like the old songs—because nobody sings them any more. Miss Blank will now play ———.

INTRODUCING A VARIETY REVUE

By Louis J. Huber

Ladies and gentlemen, as your master of ceremonies, I am about to bring to you a different kind of entertainment. It is different because it has variety. It is a variety revue.

After you have seen it you will want to re-view the revue. It is different from anything you have ever seen. The dancers will sing and the singers will dance. The comedians will tell stories that will make you cry and the tragedians tell jokes.

It isn't a very good show, ladies and gentlemen. If you are really smart, you'll go home. (Pause and a deep breath.) The reason I give them this introduction is that I'm getting even with them. They wouldn't let me be in the show.

I wanted to do comedy for them. I had a swell collection of stories and jokes. Get this one: Why does Uncle Sam wear a red, white and blue vest? Well, why does he? He needs a place to carry toothpicks. Good, huh? No? O.K.

Maybe the revue was right when they didn't hire me. Maybe I would have detracted from its greatness. I'm not mad at them. I think they will make you rock with laughter and swell with delight. I present to you the **(Name of revue).**

INTRODUCING A CELEBRITY

By Forbes Milliken

(The names in the following should be changed to other celebrities to suit the occasion.)

Adlai Stevenson was approached by an autograph hound. "Could I have your autograph, sir?" "But I have signed your book before," said Mr. Stevenson. "Yes, I know," agreed the hunter, "but when I get ten of yours I can trade them for one of Ike Eisenhower's."

There are celebrities and near-celebrities. This is what the pretty girl referred to when she said, "He not only lied to me about the size of his yacht, but he made me do the rowing."

How about the Hollywood celebrity who sends out elaborate invitations for "Bearer and One Wife"?

Not long ago a certain big-wig was bragging about Hollywood. Finally I asked, "Have any big men ever been born in Hollywood?" He said, "No—only little babies."

As I said before, there are celebrities and would-be's. We have with us this evening one whom I consider to be one of the really, truly celebrities of today. My friends, it is my great privilege to present to you **(name.)**

INTRODUCING A GIRL TRIO

By Jeff Branen

We are happy to announce that we have a girl trio to entertain us this evening. I know you will enjoy their harmony.

I love good singing, but it's just too awful if you have to live in the same house with somebody that can't sing and does sing. My cousin Dorothy lived with us awhile. Oh, what a voice! She couldn't carry a tune if it had handles. And she thought she was a finished singer. If I would have had my way she **would** have been finished. Whenever I would get all het up over her singing my wife would say, "Hold your tempo, dear, hold your tempo." I should have held my axe.

Dorothy took some singing lessons from a correspondence school, but I think the post office lost some of her mail. She said to me that she was going away to study singing. I was so happy, I said to her, "How far away?" I was in hopes it might be Singapore, because no one could sing a por-a song than she. She sang in a key that wouldn't fit anything. Sounded more like a don-key.

She threatened a number of times to go to Europe to have her voice cultivated. I told her she'd save money to stay in this country and just have it plowed under. I don't know where she got the idea that she had a singular voice. I was overjoyed that it wasn't plural. What ended it all was when she came home one day and started her screeching. I objected. She said her teacher told her to throw out her chest when she sang. She threw out her chest and I threw out her trunk.

I am just telling you these things so you will notice the stupendous contrast when you hear our three beautiful singers. Ladies and gentlemen, **(name of trio, or individual singers.)**

INTRODUCING HILLBILLY MUSICIANS

By Arthur L. Kaser

Well, folks, we shore got a treat this evenin'. A real hones'-to-goo'ness hillbilly act right straight from Skunk Holler and they don't care a scent what they do, t'other. Great place, back in them hills. I know. I've been there.

Not long ago I was talking with a true native of the hills and he was telling me he'd just been talkin' to Lem who lives across the valley. He wanted Lem to stop a-feuding with him till he'd sent to the mail order house for more shotgun shells. Another thing, he wanted to marry Emma Stump that didn't live too far away. He'd been over to Emma's the night before and says to Emma's father, "I come hyar to ask yer fer yer daughter's hand." The old man flew right up in the air and rasped, "Can't allow no sech thing, boy. Ither yer take the whole gal, or nothin'."

Emma's mother never wears shoes. The soles of her feet are tougher than a ten-year-old rooster. She was standing in front of the cabin fireplace the other day when the old man yelled at her, "Marthy, you'd better be a-movin' your foot a mite. You're standin' on a live coal." Maw said, without removing her corncob pipe, "Which foot, paw?"

The old man said to me while I was there, "Funny thing happened to me yistaday. I 'lowed 'twas gittin' a trifle warm to be a-wearin' them heavy red flannels, so I figured on takin' them off. An' do you know what, Mister? When I did take 'em off I run across a old sweater I been lookin' high an' low fer fer two years."

While I was there with this mountain family two men rode up on mules and called out to my host, "Hey, Jed, me an' Ed just found a dead man over there in the holler, an' we thought mebbe it was you." "What'd he look like?" asked Jed. "Oh, 'bout your size, Jed." "Have on a flannel shirt?" "Yup." "Red 'n' green checks?" "Nope, just sorta gray." "Nope, 'tain't me."

Now for some good old hillbilly music.

INTRODUCING AN ORCHESTRA

By Earl Jay Gilbert

My friends, next we're going to present for your enjoyment the famous ———— Orchestra, conducted by the eminent maestro, ————.

I'd like to say a few words about orchestras and music before they start. Orchestras, of course, are composed of a group playing string, wind and percussion instruments. Music is a succession of melodious and harmonious sounds, so modulated that they create a pleasing sound to the ear.

As far as we know the origin of music was probably in ancient Egypt, where it was used in religious rites and ceremonies. As a matter of fact the first use of music by all people was used for the same purpose. Even primitive savage tribes had their own types of music in the form of drums made by animal skins stretched across hollow logs, and other instruments created from the horns of certain animals. Our modern music and band instruments come from those early beginnings. Now, that's all I know about music. I just looked that up in the encyclopedia a little while ago and, friends, what a relief to get it off my chest!

Speaking of orchestras, I'm reminded of a little story. A woman took her little boy to hear a well-known orchestra, which was accompanying a famous concert soprano. Suddenly the little boy said: "Mama, what is that man shaking that stick at the woman for?" "Sh!" said his mother. "He's not shaking his stick at her." "Then what's she screaming for?" asked the boy.

Shortly after this, when the soprano had finished, a well-known ballet dancer appeared. She was wearing no more clothes than the law allowed. The little boy took a look at her and shouted: "Hey, mama, that lady's almost barefoot all over!" "Sh!" the mother said. "You mustn't talk. Just sit back and enjoy it." "I can't enjoy it," said the boy. "You said it was going to be a swell show, and I think it's lousy." The mother whispered to him: "There are two words I don't want you to use—one is swell and the other is lousy. Now promise me you won't use them." "Sure," said the boy. "What are the words?"

Well, anyway, when they started home, the mother said, "Now, Willie, didn't you enjoy the orchestra?" "Well, yes," said the boy. "All but the music." Which just goes to prove that what is music to one person isn't always music to another. However, I think you'll agree that the orchestra we're presenting to you creates music that is pleasing to everybody.

You know it takes a long time to learn to play any musical instrument well enough to qualify as a top-notch musician, such as the members of this orchestra who have all spent years of study and hard work mastering their respective instruments.

I can't help but think of the fellow who boasted of the fact that he played the piano by ear only. Someone present said: "That's nothing. I've got a three-month-old baby who plays with his toes." Another parlor comedian present said: "I can top that. I've got an eighty-year-old uncle who fiddles with his whiskers."

Well, anyway, while the members of this orchestra are all entitled to be called musical artists, it requires more than musical ability alone to make an orchestra successful. The conductor of an orchestra is principally responsible for its success. He must first choose his musicians, according to their instruments and their ability to play them, organize them into a group, select the musical numbers, attend to the musical arrangements, rehearse his group for long periods of time to bring out and develop harmonious blends until they're perfect. And then, when he appears before the public to direct his organization, someone is sure to say: "What a soft job he's got!"

Well, now we're going to let you see what this part of his job is like. It's time for our orchestra to produce those melodious, harmonious sounds we all enjoy listening to. So I'll present this wonderful combination, the ———— Orchestra and their distinguished conductor, ————!

INTRODUCING A SINGING QUARTET

By Arthur L. Kaser

We have a very pleasant surprise for you this evening. We have been fortunate enough to bring to you the famous Four Dimension Quartet (substitute real name of the quartet.) These boys have been together for some time and have made quite a name for themselves. I thought at one time I would like to be a professional singer, but a few hints from my acquaintances and friends discouraged me. A very good friend of mine once said to me, "Do you know 'The Road to Mandalay'?" I said, "Yes, do you want me to sing it?" He said, "No, take it." Another time an acquaintance told me, "If you expect to be a real singer, you'll have to sing louder." I told him I sang as loud as I could. He wasn't satisfied. He said, "You must be more enthusiastic. Open your mouth wider and throw yourself into it."

The tenor of the Four Dimension Quartet was recently arrested for speeding. When he appeared before the judge the judge asked, "Haven't I seen you somewhere before?" "Yes, Your Honor," said the youth, "I gave your daughter singing lessons." "Thirty years!" thundered the judge. Then our baritone. During one of their engagements the baritone sang a solo. A lady in the audience said to her companion, "Did you ever hear anything worse?" "Yes," said her companion, "the quartet. It's four times as bad." When the lead was first learning to sing his father would step out on the front porch whenever the boy sang so the neighbors would know it wasn't he that was beating the lad. Our bass at one time sang in a choir, but he didn't stay in it for long. One Sunday he was absent and someone asked if the organ had been fixed. However, they've gone through the rough spots and are today really recognized. The first time these boys got together they were a howling success. And now, ladies and gentlemen, here they are. **(Give their real names.)**

INTRODUCING AN ACCORDION PLAYER

By Richard Drummond

No musical entertainment of this kind is complete without an accordion number. Not only do we marvel at the dexterity of the player, but we are thrilled by the instrument—a treasure chest of melody. It is the combination of the two that holds us breathless—the accordion so full of heavenly music, and the musician to squeeze it out.

A few years ago a very dear friend of mine was doing very nicely with his accordion until he got so fat it pinched his stomach. In other words, he was getting too far out in front. He finally traded the instrument for a book on reducing in ten hungry lessons. It didn't seem to do him much good. He was a poor loser. He finally went to a doctor, and the doctor told him he was eating too much soldier food—everything he ate went to the front.

Then I got a bright idea. If my friend could play an accordion, why couldn't I? I bought a rather cheap accordion and began practicing. Two hours later my next door neighbor begged me to tear it apart and see what was inside.

However, my friends, there are many wonderful accordion players in the world, and the artist I am about to present is firmly ensconced in the upper bracket. Of course, he does make mistakes occasionally. Who doesn't? None of us are perfect. A week ago this young artist played to an appreciative audience in (name nearby town). I do not recall the number of listeners gathered there, but everybody in the room was there. Now, ladies and gentlemen, allow me to present **(name of musician)** and his accordion.

INTRODUCING A TELEVISION PERSONALITY

By Arthur L. Kaser

No doubt you have seen our guest on television many times. She is truly a television personality. We certainly should feel honored to have her with us this evening.

When television enters the telephone field and we are able to see who is at the other end our guest is going to have a lot of phone calls. She would be a television of delight. Her popularity was so sudden, too. She leaped to fame overnight. She had very little experience on the legitimate stage—her arm was in a cast once. When she first decided to become an actress she had difficulty in getting anyone to take an interest in her. She finally placed a small ad in a theatrical magazine. It read: "Engagement wanted. Small part, such as dead body or off-stage shouts."

Then one day she visited a television studio. As she entered the place her foot became entangled in a broken seat and she stumbled into television. It isn't that easy for everyone to get into television. Recently a girl was being interviewed for a lead in a half-hour drama. The interviewer was one of the producers. He looked her over carefully, and then said, "You're perfect for the part. Just the right face, perfect voice, coloring ideal—just what the script calls for. What salary would you expect?" The girl, after hearing this high appraisal of herself, said, "One thousand dollars a week." "Sorry," snapped the producer. "You're too tall."

So there you are, folks. May I present one of the most charming and beautiful girls on the T.V. today? Here she is, ladies and gentlemen, **(name.)**

INTRODUCING AN IRISHMAN

By Louis J. Huber

Our speaker, ladies and gentlemen, comes to you through the courtesy of the shamrock. I start with this blunt statement because I know how proud he is of his nationality. He is Irish.

And what more need I say? A lot more or you'd get someone else to take my place.

There is no one who can enjoy a good laugh more than can the Irish. Especially if they are telling it and the other folks can't understand it. You can always tell if an Irishman is dead or alive. Go up to him and call him a nasty name. If he's dead, you're safe; if he's alive, you'd better take to your heels.

They are a very clever race, these Irish. They can even understand English if it is spoken in Irish. Our speaker had an occasion to show his Irish qualities for upholding the weak and the downtrodden. He saw a bigger man taking advantage of a little one. He stepped right into the fray and told the bully that he should be kicked by a jackass and then he followed through and kicked the man.

When an Irishman puts his mind to something he goes through with it. Our speaker is a shining example of this. He waited up until two o'clock the other morning. He wanted to put the cat out for the night and that feline fool didn't come until then.

Yes, he's Irish. He's proud of it and we are proud of him. So, without any further words I give him to you, Mr. ———.

INTRODUCING A FRENCH COMEDIAN

By Vance Clifford

We send Statue of Liberty tourists to France and they send Eiffel Tower-ists over here. We have with us this evening a representative of that country in the person of a celebrated French comedian. He is a comedian from start to finish. However, he has one serious thought. He claims that Adam was a Frenchman. I agree with him that Adam was a Frenchman, because of the swiftness of his fall, he could have been their first Premier.

France has made a good comeback since the war. All the famous Parisian bars now have revolving doors. My uncle just returned from Paris and he swears the bars have revolving ceilings, too.

Our guest of the evening says the only difference between French girls and American girls is the Atlantic Ocean.

That uncle I mentioned—When he arrived at the Riviera in southern France he stopped at a small inn near Vichy. The clerk said to him: "It is the law you know, to fill out registration papers for the gendarmes." My uncle has traveled extensively in Europe and he says he spends half his time filling out registrations. He said to the clerk: "I'm sick and tired of filling out those things. Fill it out for me. My name is on the baggage." Some time later he returned to the desk and was handed the registration filled out. Under "name" it read: "Monsieur Warranted Genuine Leather."

Yep, it's a great country, France, and one of its greats is with us this evening. Ladies and gentlemen, Monsieur **(name.)**

INTRODUCING A QUARTETTE

By Louis J. Huber

Ladies and gentlemen, we come to the high spot of the evening's entertainment. A very proud master of ceremonies is about to produce, without benefit of anything up his sleeve, one of the best singing groups it has ever been my pleasure to hear.

This group had quite a hard time getting organized and I'd like to tell you the story. You will appreciate their talent even more after you hear the tale.

They had one tenor but no elevenor so they took a niner and added a sixer to him and thereby they came up with a threeer. Now none of this makes sense unless you get an adding machine and who wants to fool with a mechanical device tonight.

They also had a first bass but no one to play left field. So they got a pitcher and fitted it with water and put the catcher on second base because the shortstop had to go home for supper. By this time the baritone had a change of voice and he turned out to be one of the best sopranos they had ever heard. Do you know what they did? They got a deck of cards and had themselves a game of hearts.

From out of this came success in this singing world. You will know what I mean when you hear them. Their perfect blending is not mere luck. It is hours and days and weeks of hard work but it was worth it. I'll let you decide this for yourselves, but I am sure that you will agree with me. I proudly present to you the **(Name of Quartette.)**

INTRODUCING A LADY MONOLOGIST

By Arthur L. Kaser

They say that a monologue is a conversation between a wife and her husband. That goes without saying. This is proved by the answer I received to a question I asked a lady acquaintance a couple of days ago. I said, "Mrs. X, aren't you rather hoarse this morning?" She said, "Yes, my husband came home much too late last night."

These jokes are not meant to cast any reflection on our guest, a lady monologist, who will shortly entertain you.

'Tis said, "Silence is golden." Well, if silence is golden, many people will not be arrested for hoarding. Some people rattle on and on, using more meaningless words to say less about nothing. I've heard people talk so much I got hoarse listening to them. When women first started wearing men's trousers I had a hard time telling which was the husband when they walked down the street together. But it didn't take me long to figure which was which. The one who was listening was the husband.

I knew a woman who, by the end of the day, could hardly keep her mouth open. She was a woman of few words, but she kept them mighty busy.

Say, how come a woman's tongue outlasts three sets of teeth?

Friends, I want you to meet Miss **(name)**, our guest monologist.

INTRODUCING A SQUARE DANCE CALLER

By Louis J. Huber

Folks, it is now time for a part in our program that will be remembered for a long time by all of us. This is not a spot for a professional entertainer, rather it is a place where the likes of you and I hold the spotlight.

This is a surprise feature. We have brought to this gathering tonight a man who will handle it for us. Before I introduce him and let him take charge of the program I must tell you something about it.

There are many of us here who have, at one time or another, taken part in a good old-fashioned country hoedown. The old timers know what I mean. You newcomers who have been educated by way of radio and television will call it a square dance.

We have brought a caller here this evening. Those of you who know how to square dance know that there is nothing to equal its capacity for having fun. Those of you who do not know anything about it will have even more enjoyment in learning a few rudimentary steps and being a part of the dance.

The man who will show you how to do this is Mr. **(Name).** He assures us that in no time at all you will all be dancing with reckless abandon. Until you get good enough to dance with reckless abandon—whoever she is—I would like to turn the program over to Mr. **(Name).** So listen and heed, watch and learn, and swing your partner, the floor is yours, Mr. **(Name.)**

INTRODUCING A WOMAN DRIVER

By Louis J. Huber

Folks, tonight I have been given the pleasure of presenting to you our guest of the evening. Many of you know about her accomplishments in her own field but you do not know about her ability on a different level. Our speaker, folks, is quite a driver.

We can go back to her very first driving lesson. That was when she drove the instructor—to tears. He had just finished instructing her on the use of the different buttons, levers and handles when she screamed. She just noticed that the upholstery in the car did not match the color of her eyes.

It was then she turned to her husband for instructions. This was much better as many of you folks know. Especially if you have had your husband as an instructor, or if you've had the pleasure of teaching your wife. Our speaker got along quite well under the new conditions. She held out her hand when she made a left turn. Her husband was pleased. To this day he doesn't know that she did this to dry the polish on her nails. Let me inject right here that it is not true that women drivers are not as safe as men. Statistics prove that every automobile wreck in this country has involved one or more cars driven by a driver who had his hand on the starter button at the beginning of the trip.

INTRODUCING A COMEDIAN

By Louis J. Huber

Ladies and gentlemen, the next spot on our program has been allotted to a comedian. He is a funny fellow who will make you hold your sides, especially if you have broken ribs.

You will hear, from the jokes and stories that he tells you, that his material has been written by a very clever fellow—me. Each time you laugh I will laugh with you because you make me very happy.

He has a great joke for the opener. When he comes on he will ask a simple question. This is what he will ask: Is there a doctor in the house? One of you must stand up and say: Yes, I'm a doctor. He will then give you the punch line. Like this: How do you like the show, doc?

Isn't that a dandy piece of humor? Of course it is, I wrote it. He will also ask this question: How would you like—?

(Looks to the side) What is it? Oh, the comedian won't appear if he must use my stuff.

All right, let him use his own and see how far he gets. I know that I won't applaud. Not unless my hands get cold and I'm forced to do it to keep them warm. I must be a little silly, I'm getting cold. (Starts applauding.) And you'd better do the same as I present to you one of our really great comedians, Mr. ————.

INTRODUCING AN OLD-TIME ENTERTAINER

By Louis J. Huber

At this part of our proceedings, ladies and gentlemen, we come to a spot that makes me very happy. First, because we are going to witness a performance by a man who has been in this game of entertaining for a long time. Second, because I have the honor of introducing him.

A good entertainer, ladies and gentlemen, is like wine. It gets better with the years and yet it keeps the taste that started it on its way. Our guest is such a person. He has withstood the ravages of new mediums and he is still head and shoulders above many of them.

Let me tell you a bit about his past. Some twenty-odd years ago he gave a command performance. It was one of his off days. He got a second command before the performance ended. He was commanded to beat it.

Came the day he was awarded a part in Ali Baba and the Forty Thieves. He was told he could be one of the pickpockets and he went about it with a great interest. He got so interested that he got caught. The judge explained to him that Ali Baba had no pickpockets in his story.

Since then he has learned better. He has also learned the secret of successful entertainment and he will prove my words. I am proud to present to you, an old-timer who will always be new, Mr. ————.

INTRODUCING AN ANIMAL IMITATOR

By Louis J. Huber

Woof, woof. (Barks.) Does that sound like a dog? It does? Then I'd better let the next entertainer introduce me and I'll take over his act. (Pauses.) No takers? All right, folks, you had your chance to see me and to hear me making animal noises.

Which is exactly what our next act is going to be, an imitator of animals. Is he good? I'll leave that to you, but I'll do it only after I tell you something about him, and about myself and my abilities.

He is one of the few men who can imitate a fish out of water. I can do it but I don't want him to see it. He goes like this. (Imitates a fish swimming.) There was a time when I could also imitate a sardine but I got that squeezed out of me at the last bargain counter sale at the (local department store).

There was a time when I imitated a duck. That was when a certain individual threw a stone at me. Now wasn't that a dandy quack? I wish you folks would imitate a hyena and laugh a little at my jokes. Isn't that a foxey way of asking for applause?

All right, so you won't applaud me and I don't blame you. But you will applaud the merits of this next act because it is the type of entertainment that just makes you want to move your hands and give credit. I present to you, Mr. ————.

INTRODUCING A MAGICIAN

By Louis J. Huber

Ladies and gentlemen, tonight it is my great pleasure to introduce an entertainer who will mystify and astound you. He will also amaze and amuse you and for fifteen cents he will make your mother-in-law disappear. The line, gentlemen, forms at the right.

To give you an idea of the type of act that he will bring to you I have graciously consented to preview a bit of prestidigitation. I will prove that the hand is quicker than the eye. Have you ever seen a man with a black eye? There's your proof. If his eye had been as fast as the hand—you see what I mean.

Here, folks, I have a deck of cards, a full deck. (Holds them up.) Please take one card. (To someone sitting near.) Now give it back to me without looking at it. (This is done.) I will return it to the deck and shuffle. Ah, just right. You, sir, had the ten of clubs. Right? You don't know because you didn't look at it? Take my word, sir, that it was the ten of clubs. It will save a terrible argument.

Oh. what's the use? I practiced that trick for days and I still didn't get it. But we have an entertainer who can do it and many others. Ladies and gentlemen, that great Master of Magic, Mr. ———————.

INTRODUCING AN IMPERSONATOR

By Louis J. Huber

Perhaps, ladies and gentlemen, there is no greater art in the entertainment world than the type you are about to witness, an impersonator. It is a knack of studying the traits and characteristics that belong to another and then doing likewise.

The reason I know it is not an easy medium of entertainment is that I did a little of it. I can recall the day I was in a local restaurant doing an imitation of a waitress. Someone came along and gave me a tip. Which was all right only it happened to be the tip of his shoe.

Imitation, they say, is the sincerest form of flattery. I wouldn't know about that because no one ever flattered me because no one is brash enough to imitate me. And if they don't imitate they can't possibly impersonate.

I did have one successful impersonation. That was also in this same local restaurant. I imitated a hat rack. This was easy for me because of my ears. Within two minutes they had hung four hats on me and my ears. Easiest money I ever made because I sold them for five dollars each.

Enough of this balderdash. I want you to meet a man who can do all the things I'd like to do. A man who can imitate my wife's cooking by buying a new can opener. A man who can imitate many people and many things. It is my pleasure, ladies and gentlemen, to bring him to you, Mr. ————.

INTRODUCING A BACHELOR

By Louis J. Huber

Ladies and gentlemen, tonight it is my pleasant duty to bring to you, as our speaker, a man with many accomplishments. You know of many of these. Just as you know that one of these claims to success is the fact that he is a bachelor.

A bachelor, according to scme scientific sources, is a man who always took no for an answer. Many of you will agree with me that, in this day and age, it takes a smart man to remain single. Our speaker has used his head. All he did was shake it sideways instead of nodding it up and down. The difference between yes and no.

There was, at one time, a very ugly rumor that he could have married anyone he liked. The trouble was that he didn't like anyone. One lady friend wrote to him and asked him to be her soul mate. He is quite a bad speller and thought she was talking about the sole of his shoe. So he sent her to a shoemaker. They are happily married.

Another young lady asked him to be the light of her love. He tried it for a few days and then sent her a bill because he disliked being used as a utility company. He found a good way to keep from holding hands. He always sat on them.

Despite all the wrong things that have been said about him, all of them delightful untruths, we like the boy. So we give him to you and we know you will also like him. Mr. ————.

INTRODUCING A LOCAL ORCHESTRA

By Arthur L. Kaser

We are happy to welcome to our stage this evening the **(name of the orchestra)**. All the members of this musical organization are localites, and no doubt most of you know them personally. I think we are going to have a very enjoyable evening.

I'm a nut about music. In other words, I'm a musical nut that bolts to every concert. Some time ago I went to see Paul Whiteman's wonderful orchestra. The next day a friend of mine asked me, "How did you find the orchestra last night?" I told him Paul Whiteman stepped aside and there it was. The pianist in that orchestra was marvelous. He played just like Paderewski — he used both hands. Those musicians surely have it easy. All they do is play around. And those violinists — they were out of this world, their violins were Stradivarius. That is something you can't say about all chin music. There is one thing I'm not quite clear on — if there is music in heaven, where do the violinists go to tune their instruments? They also say that violins have souls. Some of them sound like the lost variety. Most professional violinists dedicate their music to the cats who gave their lives that the violins would have strings.

The orchestra's drummer started his career in a rather odd way. He was a mousetrap salesman. That's how be became a trap drummer. Every time he called on a prospect he was told to beat it. He's been beating it ever since.

Ladies and gentlemen, the **(name of the orchestra)**.

INTRODUCING A NEWLYWED

By Louis J. Huber

Friends, it is my great pleasure to bring to you this evening, a speaker who needs no bringing because he has just been brought. What I am saying, in a long and roundabout manner, is that he has been brought—to his knees. In short, he has just been married.

As usual he has the same troubles that befall any man who has taken a wife. There is mother-in-law trouble and there is —no, let's get back to what we started—mother-in-law trouble. Our man has not yet reached a speaking acquaintance with her. So far he is still at a listening distance.

His wife told her mother, just the other day, that our speaker gives her everything that she asks for. The mother quickly changed that kind of thinking. She assured her daughter that she isn't asking for enough or she wouldn't be getting all she asks for. Our man has also learned to use the phrase "I must say so." He now speaks like this: "I must say you're wonderful, my dear mother-in-law. . . . I must say that you are masterful, my dear mother-in-law. . . . I must say that I am the luckiest man in the world, my dear mother-in-law."

Yes, he must say all that or suffer the consequences. We don't know what he must say tonight, but you are now going to hear what he will say. May I present Mr. ——————?

INTRODUCING A CHILDREN'S ACT OR A CHILD ENTERTAINER

By George A. Posner

I became an emcee at the urging of thousands—of hundreds of people—a number of folks—a couple of friends—O.K., THEN!!!—my mother—.

I guess I inherited my talent from my dad. I got everything else he had. His old shirts, his old ties—ah, those dear old family ties—his long underwear—(can't I ever learn to keep my trap shut?) His blue serge pants—that's where I shined.

I remember one day I saw Dad in the bathroom, shaving. And the way I started to bawl.

"What's the matter?" asked my mother.

I pointed my finger at Dad shaving and howled, "Look! Now I suppose I'll have to wear those red whiskers!"

O.K. To business. I'm supposed to introduce these children to you proud parents gathered there. What's the matter, don't you know your own children?

The little children, bless their little hearts. What a comfort they are to us in our old age—and how swiftly they help us reach it!

When they're young, they want to get older. When they're old they want to get younger. When they're females, they just want to get, period!

A man works hard to keep the wolf from the door. Then his daughter grows up and brings one right into the house.

The men work hard and save their money so their sons won't have the problems that made men out of their fathers.

The little itty-bitty kiddies. Try making them eat spinach. The only way I know to make them eat spinach is to tell them it's mud.

Don't get me wrong. I love babies. Those born twenty years ago, and sopranos.

Never mind. Some one has said that children are little people who aren't allowed to do what their parents did at their age.

The children I'm introducing tonight are musical children. I don't know what key they're in, but they're musical.

I was a musical kid, too. By nature. I was born with drums in my ears—(don't shoot!).

I was an only child, a small litter. My parents were so poor, in fact, the neighbors had to have me.

As I grew up I acquired quite a musical background. My father used to spank me with a mandolin. Man, how he picked on me! He made some spanking good music. That's where the term "hot music" came from. I was plenty hot. It was the real be-bop, the way he bopped me.

Later, when I grew up, I played the piano by ear, while my father fiddled with his whiskers. (Not only my father, but the joke in this case, has whiskers.)

My music teacher did his best to make a finished musician out of me. The neighbors tried to help. They almost got me, too.

They did say I played with a lot of feeling, but not for the neighbors.

Finally the neighbors offered to send me abroad—since they could find no other way to deport me.

I learned to play the piano in no time. No time at all—that's what the neighbors complained about.

Yeah, I was a musical fellow, all right. I went out for the school band. I went out for the school choral society. Yep, whenever they wanted any errands done, I went out for them.

Then the war broke out and the army got me. I was really too young for the army, but my dad was on the Draft Board.

In the army, I went out for the band. First they gave me a flute to play. I said: "See here, I can't play this thing—it's full of holes."

Then they issued me a **slide** trombone. You know, one of those things with a big slide you push in and way out. That was better. It was nice, marching in the parade, with the sergeant, his back to me, marching ahead of me. Every once in a while I managed to get him inside the range—gosh!

And when we finally got to France, I would have had a medal, too—only they couldn't find a French general brave enough to kiss me.

Never mind. After I'd been doing this musicianing and emcee-ing for a while, I was certainly a sought-after man. Of course sometimes it was with bloodhounds.

Anyway, it's time to introduce to you what you really came to hear—the little darlings—the future Glenn Millers, Ezio Pinzas, Bob Hopes, and your hopes—

ADDITIONAL MATERIAL

Speaking of children: My young son came home the other day with an alley cat in his arms. He said: "Oh, Daddy, look at this great, big, poor, homeless cat I found. Couldn't we please keep it, Daddy, couldn't we?"

I looked at the cat and I could see at a glance that if we adopted that cat we'd not only have a cat but some kittens, too; very, very soon. I'm psychic that way.

But he pleaded so hard, the little feller, I finally gave in.

A day or two later the kid came running in, crying as if his heart was going to break. And I said: "What's wrong, sonny?"

So he says: "Oh, Daddy, it's the cat!" And he wailed, "Oh, Daddy, something terrible's happened to her!"

"The cat?" I asked. "What happened to her?"

"She went into mummy's closet, and then just fell apart! In seven pieces!"

* * *

We were traveling by train overnight and had put our little girl to bed in her upper berth while we sat up to read awhile. She kept crying, she felt afraid, and lonesome up there alone, and her mother would tell her not to worry, because God would take care of her.

"Mother," came her voice once more, "are you there?"

"Yes, I'm here."

"Daddy, are you there?"

"Yeah—"

A fellow passenger in another berth lost all patience at this point and bellowed: "We're all here! Your father's here. And your mother's here! And your sisters, brothers, uncles and cousins. All here! Now for God's sake, go to sleep!"

There was a pause, then very softly: "Mamma!"

"Yes, dear."

"Was that God?"

* * *

I was at a lecture the other day, and I said to my little boy: "Sh-h-h, Johnny, the speaker's going to the rostrum."

He answered: "But, Daddy, why must I be quiet just because someone's going to the rest room?"

* * *

My little son went wading with the little daughter of the family next door. Pretty soon they decided that the only way they could keep their clothing dry was to take them off. My little boy stopped to look the little girl over. "Gosh," he remarked, "I didn't know there was **that** much difference between Catholics and Protestants!"

* * *

Speaking of kids—a woman was driving down Hollywood Boulevard the other day in an antiquated jalopy filled with about nine kids of variegated ages and sizes, and at Vine Street she drove through a red light. A whistle from the traffic officer brought it to a halt. He came up, looked grimly at her for a minute, and said:

"Don't you know when to stop?"

"These kids aren't all mine," she answered calmly.

There have been a lot of mistakes . . . in connection with kids . . . No, I'm thinking of the story of King Christian X of Denmark, at the time he was making a tour of his domain and entered a town in which he had never been before. He was greeted there by a great multitude of cheering children.

"Where," asked he, "did all these children come from?"

Explained the Mayor: "Your Majesty, we have been preparing for this great day for years."

* * *

"You say that you were afraid to have any more than four children in your family?"

"Yes. We read that every fifth child born is Chinese."

* * *

When their kids reach eighteen the parents quit worrying how their kids will turn out. They begin to worry when they will turn in.

* * *

I saw a stern-faced woman walk up to a tough little kid of about ten, standing on a street corner, smoking a cigaret. She said to him:

"Young man, does your mother know you smoke?"

He replied: "Lady, does your husband know you stop to talk to strange men on the street?"

* * *

Some kids take after their father. Some take after their mother. This kid took after his nurse.

* * *

The kid sure wasn't long reaching the awkward age. Too young to leave home alone, and too old to trust with baby sitters.

* * *

My kid was on the front porch the other night, uttering a series of heart-broken howls. A neighbor stopped to inquire about the trouble.

"Oh-h-h-!" said the boy. "Daddy and Maw went to the movies and didn't take me. And I want to go—go—o—oo—oo. Wowowowowo!"

"But don't cry so," said the neighbor. "Do they ever take you when you cry like that?"

"Sometimes they do and sometimes they don't," explained the boy. "But it ain't no trouble to yell!"

* * *

A small boy living down the street from us was having an argument and using some pretty strong language.

A woman, who was passing, stopped and said to him in a shocked voice: "How do you think your mother would feel if she heard you?"

"She'd be tickled to death," replied the boy. "She's deaf."

* * *

Little four-year-old Johnny, being told to pray for his absent father, for his small brother who was ill, and for the servant who had sprained her ankle, did so.

Then to his mother's astonishment he concluded: "And now, God, please take good care of yourself, because if anything happens to you we will certainly be up against it for fair."

* * *

The other day it was raining and I heard the wife shouting to my small son: "Johnny, let your sister in. Don't you see it's raining?"

"I can't help it, Ma," he shouted back. "We're playing Noah's Ark, and she's the sinners. She's got to stay out in the wet."

* * *

The other day she was saying to him: "You've been naughty, Johnny. Fighting again!"

He answered: "No, I haven't been naughty, Mother."

"Then how did you get your face all scratched and your clothes muddied and torn?"

"I was trying to keep a bad little boy from hurting a good little boy."

"Oh, that was noble. Who was the good little boy?" she asked.

"Me," said he.

* * *

The other day I said to the wife: "That boy has taken some money out of the pants I had hanging over the chair there!"

"How can you say that?" she protested. "Why, I might have done it."

"No," I said positively. "You didn't; there was some left."

* * *

Which reminds me, there were two little boys passing a nudist colony, and noticed a hole in the fence. Being curious, they stopped and one of them peeked through the hole.

"Gosh, there are a lot of people in there," he said.

"Men or women?" asked the other little boy.

"Dunno," said the first. "They have no clothes on!"

* * *

Some friends came to visit us for the week-end and brought their little boy, Johnny. Our dog came up and licked his hand. The boy began to cry.

"The dog's going to bite me!" he cried.

"Don't be silly," we told him. "What makes you think he's going to bite you?"

"Well," he said, "don't you see he's already tasting me?"

INTRODUCING A MINSTREL SHOW

By Earl Jay Gilbert

Folks, we're going to have a lot of fun tonight watching an up-to-the-minute minstrel show. You know, the kind that's filled with singing, dancing, comedy, music. We've got a lot of talent who are going to strut their stuff. A lot of these boys would click in a big way in the professional field. A good minstrel show is something for everybody to enjoy—men, women and children. It contains all the elements necessary for general entertainment.

Outside of productions like this you seldom ever see a minstrel show any more. It hasn't been so many years ago that there were dozens of professional minstrel shows traveling all over the United States, playing everything from one night stands to periods of several weeks and longer in one place. Most of the members of those troupes got their first experience in home town productions like the one you're going to see tonight.

The minstrel show as we know it is strictly an American institution. Of course there were minstrels in medieval times, who traveled from place to place. They composed their musical numbers and sang and played their own compositions on harps and other musical instruments. During the days of chivalry they were welcomed and highly honored everywhere, but as the chivalric age passed, for some reason or other, their popularity declined, and during the reign of Queen Elizabeth they were classed as beggars and vagabonds, and as entertainers they practically vanished from the scene.

I wonder what those oldtimers, who actually composed and played their own songs and music, would say if they could come back and see some of their present day counterparts—like the singers who moo like calves and howl like wolves and get paid big money for it—or the guys who calmly appropriate the music of the great composers and earn five thousand a week or more as song writers and composers. Bach, Beethoven,

Mozart, and the other old masters must be dizzy from turning over in their graves!

Well, anyway, no other country in the world has ever had anything in the entertainment field like our own American minstrels, who owe their origin to the early Negro community groups. In the slave days when Negroes relaxed after their day's labors, they used to sing and dance and tell jokes and play instruments — mostly strings, banjos, and similar instruments. From these early Negro groups, with their spontaneous gaiety and natural humor, and ever-present infectious laughter, developed our minstrels. The members blacked their faces, usually with burnt cork, and imitated Negro dialects.

I am reminded of the Frenchman who excitedly rushed up to a friend and exclaimed: "Oh, Jules, the mos' taireeble theeng 'ave 'appened! I go 'ome. The door she is locked. I cannot enter. I look in window. There I see my wife—my Mimi—she is with Americain Negro G. I. soldier! What shall I do?" "Restrain yourself, my dear Alphonse," said Jules. "Why not put some shoe blacking on your face and return to your 'ome? Maybe then your wife will admit you!" Clevair race, thees French!

But to get back to the old time minstrel show. They were not as good as our modern minstrels, but they were really something to see. The entertainers sat grouped in a tier of seats, arranged in a semi-circle. The interlocutor, or master of ceremonies, who did not black up, sat in the center and introduced the acts and announced the musical numbers and cracked jokes with the two endmen, or comedians.

An endman would say, "Mistuh Interlocutor, kin you tell me why a fireman wears red suspenders?" and the interlocutor would answer, "No, Mr. Bones, why does a fireman wear red suspenders?" and the endman would reply, "To hold his trousers up!" That was always a sure-fire gag, no matter how often an audience had heard it.

However, I understand our boys have got some newer jokes for tonight. Although most comedians will tell you that if a joke is really funny, its age doesn't matter, especially if you've never heard it before.

It reminds me of the fellow who went to a minstrel show in the old days and heard so many old jokes that he got disgusted and got up and walked out. A man stopped him outside the theatre and said: "Sir, will you give me five dollars to bury an old time endman?" The disgusted theatre patron said: "Here's thirty. Bury six of them."

And then there's the story about a minstrel show arriving in a small town at about three o'clock in the morning on a very dark night. They were met at the station by an old man with a lighted lantern. He was a typical old Rube, as they used to call them — you know, with the chin-piece. He said: "Boys, I run the hotel. Jest get in line behind me and we'll go right up. Be kinda careful of that sidewalk. There might be some loose boards in it." They tramped along, following him, for about twenty minutes, when finally one of them said: "How much farther is this hotel of yours?" The old man said, "Only 'bout ten minutes more. We'll get there directly." Eventually they reached the hotel. The old man lighted a kerosene lamp in the lobby and called up to his wife: "Hey, Ma, here's them actors." She called back: "Where we goin' to put 'em? We ain't got no empty rooms!" He yelled back: "Some of 'em can double up in them salesmen's trunks in the sample room. The rest of 'em can take turns sleepin' on these three chairs here in the lobby!" One of the troupers said disgustedly: "Say, Grandpa, is this the only hotel in town?" The old man said: "No, it ain't. There's another one right around the corner, but you boys wouldn't like it. It ain't a nice place." Then he lowered his voice and whispered significantly: "It's rumored about town that they not only sell liquor, but they also harbor wild women!" The lobby was emptied in two seconds flat.

Well, folks, the original minstrels have long since vanished. But as long as people love music and singing and dancing and comedy, we'll always have new ones. The one you're going to see now is the latest and most modern version of the old-timers. So prepare for an evening of good entertainment and laughter brought to you for that purpose by our own minstrels. Let's all have a happy evening!

SECTION THREE

THE EMCEE AT SPECIAL OCCASIONS

In this section we have selected material that will provide the necessary patter for the many special situations that require up-to-the minute and alert treatment by the emcee. Usually he has the responsibility of establishing a happy atmosphere at the gathering and assuring the right kind of audience to the guest of honor. Here again experienced emcees have contributed a large amount of the material in this section.

Much of the material is lengthy in treatment so as to enable the emcee to select the parts of it that can be adapted to the requirements of the situation. There can be an interpolation of stories and incidents that are appropriate for the occasion.

THE EMCEE AT AN ARMY BUDDIES' REUNION

By Arthur L. Kaser

When you are in the army and bunked close together, and you eat close together, drill, work, fight close together, you get —Well, you become pretty close buddies, and this reunion should bring back some happy remembrances, and some perhaps not so happy.

This is a good opportunity to tell you veterans how you can get a good substantial additional bonus. Just move to France or England. Congress will think you are foreigners and pay you handsomely.

Can anyone here tell me who the wise guy was that said, during our fight with Japan that the Jap Zero planes were just like step-ins, and it took just one Yank to bring them down?

Perhaps it doesn't seem so long since we were in the service, but great strides have been made in our weapons. Did you know that we now have a new rifle that fires so rapidly that it shoots eight times before you didn't know it was loaded?

Speaking of speed, did you hear about the new WAAC who said to the sergeant: "I'm a hungry gal. Where do I eat?" The sergeant said: "I suggest that this first evening you mess with the officers." She said: "Oh, I've done that already, but I tell you I'm hungry." Well, she ate with the officers, and what an eater! When she had speared her fifth pork chop and ninth boiled potato the officer next to her said: "Sister, you sure do like your food, don't you?" Between bites the WAAC said: "Not particulary. It just happens I am passionately devoted to bicarbonate of soda."

One of the best-liked men in our outfit was so dumb that when he couldn't manipulate his rifle successfully during the manual of arms the sergeant roared: "Can't you find the balance of your rifle?" The rookie replied: "I thought it was all here. It's all they gave me." On the rifle range, when the command was "Fire at will," he asked the sergeant, "Where is Will?" When this chap, Jones, first arrived with us and was on the drill field marching close order, the sergeant yelled, "Halt!," Jones kept right on going. "Jones," asked the sergeant, "what were you before you got in the army?" "I took care of horses," said Jones. They started marching again. The sergeant yelled: "Squad, halt! Jones, whoa!"

One day I saw Jones when he was so sad that he was nearly crying. I said to him: "Jones, what's the matter?" "Homesick," he confided. I said: "We all get that way." He replied very sadly: "It's different with me. My father has a tavern."

Attention! At ease. Anyone desiring a discharge will make application at H. Q.

THE EMCEE AT A MERCHANTS' BANQUET

By Forbes Milliken

We never realize how many merchants there are in our city until we all get together. And thereby hangs a sale. When Noah built the Ark there was no lumber companies to furnish him the materials. He had to cut his own timbers. There was no government tacks in those days so he had to use wooden pins to hold his ship together. He could hire no union shipbuilders because he had no money to pay them. He couldn't float a loan so he called in his wife and animals. Today it is different. We have lumber companies everywhere; men can be hired if we have the money. If we don't have, it isn't so difficult to float a loan and we don't have to make wooden pins to hold our business together. The government has plenty of tax for us.

Today, however, we must advertise to survive. Competitive advertising can be both profitable and interesting. A certain owner of a haberdashery hired a very beautiful girl to make men's ties in the store window. Big crowds of men were constantly blocking the sidewalk to see her. The following day a competitor placed an attractive girl in his store window making ties. But her back was turned to the street. The crowds of men that wanted to see her had to come **inside** his store.

I was in a local store not long ago when a lady entered and asked about yarn to knit a sweater for her dog. "How large is the dog?" asked the sales girl. The answer was so vague, she said: "Why don't you bring the dog in here?" "Oh, no," said the customer, "that wouldn't do. You see, I want my dog to be surprised."

And speaking of advertising, how about this ad in the local newspaper: "For Sale—Bakery business, including large oven. Present owner has been in it for years. Has good reason for leaving."

My little nephew noticed for the first time a very vivid rainbow. "Uncle," he asked, "what does it advertise?"

An old codger from way, way out stepped into one of our clothing stores and stood for some time watching a clerk unpack a box of men's gayly colored pajamas. Curiosity, getting the better of him, the man asked, "What's them?" "Pajamas," said the clerk. "Pajimmies?" echoed the man. "What are they for?" The clerk explained: "You wear them at night. Could I sell you a pair?" "Not me," said the old codger. "I never go no place at night 'cept to bed."

This was heard in one of our jewelry stores. A man was gazing with rapture at a display of diamonds in the case. "Beautiful diamonds," he said to the clerk. "I'd love to smother my wife in diamonds." The clerk shook his head. "Isn't there a cheaper way?" he said.

And now, ladies and gentlemen, our speaker, who made the fatal mistake one time by beginning his speech: "As I look over the audience I see many faces I should like to shake hands with," Mr. **(Name of the speaker.)**

THE EMCEE AT A PLUMBERS' CONVENTION

By Jeff Branen

I was almost late getting here this evening. I bought a used car this afternoon and had a flat this evening. I had to borrow a jack. That car must have belonged to a plumber. No tools came with it.

A plumber, though, shouldn't be blamed for everything. A lady who was getting up a group for an afternoon picnic called the weather bureau, and asked: "Any chance of a shower this afternoon?" The weather bureau man said: "Lady, if you need one, take it."

A lady called me to fix a leak in her kitchen sink. I was under the sink when her husband came home. He looked at me and then yelled: "Helen, who put this homely statue under the sink?"

When I had finished I charged him eleven bucks for a four-dollar job, and did he holler! I said to him: "Mac, remember what Shakespeare said in MacBeth, 'He who dances must pay the piper, and he who pipes must pay the plumber.' "

FOR THE EMCEE AT AN OFFICE PARTY OR CEREMONY HONORING A MEMBER LEAVING FOR ARMY SERVICE

By George A. Posner

THERE IS A SOUND OF "REVEILLE" PLAYED ON A BUGLE, THE PIANO, OR HUMMED BY THE MASTER OF CEREMONIES.

I was wondering why the girls in this building were looking so depressed lately. I just found out. It seems we're about to lose the Beau Brummel, the Casanova of the office—shall we say the Joie de Vie of the girls' lives? I'm always the last one to find out these things. Gosh!

He has a letter here, from the **President,** and it starts, "Greetings, Greetings"—well, what do you know?—a close friend of the President's, asks that he "come up and see me some time soon." Well!

THE M.C. HUMS "REVEILLE" AGAIN. SAYS TO THE INDUCTEE:

A beautiful piece. You'll hear it often. In fact, you will find you just can't start your day without it.

Well, when a fellow gets to be the age of our hero here, it's a question as to which he'll be answering first—the military or the wedding march. But what's the difference? You're going to battle either way.

There's just one sure way to keep from going into the army, for a young fellow like you. Wanna know? Join the navy!

But it won't be so bad. I look back on my own army days with a kind of nostalgia. You know I came from a family of fighters. I should say fighters ran in my family. Yeah, they were fighters from away back. The further back they were, the better they liked it.

Don't think they didn't fight. They fought and fought,

and fought and fought. My, how they fought! But they had to go anyway.

That's all right. I've got an uncle, a war casualty. Completely shattered nerves. Because of the war. No, he didn't go; it was his fear of being drafted.

But I had another uncle who wanted to go. However, his employers made a pathetic plea to the Draft Board. I'll never forget that letter; word for word I remember how it read: "Will you please grant him deferment? He's the only man left in our plant, and at the present time he's carrying on with twenty inexperienced girls."

Don't worry, my boy. I was in the army myself, and it wasn't too bad. Roosevelt guided us. We said, "Hurray, Teddy—up San Juan hill we go!"

It wasn't much different with the Draft Boards in those days. If you could see lightning, and hear thunder—you were in, boy!

Here's how it will be, son. There will be the medical exam at first by those army doctors. But they're really a jolly bunch. Always there with their funny digs—with this needle and that needle. They're good. You've got to take your hat off to them. Also your shirt, your shoes, your sox, your pants.

First they'll want your blood. A sample. I'll never forget how they went at me. They dug the needle in here, they dug it in there. And then, here and there. Nothing, nothing happened. Finally they said: "We give up; where do you keep it?"

They finally had to give me a blood transfusion to get some.

I was a wreck. Stomach trouble, too—I had no guts.

They said: "Now read that eye chart." I said, "What chart?"

That almost got me out. But that night, while I was sitting in a movie theater, who should come in and take a seat next to me but the eye doc who had examined me.

But I was a fast thinker. I turned to him and said: "My good man, does this bus go to San Pedro?"

It didn't do much good....

Next thing they'll send you to a psychiatrist. Know what a psychiatrist is? It's a guy who is paid to do what any man's wife does to him for nothing. You know, you married guys?

But before you know it, you'll be in. They'll give you one of those G.I. haircuts. That's short for "G. I. Can't-Believe-It. Is- **That**-the-Way-I'm-gonna-Look!" Yeah, it's the same old army.

I well remember the day they outfitted me with my new uniform. They have good tailors in the army. The sergeant looked me over and said: "The trousers are a perfect fit, sir. The blouse is a perfect fit, sir; the jacket fits you perfectly—looks nice in the back, too.

I said, "Heavens, you don't suppose I'm deformed, do you?"

They assign a sergeant to you, you know, as soon as you get into the army. He's a kind of valet, or something.

First thing in the morning he'll awake you, with a gentle shake, and say: "Sir, will you have your breakfast in bed; or are you getting up to eat today, sir?"

You'll gain weight in no time at all in the army. Soon I had gained sixty pounds—two pounds of flesh and 58 pounds of equipment.

But those happy training days are soon over, and there you'll be marching down to your ship for embarkation. Marching between lines of people standing there and cheering. Who are those people cheering? They are people who aren't going.

You'll love the ship. I well remember my first time aboard a troop transport away out at sea. I could hardly contain myself! Boy, how I whooped it up.

Ma de mer is what this is called. That's French for "You Can't Take It With You." It's all right so long as you don't—as did one fellow—get seasickness and lockjaw at the same time.

You'll always remember, as I did, how sweet and beautiful your girl looked there on the dock waving goodbye to you, and crying. I remember how I shouted to her, "Don't cry, dear. I won't be lonesome. There will be girls over there, too."

And my girl said, "I know. Why do you suppose I'm crying?"

It's all right. The army will make a man of every one that goes into it. Except, of course, it will also make a lot of Wacs. But is that bad?

Yeah, our Harold's place is going to be hard to fill. Hard to fill. Who can kiss like he does—like a man siphoning gasoline?

Before I finish, and before I forget it, I want to be the first to put in my bid for your little black address book!

It's all just kidding, of course. We're really going to miss you a lot around here. You've been a good worker, and a good guy. And when you've finished doing your duty and are ready to come back to us, your job will be waiting, we'll be waiting, the girls will be waiting (we hope) to welcome you back. God bless you!

ADDITIONAL MATERIAL

My grandfather told me a good army story. He was in the Confederate Army during the Civil War.

It seems there was a certain Confederate town that was attacked by Northern troops, and sent for aid from the mountain volunteers. Before the aid could arrive, however, the Southern troops were driven out of the town by the Federals.

So in the night, the Southern reinforcements arrived, my grandfather among them, and found the town deserted. It was the first time they had ever been there, so they decided, as they saw the enemy returning, that discretion was the better part of valor, and left by the rear gate just as the Federals entered by the front. Scouts reported it was a large force.

So the Southerners, seeing before them a fine smooth road, with tall white fences on either side, let themselves go for all they were worth on a "Sheridan 20 miles away" ride for more aid. But they rode and rode all night, and never a sign of civilization did they see. It seemed as though the whole state was deserted. At last the sun peeped over the mountains, and found them still galloping, with the dust in clouds behind.

Then to the amazement of the troops the colonel suddenly drew up, and with a strange look, turned to his lieutenant.

"What's the matter, suh?" asked the lieutenant.

"Matter? Why, suh," roared the colonel, "we've been galloping around a race-track all night!"

* * *

The draft board in my town was just about the easiest-to-please draft board you ever saw. We heard rumors that the official dictum from Washington was, "If they can hear thunder, and see lightning—they're in!" We don't know how true that was, but what a dickens of a time one neighbor of mine had.

He kept expostulating to the board that he was unfit for service, but it seems they wouldn't take no for an answer; and when he arrived at the army recruit camp depot at Riverside, California, he was still arguing.

And finally he says to the sergeant who took him in charge: "And to cap it all, I have no arms. Now can you see why I would be no good for the army?"

"No good!" replied the sergeant, joyfully. "Why, you're just the man we've been looking for!"

"What do you mean?"

"You see that guy over there pumping water?"

"Yes."

"You stand by him and tell him whenever the bucket is full," said the sergeant. "He's blind."

* * *

A huge army supply depot, fronting on a well-traveled highway, was patrolled by guards mounted on motorcycles. One night an old sergeant was showing a recruit where the limits of his beat would be. Said he: "You patrol from here to that third red light you see down there on the highway. Now get going—it's midnight now, and you should make forty round trips by the time you are relieved in the morning."

Next day the corporal of the guard reported the rookie as missing. And this rookie didn't show up again for three days. Then one morning, there he was, all bedraggled, dusty and weary.

"Where in heck have you BEEN?" demanded the sergeant.

"Well," said the recruit, "you know that third red light you pointed out? It was on a truck on its way to Salt Lake City!"

* * *

But that's nothing to what happened to another rookie I know. His company, all raw recruits, had gone on their first long hike of twenty-five miles. At the end of that twenty-five mile hike they were to meet a flock of trucks which were to take them back to the camp from which they started.

So here they were at the end of that hike they had made (with full packs, too); and before the trucks could come up their captain said: "You know what? That was a wonderful hike, and I feel wonderful." Why shouldn't he? He was on a horse.

"I feel just wonderful," says he, "and you know what, I really believe it would be fine if we **hiked** back instead of riding. But anybody who doesn't want to hike, take two paces forward."

The whole company stepped forward, except one little private. The officer came up to him, patted him on the back, and said: "I'm proud of you. I'm glad there's one man ready to go twenty-five miles more."

So this private wearily lifts his head and said: "Captain, I'm so tired I couldn't even take those two paces forward!"

* * *

A Negro draftee, seeking exemption, entered the Draft Board office and asked another Negro waiting there:

"Am dis whar de redemption board is?"

"Sho' is," answered the other. "But de blessed redeemer done gone out fo' lunch."

* * *

When during the war the draft age limit was set at 26, a certain fellow called before the draft board claimed exemption, saying he was 27.

A few months later the age limit was set up to 36, and he was called up again.

"I'm above the draft age," said he. "I'm 37."

A member who had served on the board when this young man had been previously called thought he remembered the face, and he asked:

"Weren't you in here a few months ago? As I recall you claimed then that you were 27."

"I know," he replied blandly, seemingly undaunted. "But I aged 10 years when I heard I was called!"

* * *

During a dust storm a recruit took refuge in a cook tent. The following dialogue occurred:

Recruit: "Say, cook, if you kept the lid on that pot you wouldn't get dust in it."

Cook: "Your business, young man, is to serve your country."

Recruit: "To serve it—yes! But not to eat it!"

INTRODUCING A BATHING BEAUTY CONTEST

By George A. Posner

Attention . . . Attention! . . . Attention, please!

Hm! . . . Can some one find the time to spare, to look at me? I'm an optimist . . . Honest, fellows, the girls will be here for a while longer. Believe me!

Hm! . . . Anybody got a bathing suit I can wear? A size 52? Well, don't laugh! You should see me in a bathing suit! I'm really a knobby sight. The suit's being fixed at present—the trap door flopped. Well! Thank you!

Really, I won a cup in a bathing suit contest. President McKinley and Lillian Russell were the judges. I was Mr. United States. Was I pretty! A little bulgy around Iowa, maybe. And maybe around Lower California. But not so bad.

I had what we called an hour-glass figure in those days. Tsck! The sands of time run down—mostly to the bottom. Darn it! A million dollar figure to start with, then inflation had to set in.

You should have seen the bathing girls of my day. When they put something on they weren't stingy. They dressed like Mother Hubbard. Now they look more like Mother Hubbard's cupboard.

In those days the mosquitoes certainly didn't have the breaks they have today.

Well, look at our girls of today. Aren't they beautiful? God dress—I mean, bless 'em! . . . Um! . . . What happened to the old-fashioned girl—who had hidden charms? What **happened** to the old-fashioned girl—thank God!

You know, all my life I've been hearing women complaining that they had nothing to wear. Now I'm beginning to believe it. But why complain? On these girls it looks good.

These suits, they tell me, are called the Withholding Tax Type. They cover about twenty percent. Twenty percent, indeed! I just wish my taxes were that small.

Hm! . . . I hope there aren't any moths around . . . With a moth or two there could be a situation!

Ladies and gentlemen! Here are the entrants to our Bathing Beauty Contest. In these bathing suits the girls are showing a lot of style. And the styles are showing a lot of the girls.

So take a look at the girls, and at the styles. Hurry! The way the styles change it won't take long for these bathing suits to go out of style—and out of sight, too. The prices are already out of sight.

You know the definition of a style expert? It is one who can get the women to pay more and more for less and less.

We've got a lot of good lookers here. Not only on the stage, but in the audience. . . . Say, are those eyeballs there on stems? . . . Press them back in, please. If you can. The cat might get them.

Photographers! Don't shoot until you see the whites of their thighs!

Well, girls, you know the rules of a contest. All entries become the property of the company. . . . What am I thinking of? . . . No, I'm kidding. The rule doesn't apply in this case. So, you judges, get that look off your faces!

Let's look at our first entrant. Do I have to ask? Beautiful! Beautiful! Can you imagine an ocean decorated by this little beauty? The tide would come in and refuse to go out.

And this little girl here. Doesn't she look like a million? . . . No wonder so many men are trying to make millions!

And here is Miss ————. M-m-m! Do you know a girl like this could be a menace to society? One look at her, and men may go home and shoot their wives.

You know, the last time I emceed a bathing beauty contest my wife got me aside and yipped: "Down, boy, down! You look at a few girls in bathing suits, and immediately forget you are married." How wrong she is! Nothing reminds me of the fact so forcibly! No, I'm just kidding. We're really a happy married couple. My wife's happy, and I'm married.

And this is Miss ————. They say the town she comes from is just a whistle stop. I can understand that. How do you like that swim outfit? There is a girl worth wading for.

Here would be the girl to marry, fellers. You'd **know** what you are getting.

And it wouldn't take much to keep her in clothes. Clothes. What clothes? Anyway, who sees her clothes?

And this little girl. Oh, my, I'll bet when she gets on a street car, the advertising's a total loss.

I mean, even without that bathing suit! No, I don't mean that, either. You know what I mean. I mean she's beautiful. Isn't she?

She says, "Thank you." Don't thank me, just for complimenting you on your suit. It's really nothing . . . nearly nothing . . . The girl's been well-reared. . . .

Looks good from the front, too.

What do you think of this little girl, and this outfit? Isn't it wonderful? Thank you. You can thank them, Miss, but please don't bow. The suit may change from wonderful to sensational.

Hm! I'd say she looks like a rail. I mean a third rail—dangerous when exposed. This is what you might call a daring costume. If I could only take a dare.

They do say women are braver than men. They show a lot more backbone, anyway.

Women! Women! Women! What's the philosopher say? They're just a rag, a bone and a hank of hair? Well, meet a happy junk collector!

You know the story of the school teacher asking little Herkimer, "Under what gender would you classify women—masculine, feminine, or what?" And the boy answered, "The nuder gender?"

Never mind. Imagine having a wife like that to come home to. Taking your shoes off with her own little hands—when you want to go out with the boys?

Who'd want to go out with the boys? Not for a long time, anyway.

Well, girls, are you sure the material in those suits is guaranteed against shrinkage? Anyway, don't go in the water. As they said in the war. "Trust in the Lord, but keep your powder dry." . . . G-r-r! Pass the ammunition! . . .

Let's go on with the judging.

THE EMCEE AT A TESTIMONIAL FOR A LONG-TERM EMPLOYEE

By Earl Jay Gilbert

My friends, this, as you know, is a special occasion. I'd like to say first that ours is a good company to be connected with. I don't think anyone will disagree with that statement. So it isn't surprising that we have an employee who's been with us for ——— years, nor that we're here to pay our respects to that gentleman, whom we all regard with admiration and affection—admiration for many years of unquestioned loyalty and service to his employers, and affection for the many qualities he possesses which have made him so many friends. His entire career has been a symbol of faithfulness, of trustworthiness, of integrity.

When he started with this organization his first job might not have been considered by some people as being highly important, but by his own efforts and diligence he made the job important, and ever since then, no matter what undertaking or commission has been given him, he has applied himself earnestly and industriously, and his record shows that he is entitled to and worthy of all the appreciation we can give him.

To digress for a moment, I'm reminded of a story. It has no connection with our friend or with this company, but I think it deserves to be repeated. It seems the president of a certain firm, who was not noted for a decent appreciation of his employees, sent for an old employee. He said, "Mr. Jones, we're laying you off indefinitely." "But," said the old man, "I've been working here for sixty years." "I know," said the president, "but because of age limitations we'll have to let you go. Your work here has been pretty fair, although your attendance has not been what it should have been. You lost two days in January, 1922, and in March of that same year you were twenty minutes late one morning. However, we'll overlook that. Unfortunately we have not been able to give you the increase in salary you have asked for from time to time, but we want you to know that we feel that you've been worth the thirty dollars a week we've paid you. And, as a token of our regard and as a reward for long service, we're presenting you with this check for twenty-five dollars." As the old man looked at the check, the president leaned over and whispered in his ear, "Don't put that through 'till Thursday!" The next day's paper carried this news item: "Judge reprimands old employee for stuffing check down employer's throat and wrecking office." Well, it might have happened.

Now, to be serious, we all know that success in life means different things to different people. We're all striving for some form of success, in accordance with the way we each measure success. Some people rate success in terms of fame, of power, of money—and don't misunderstand me—I've got nothing against money. It comes in handy at times, as most of us have discovered.

But I think that a man can call himself successful when he knows that he's always done a good job, and it isn't so much what a man does, it's how he does it, that counts. When a man does a good job, and knows that others appreciate it, that's a most satisfactory feeling, my friends—one of work well done.

And as our friend looks back over the years he must feel a deep pride in the rewarding thoughts that in addition to any possible material gains, he has not only achieved his measure of success, but has also won the sincere respect and friendship of his fellow men. His career should be an inspiration to all of us. And now, I think we should hear from him.

(Or, if a presentation is to be made)

And now, on behalf of the company and your fellow employees, we want you to accept this gift with all of our best wishes, in commemoration of your ——— years of service.

FOR AN EMCEE AT A BRIDAL SHOWER

By George A. Posner

They asked me if I would like to talk at this bridal shower. Asking a woman if she'd care to talk! That's like asking a bedbug if it would like to bite.

It reminds me of my little one-year-old brother. They keep asking Mother and Dad, "Have you taught him to talk yet?" And my folks always answer, "Have we taught him to talk yet? We're already teaching him to shut up!"

Maybe you people will wish you hadn't started **me!**

Our little queen, Irma, is going to be married. And so we are giving her a shower. Shower! That's symbolic, little queen. It signifies the beginning of a reign. Until maybe a year later, a little Prince of **Wails** comes along, and takes over.

Well, I say go ahead and marry your man. What advice, marry your man! What else is there for us girls to marry? But isn't it a shame a girl can't marry without dragging some poor innocent man into it. What have men done to deserve being made husbands?

Poor innocents! They see a pretty girl. A pretty girl is like a melody, they are told. So the boys whistle at her. And first thing they know they're facing the music. At the halter—I mean altar. Getting the last rites from the minister. For most of them it's the last rights they'll ever have.

But be sure you get the right one, girls. Because the saying goes that if he isn't, the rites won't right him, or the altar alter him.

He thought it was just a harmless flirtation at first. Well, he found out differently, didn't he? Oh, of course we girls don't chase the men, do we? No. Neither does a mouse trap chase the mouse. There are two kinds of men—the quick and the wed. Mencken said, "Love is the star a man looks up to; and marriage is the coal hole he falls into."

The poor boys spend the years between twelve and twenty-one waiting to become their own boss. Then they get married.

Before marriage, they think a man should be the master in the house, or know the reason why. After marriage they **know** the reason why.

Of course, as a husband, he is entitled to lay down the law to his wife. But, boy, how she can repeal them!

The men say marriage is a lottery. Poor suckers. You have a **chance** in a lottery! But the girls believe it's a lottery. Don't they give the boys their numbers?

Well, Irma says this man is really an ambitious fellow. Always trying to go places. Yeah, but what places, please? Maybe he's like the one I was out driving with the other night. Did **he** want to go places! It was all I could do to stop him!

He parked at the roadside, turned off the ignition, and said he was bugs about me. Then I guess I'd call him a **bedbug,** because the minute the lights were out he started to get busy!

Yeah, did he want to go places! Wish I could tell you the places I told **him** to go. That devil.

You know a woman is like a typewriter. Press the wrong places and you get terrible words.

In the days of Adam and Eve, a woman was a man's rib. Now he wants her to be his neck!

But to get back to Irma. Remember, Irma, it's up to you. Marriage can be anything from "Love's Old Sweet Song" to a "Hot Time In the Old Town Tonight." So be on the watch. Especially while on your honeymoon, don't be **napping.** A husband is like a furnace. If you don't tend him, he'll be going out. You know husbands are only little boys after all. After all they can get!

Men! Before marriage they swear to love. And after marriage—they love to swear! That's why God made women beautiful but dumb. Beautiful so that the men would love them, and dumb so that they would love the men.

So don't forget to hug him once in a while. Wind your soft little arms about his waist. It will make him feel wonderful. He'll feel wonderful when he feels his pocket and finds his money is still there!

Remember, all men have a sense of humor. The more you humor them the better they like it. Not that the women can't take a joke. Look at some of the men they marry.

Remember the way to a man's heart may be through his stomach, but there are other ways of stuffing him. I once read a recipe for a happy marriage. It said: "Take a rich duck. Stuff with balogna. Baste with banana oil. Add apple sauce. Service while hot."

But remember, there's a difference between women and men. The beasts! If a man attends a club it's because he needs social recreation. If a woman does, it's because she loves to gossip.

If a man smokes, it's because he gets solid comfort out of it. If a woman uses cigarets, it's to be smart.

If a man has an accident with his car, it's the other fellow's fault. If a woman gets her car tangled up, it's because she's a poor driver.

If a man gets drunk, it's funny. If a woman does, she's degraded.

If a man is nervous at the end of a day, he's overworked. If a woman complains, she's worried herself into it over nothing.

If a man refuses to adopt the new styles, he's conservative. If a woman does, she's old-fashioned.

An old preacher—a man, of course!—said that a wife should be at once like and unlike three things. First, she should be like a snail, always within her house. But she should not, like the snail, carry all she has on her back.

Secondly, she should be like the echo, speaking only when she was spoken to. But she should not, like the echo, always have the last word.

Thirdly, she should be like the town clock, always on time. But she should not, like the town clock, speak so that she is heard all over town.

There you are. Aren't men the beasts? But we women—darn it!—all love animals.

Never mind, Irma. You know, of course, I'm just kidding, and this is all in fun. Go ahead and marry him, God bless you, and in all seriousness.

Maybe that's why I never married. When a woman wants to catch a man she must learn to keep her trap shut.

Let me introduce to you our lovely guest of the evening, a girl whom it's been my great pleasure to call a friend—Irma!

ADDITIONAL MATERIAL

By George A. Posner

As for your husband, remember they're all the same. Give them a free hand, and they'll have it all over you. So beware! Be on the watch!

Ever hear the story of Angela MacDoughal? Well, he told her he was going to take her to all those far-away exotic places you hear about on the disc-jockey programs, after they were married—so she inferred from the line of talk he fed her.

And where does he take her on their honeymoon? Coney Island, for three days. "That's only the beginning" says he.

After that, he says to her: "Angela, if you'll be a good wife to me, a frugal one, which is one who is economical always, we could save up our money, and some day have our reward in a nice trip to Europe, and maybe around the world."

That sounded wonderful to the wife, and she bent herself to the project in view. She scrimped and saved, denied herself any fripperies in clothes, ate very simply and did away even with "such follies as shows or movies," which her husband seemed to frown upon.

From time to time she'd say to her husband, Andrew, hopefully: "How am I doing? Are we nearly there yet, dear?"

"Well, not quite," Andrew would answer. "But be patient, dear, we're certainly getting there."

So years wandered by. Ten years; fifteen years; and finally it was twenty years; and she was beginning to feel and look pretty discouraged. So she finally said: "It is twenty years now, Andrew. Have we enough for the trip maybe to Europe?"

This time he gives her a pat, a big smile, and says: "Cheer up, dear. I've got good news for you, Angela. Finally we have enough money to go to Europe!"

She could hardly believe her senses. "Wonderful, wonderful!" she trilled, and began to flutter around like a bird, getting ready for the long-awaited journey. "When do we start, dear, tomorrow morning?"

"Ah, now, wait dear, listen! I'm trying to tell ye; now we gotta start savin' for the trip back!"

So watch them! Watch them, the beasts!

There are lots of ways to find out what kind of a husband you are going to get, before you take the fatal step. But be on the watch; don't let them fool you. They're clever, the beasts!

There was a girl named Linda in our block, who owned a pet monkey. She also had four suitors, and she didn't know which one she would pick for the one to shackle. Then one day she got a bright idea.

"Monkeys are imitative," she thought. "They imitate what people around them are doing. So, since I have four suitors, and don't know which one will make the best husband, why don't I do this? I'll let each of the men take care of my monkey for a couple of weeks. Each time, when the monkey is returned to me, I'll study its habits. Then I'll know what the habits of the man who had him were."

So she told the first suitor: "Alfred, I'm going out of town for a while. Would you mind taking care of my pet monkey while I'm gone?"

"Of course," he answered. "I'll take care of him."

When the two weeks had elapsed, and the monkey was returned to her, she noticed that it chased every woman it saw.

"Aha!" said Linda. "A woman chaser!"

She scratched that suitor off her list.

When the monkey returned after its stay with the second suitor, Linda found that he would grab every bottle he saw, pull out the cork, and guzzle its contents.

"Oho! A habitual drinker!" And off her list he went, too.

When the monkey returned after a couple of weeks with the third suitor, Linda found he would grab every deck of cards he saw, start shuffling them, and then dealing them around the table!

"Well! Tim's a gambler! I'm glad I found that out!" And she scratched **him** off the list.

Now when the monkey returned from its stay with the last of the suitors, Otto Schlesel, it was the neatest, most orderly, most methodical little thing she had ever seen! He was constantly cleaning up the place. If he saw a crumpled, discarded garment he picked it up, folded it neatly and put it away. If there was lint or dust on it, he carefully brushed it. The house was soon in meticulous order.

"Well!" exclaimed the delighted Linda. "There's the man for me. He's a paragon of neatness and efficiency!"

And so she married him.

After their marriage, she found that not only did he chase women, but he was also a habitual drinker, and a gambler besides. And so shiftless and thoughtless regarding her that at the time she had loaned him her pet monkey for safe keeping he had shifted the whole thing over to his butler!

So watch them, girls; watch them, watch them!

THE EMCEE AT A BASEBALL FAN CLUB DINNER

By Bob Royce

Ladies and gentlemen, our speaker today I think will speak on diamonds; diamonds of four facets encased in a mounting of tiers and bleachers. In other words—baseball.

We think of the game of baseball as a more or less modern game. But, my friends, it goes back farther than you think. For instance, we read in the Bible where Isaac met Rebecca at the well when she was walking with a pitcher. Again we read where Samson struck out when he beat the Philistines. We can find two records of Moses as a baseball player. He made his first run when he saw the Egyptians. Then when he shut out the Egyptians at the Red Sea. You have read about Abraham making a sacrifice. And how about the prodigal son? Didn't he make a home run? We are not sure about Noah. He was hampered so much by wet grounds. And then during the heyday of the Romans—we are certain they played baseball until the fall of the Roman Umpire.

But the game today is an international sport. It is played everywhere. That may account for the world being all balled up.

My wife could never understand the game. Just once did I take her to a game. When I got a little excited when a man slid safely into second base, she said: "Why are you so delighted because he fell down? Do you know him personally?"

Everybody's eyes are turned in the direction of the ball park during the baseball season. One employer posted this sign over the punch clock: "Any workman desiring to attend the funeral of a near relative will notify the foreman before 10 A.M. on the day of the game ."

Now, ladies and gentlemen, our speaker, **(name of speaker)** will pitch the next inning.

THE EMCEE AT A RETIREMENT PARTY

(After Thirty Years of Service in an Office)

By George A. Posner

The smiling gentleman you see before you has completed thirty years with our company. You notice I didn't say thirty years of **work** with the company. Sometimes I don't feel so sure!

Thirty years! Time certainly does fly.

I remember when he first came to me for a job. What a gay, handsome young buck! There's another thing called a buck that's depreciated quite a bit since then—the dollar. It's worth 50 cents now, is it? Something like that. But **our** young buck became steadily more valuable . . . I think! We sure kept paying him more money!

I well remember that morning he came in here for a job. He came in without closing the door behind him. And that didn't make me very happy, that cold day. So when he said: "Have you an opening here for a young man . . . ?" I said: "Yes, and close it as you go out, please!"

Then I guess I softened, and I said: "Young fellow, I'm sorry I don't have something for you. But we don't have enough work for the men we have."

He was persistent, though. He says: "Surely you could find a place for me—the little bit of work which I'd do?" Well, something like that. I don't recall the exact words.

But we both laughed, I remember, and then I said: "Considering how much time Mr. Jessup here seems to have to kill, he'll probably need an assistant to help!"

Finally I said: "Come to think of it, there is a little work accumulated in the file section. But I think I ought to tell you there's only two weeks' work there. Want it?"

He took it, and here he is, still with us, after thirty years. And you know, I've often wondered: Was it that I was that much of a slave driver, or a nincompoop, that I figured that what was really a **30-year job** could be done in **two weeks.** Or did our friend here take **30 years** to do a **two-weeks'** job?

I've laid awake nights worrying about that!

Anyway, it's too late to do anything about it—that's for sure. He's got us nicked for a pension, and that's that.

When he started with the firm he was quite a favorite with the ladies. He was a good-looking fellow. Still shows that, doesn't he? The girls called him "Tall, Dark and Hands." I wonder why? He was really tall, even at that young age. Say, is it true you have to stand on a chair to brush your teeth?

He was so popular, the thirtieth girl on his list, which he kept alphabetically, was Alice Adams. He sure got them. They say he used to drive up in his Chevvy coupe, and say: "Chicken, here's your coupe," and in she would get. And they say he and his old coupe were parked so often up there in a certain spot on Lovers' Lane, they were thinking of putting him on the road maps.

Well, it wasn't long before one of the gals had our handsome Romeo roped in. And soon they were playing the Prisoners' Song—er, I mean the Wedding March, over him. You know you can't play with matches, and not get burnt. No, I'm kidding, of course—he made a good match. A fine gal.

And then the kids began to arrive. I knew every time there was a new one. I'd look up and see him standing before the desk—"Sir, I think I should have a raise." Gosh, he nearly broke us! I don't think the stork made trips to that house—he boarded there!

I remember one day I was invited to dinner over at his house, and just as I got to the front stoop, something that looked like a duck suddenly came rushing through my legs and upset me. When I got up, I asked: "Heavens, that duck surprised me. I didn't know you had them here."

He answered: "That wasn't a duck, sir. I think it was the stork, with his legs worn down!"

He was always such a civic-minded, patriotic guy. He's always doing his best to support the special weeks or days. Comes the annual Poppy Day, he never fails to buy a poppy to help the veterans; comes National Apple Day, and he goes out and buys an apple; Mother's Day, a carnation. And he has a houseful of youngsters, strapping kids, good-looking and well-behaved.

I loved to watch him giving a new baby of his its bath. He had a method of his own for testing the water temperature. First, said he, you put the baby in the water. If he turns blue, the water's too cold. If he turns red, it's too hot. And if he turns white, then he needed the bath!

One day when he was giving one of the babes a bath, I put my hand in the water, and then said: "Heavens, man, with the temperature of this water, you're practically boiling that baby!"

He said: "That's just it. See this?" And he showed me a book on child care, pointed to a place where it said: "Health Hint: If the baby doesn't thrive on fresh milk it should be boiled." Oh, that man had his systems! Bless him!

Well, there's been water under the bridge since then; the kids have grown up and married. The world rolls along. You know the saying:

When she laughs at your every word—you're a bridegroom.

When they listen to you, and then do as they please—you're a father.

When you have to shout to be heard—you're a grandfather.

Our friend here, I am sure, has progressed through each of those states of the drama and comedy of life.

He has fulfilled his duty to his community, his job and his family in a manner deserving of respect and commendation. I am certain he has earned love and friendship of those with whom he has been associated. While he hasn't become anything like a rich man in the process, I feel he must have a good feeling of satisfaction and happiness. He has run a good race and he has the reward of accomplishment.

After all, what is money? It is certainly no yardstick with which to measure success.

It reminds me of another story which I'll have to give to you, before I close.

It seems there was a man named Patrick O'Houlihan who was busy digging away at the bottom of a ditch, when the foreman appeared at the top, and shouted down: "Patrick, you lucky divvil! Word's just come that yer uncle's dead and lift ye twenty-foive thousand dollars!"

So Pat threw down his shovel, and quit the job, but quick.

Pat drew the money, and went on a binge that lasted for months. Carousing. All day and night parties. Celebrations. And then even his home town wasn't good enough for him, evidently, for he disappeared from sight. But from time to time word came from people who had seen him on his travels. He knocked around all over the world. Then finally one day, months later, he showed up, his clothes tattered and torn, and himself looking tired, worn and humble. And asked the foreman for his old job back. He hadn't a dime.

So there, a couple of days later, he was, digging away, when again the foreman's face appeared at the top of the trench, saying: "Pat! You lucky, lucky, lucky, son-of-a-goon! If it ain't happened again! Another relative of yours died and left you thoity thousand dollars!"

And Pat leaned on his shovel, and groaned: "Oh, Lord! Do I have to go through all that again?"

That's supposed to be a funny story, but it contains a truth I am sure we can all see and agree with—that money isn't everything. It certainly can't take the place of nor compare with the basic essentials of happiness—the love of your family, the respect and good will of your friends and associates, peace of mind, a clear conscience, and your own inner realization that you have tried well, and have done the best you could with the equipment God gave you. All this, I am sure, is yours. And, believe me, it's a great deal.

I have here some gifts, from the company, and from your friends and associates—something to help you think of us occasionally, as I am sure we will of you—and to remind you to drop in and see us once in a while. Come as often as you like, will you? We'll always be happy to see you.

THE EMCEE AT AN AUCTION

By Louis J. Huber

All right, ladies and gentlemen, gather in here around my platform and I will assure you that you will be given the time of your life. That's what the judge said when he sentenced my uncle. Poor uncle! Little did he know that the time of his life would last for life.

All right, all right, come on closer, ladies and gentlemen. Let those people with a lot of money stand in the background, please, because people with much gold won't be given the opportunity of getting in on the bargains that I am about to sell at auction.

You, young lady, how would you like to buy a grandfather's clock for the small sum of one dollar? Of course, you'd like it and we have that very piece. And we are going to sell it for one dollar. If, and I say IF, we can get grandfather out of it. He's been living in it for the past forty years. Poor grandpa. Little does he know that you can't live on borrowed time and that the clock must go back to the store unless he makes the payments.

And who among you wouldn't like to buy a television set for two dollars? Everyone would like to own a TV set and only pay two bucks. Everyone and that includes me. So if any of you good people know where I can purchase one for two dollars please let me know. Now, while you folks are getting in closer, I'd like to show you a bit of tomfoolery and I'd like to entertain you with it. Is there anyone here named Thomas? Anyone who has any relatives named Thomas? Good. I had a joke that fitted into this spot and now I've forgotten it. It had something to do with tomfoolery.

But I have not forgotten why I am here and so I go on with the business at hand. And that business happens to be this genuine eight-day alarm clock. It takes this clock eight days before it gets alarmed. I wish I could remember that joke about tomfoolery.

Really, folks, this is not tomfoolery. The clock I hold in my hand has a retail value far beyond the price for which I am going to release it. I released one of these the other day and it broke into a thousand pieces.

A thousand, do I hear? Of course, I hear a thousand because I said it. Do I hear two thousand? Certainly not. This article is not worth that much and I will be the first to admit it. You good people will also admit it and so we are of one mind.

While we are of one mind let us start the bidding for this magnificent piece of merchandise. This is the ideal of the clockmaker's craft. The man who made this masterpiece spent many hours on it. That's why it is a little flat; he spent TOO many hours on it.

Do I hear a bid? I do. The gentleman bids ten cents. Ten cents for this work of art? One thin dime for this creation? Is that all? All right, I'll take it. And now do I hear twenty cents, twenty cents, twenty cents? I hear it. Twenty cents.

Twenty cents I have been bid. Shall I let this lovely article go for such a small sum? I shall not. If I did, my wife and children would never speak to me again. Would you people want that to happen? Certainly not. Do I hear thirty cents? I hear it. Thirty cents. (Keeps on trying to get more money for the merchandise until he feels he has reached the limit.) We are at one dollar, one dollar, one dollar. One dollar once, one dollar twice—and here is your last chance—one dollar three times! Sold to the gentleman, for the give-away price of one small dollar. Now the next piece of precious merchandise that we will award to the lucky bidder . . .

THE EMCEE AT A RAFFLE

By Louis J. Huber

Gather 'round, gather 'round, ladies and gentlemen, I am about to unfold the greatest event of the evening. This is not a daring exhibition of skill and courage. This is not an event that will see a man-eating lion being put in the same cage with a woman.

Which brings up an interesting question: What would a man-eating lion do if he were put in the same cage with a beautiful girl? What could he do? Well, as the man said just before he jumped off the sidewalk, he could change his diet.

But we are not concerned with lions and diets right now, ladies and gentlemen, we are interested in disposing of a certain number of pieces of merchandise that will make you wish that you were a millionaire and that you could buy each and every one of them for yourself.

Yes, a million dollars would come in mighty handy many times. But not right now, good people. You do not need a million dollars, you do not need a thousand dollars, you do not need a hundred dollars to own one of these fine pieces of merchandise.

Let me show you the articles in question. Here I hold in my hand a package. (Does this.) The box is sealed and no one knows the contents. Starting this very minute I will send the young ladies among you and you may purchase as many chances on this article as your heart desires and as your wallet permits. All right, girls, let's go. Give these lucky people an opportunity to participate in this raffle. (Girls mingle with the crowd to sell chances.)

That's right, young man, step right up and buy an opportunity to win this wonderful prize. One moment, young lady. (Calls one of the girls.) Let me have five thousand chances on this article. Oh, I beg your pardon, according to the rules I am not permitted to take a chance myself.

Oh, you lucky people, you who are so fortunate and are not barred from being in this grand and glorious event. I take this opportunity and congratulate you on your good fortune.

Yes, young man, do take another chance. Let the world see that you are a daring man, a man who risks one thin dime after another just to learn what I have in this package. Sell the young man another chance, lady. He knows that this opportunity will never come his way again. (He keeps up this patter, congratulating the people, telling them how lucky they are, how he envies them until all the chances are sold.)

All right, all right, folks, the time has come. Bring those stubs to me, girls, and I shall put them in this hat. This hat has been used for many things. It has been used as a head warmer and many times, when I felt like talking through my hat, I have used it. This, of course, is not one of the times.

For at this time I bring to the recipient of a lucky ticket the good news that they have won. No, no, I can't do this yet. I want to let this minute linger long. I want it to last forever. I feel quite privileged that I should be allowed to break this good news and I don't want it to end abruptly. Hold everything for one moment, please, while I draw out the lucky stub. (He draws the stub and just leans back and relaxes.)

Now I have gathered the strength to inform the holder of the lucky ticket that the time has come. Here it is: Number (Reads this.) Here is your award, friend. May you have much success with it. And now let us go on to an even greater prize and continue with the next article which is to be raffled here this evening. Ladies and gentlemen, this is the marvel of the age. In this box I hold one of the wonders of the universe, etc. **(On to the next article.)**

THE EMCEE AT A SILVER WEDDING ANNIVERSARY PARTY

By Louis J. Huber

To this house tonight, ladies and gentlemen, comes a celebration that deserves just what it is getting—our highest esteem. I would like to be so bold to suggest that I, your emcee, be permitted to point out a few things that make this a wonderful occasion.

A quarter of a century of wedded bliss is no simple accomplishment. We can repeat that for you but it would sound just the same. It is no easy task when one considers the divorce courts. When one considers that so many who take a mate for better or for worse, find it simple to untie the knot.

Actually, folks, I want to make my voice and manners sober and sincere because I'd like to tell you something so very few of you know. Despite the fact that Helen **(Name)** and Joe **(Name)** have been married twenty-five years he is her fourth husband. Even he does not know this and I hate to think of how he feels now that I'm forced, because I am twisting my own arm, to divulge the secret.

It's a sad story, good people, so lean back and be ready to cry. It seems that Helen had three other husbands. They all turned out to be a little on the seamy side and had to be sent to an institution for treatment. Not one of them ever got back. So she married Joe. She was bound to have a safe and sane fourth.

Now that I've told a fib about Helen it is only fair that I do the same thing about Joe. Some of you know, because you were at their wedding those many years ago, that Joe was given one dollar for a wedding gift. He invested it wisely. On their honeymoon he used it to make a telephone call home for more money.

We may joke about such matters, ladies and gentlemen, but there is also a time and a place to be serious about it. Let us now take that time. To be married for a quarter of a century a couple must have many ideas and ideals.

There must, of course, be love. For it is still love that makes the world go 'round. And I'm being square with you when I tell you that simple truth. So what is love? We can turn the pages of many books and find many silly answers. The word deserves a better treatment.

In "Romeo and Juliet" there is a line that, to my way of thinking, defines most of the aspects of the word. Shakespeare wrote it into the second act of the play. See what you think of them: "My bounty is as boundless as the sea, My love as deep; The more I give to thee the more I have, for both are infinite."

If we take but a moment to analyze these lines, we have the answer to a quarter of a century of love. The important words are in the middle of the quotation. Let me repeat them for you: "The more I give to thee the more I have."

Then there must be understanding. What is understanding? Voltaire wrote that when he to whom one speaks does not understand, and he who speaks himself does not understand, this is metaphysics. I'd like to rearrange those words to sound like this: When she to whom one speaks does understand, and she who speaks herself does understand, that is a silver wedding day.

That is why we are gathered here today. To help celebrate this anniversary so richly deserved by two of the most wonderful people. We would like to add a short toast to our tribute. May the silver memories of this day add to your golden happiness. And when your shadows grow bigger may it come from the fact that the sum of contentment is closer than ever. We salute two very happy people because they deserve every bit of it! Joe and Helen, what do you have to say about it?

THE EMCEE AT A CAMERA FANS' MEETING

By Arthur L. Kaser

It certainly is pleasing to see so many camera fans gathered here.

This morning I ran across a snap of me taken when I was a very young baby. I showed it to a friend, and he said: "You sure were a baldheaded kid." I said: "Wait a minute. You've got the picture upside down." Then he began talking about his new girl friend. He said: "You've never seen her. I'll send you three pictures of her." I asked why should he have to send me three pictures. He said: "She isn't all in one picture."

In court the other day the judge asked: "What is this man charged with?" The arresting officer said: "He is a camera fiend of the worst kind, sir." "But," said the judge, "he shouldn't have been arrested just because he has a mania for taking pictures." "It isn't that," said the officer, "he takes the cameras."

A man went to a photographer and asked: "How much do you charge for taking a family group?" The photographer said: "Twenty dollars a dozen." The man thought a moment and then said: "I'll be back in two years. There are only ten in the family now."

Camera fans, it's fun to snap one another, but please don't snap **at** one another.

THE EMCEE AT A "DO IT YOURSELF" CLUB

By Jeff Branen

This "Do it Yourself" has swept the country like a new broom. Personally, I think it is a wonderful thing. I remember when I was a small child we had hobby horses. Now we have hobby houses. This new hobby has many good points. For one thing, it has transferred a lot of married men from debasement of taverns and pool rooms to de basement of their homes. It has changed the buzz of street corner buddies to the buzz of table saws, jigsaws, bandsaws, buzzed fingers . . . And just look at what is being produced in these basements: intricate hanging shelves for clinging vines and whatnots, beautiful scalloped hinkeybobs for kitchen cupboards, decorated mousetraps, and many other things that drive the housewives batty. The same girls that awhile back were bobby-soxers are now hobby-dodgers.

I just bought myself a new table saw. Boy, does that saw travel. The blade goes around faster than a harmful rumor. The saw is wonderful. Of all the saws I ever saw saw I never saw saw like that saw saws. You ought to saw it. I wanted to make something for my wife. I wanted to make something both beautiful and functional. I gave it a lot of study and finally hit upon the idea of a shoe cabinet. It was to be a surprise for her.

I sneaked in some two-by-fours and one-by-sixes, some nails and a gallon of red paint. I worked feverishly on that shoe cabinet and finally it was completed. I proudly led my wife to the basement to view my handiwork. She clapped her hands with glee, and exclaimed, "Oh, what a beautiful dog house!" I was momentarily crushed, but I didn't let on. Instead, I went right out and bought a dog about the size of ten pairs of shoes.

I understand that it is the medical profession that really inaugurated this do-it-yourself hobby. They claim it is a real stimulant for tired men, and then, too, there's quite a good-sized fee for replacing thumbs and fingers.

Some time ago I visited a friend who had just purchased a new power saw. As soon as I arrived he led me to his workshop to see his new saw. Then I noticed one of his fingers was decorated with a large bandage. I said to him, "What happened?" He started his saw. "It was like this," he said. "I got my finger too close to the saw just like this—OUCH! There goes another one!"

Gentlemen, I've had my say. From here on you do it yourself.

THE EMCEE AT A BRIDAL SHOWER

By Louis J. Huber

Ladies, there has been placed on my lovely round shoulders a burden that I carry with extreme pleasure. Now that Mary (the bride) has been surprised it is up to me to put the matter into motion. We could say that I've been delegated to shut off the shower but that would be an awful wet pun. And no one likes wet puns; they're usually very soggy.

Mary must know by this time that we are here for the purpose of showing our love and loyalty to her. It would be too much to ask her to show her love and loyalty to us because she has reserved all that for her future husband.

Most of you know Fred. (The husband-to-be.) Let me tell you a little about him. He was turned down by every girl in this room at one time or another. He had proposed to almost fifty different girls before Mary came along and saw the fine points in his character.

Many of us are wondering what she ever saw in him. He's not handsome and he's not brilliant. He has a very ordinary job and he's been known to stay out all hours of the night playing poker with the boys. He has every attribute that would make him a delightfully incompetent man of the house. (Stops shortly.)

Yes, that's how it is NOT. Mary, you knew all the time that I was saying just the opposite of how we all feel about Fred. You are a lucky girl because he is a fine boy; he is a fortunate fellow because in you he is finding a wife that will make him extremely happy. And anyone who wonders what you two ever saw in each other had better do something about their own eyes.

This is a shower. And a shower without gifts would be like a shower without rain. It would be like stepping into the water and not getting wet. So, Mary, we girls have bought and brought a few things for you.

First, we have some things that are slightly on the lighter side. A shower must have its dry moments. Jane has something for you that will come in mighty handy at times. Jane has a small padlock, with a key. You can use this at any time your Fred decides to go out with the boys instead of staying home. Just put it on the door and he'll be forced to spend the evening with you. **(Presents the gift.)**

Alma also has a gift for you, Mary. This is a small bag of onions. If, at any time, you think Fred is going out for the evening and the padlock won't work you can use these onions. Just feed them to him for supper. They are extremely strong onions. They will serve your purpose in two ways. First, they will enable you to trail him just by sniffing the air. Secondly, there won't be any point in Fred going out because, with that onion smell about him, no one will want anything to do with him. Seems like kind of a strong trick, Mary, but a girl has a right to these things if it will keep her husband in line.

We have still one more present that you can use to accomplish the same goal. There are times when a strong onion or a padlock might not do the job. However, this third gift is the one that will clinch matters for you. Harriet has it. It is a bottle of glue. Don't use it as you would an ordinary glue. This glue works best when it is put in food. You cook it with the evening meal.

After Fred has eaten the first few bites he won't be able to open his mouth. Now he can't ask your permission to go out. So long as he can't ask you don't need to give it. Of course, his kisses will be mighty sticky but that's not so important. Now we have other gifts. **(They may be presented individually or in a group.)** These are of a saner nature and really meant to be useful. Girls, the gifts.

THE EMCEE AT A GOLDEN WEDDING ANNIVERSARY

By Earl Jay Gilbert

My friends, I'd like to go back to an event that occurred a number of years ago. Let's try to visualize the scene. On that memorable occasion a young couple, obviously happy and perhaps a trifle self-conscious and nervous, stood before a padre and heard him pronounce a few words that made them one. That was fifty years ago — and they're still one — more so than ever, if such a thing is possible.

That's why we're here now. To help celebrate the Golden Wedding Anniversary of that wonderful couple. Of course, the fact that in these days any couple that have managed to stick together for so long is wonderful in itself. But if there hadn't been something fine and great about these delightful people we wouldn't be here today to help commemorate this event.

Just think, my friends, fifty years of wedded bliss — maybe it wasn't all bliss — but there was at least enough of it to carry them through the years. Fifty years of joys and sorrows — of peace and discord — and they're still together — held by bonds of love and affection that have grown stronger with each passing year.

Someone once compared a married couple with a pair of scissors — two separate parts that are joined together as one — pulling apart at times, but always coming back together again — and anything that tries to come between them is punished.

In the fifty years that our dear friends have been together the whole history of the world has changed. Great nations have fallen, small nations have become great. In that period powerful tyrants and despots have grown more powerful and have wielded almost unbelievable control over the lives and destinies of millions of people and have been eliminated. Plagues and epidemics that formerly wiped out thousands and thousands of human beings were conquered by the tremendous advances of medical science. Today we accept as commonplace the miracles of science that were looked upon as ravings of madmen fifty years ago — the radio, the airplane, atomic power, to name a few.

This lovely couple have seen these miracles born and develop and grow, and have looked and marvelled at these things and accepted them into their lives as part of their own growth and development into the peaceful understanding and serenity that now envelop them.

We all know that youth has always been impetuous. Youth craves excitement, adventure, romance — and they want it all at once — sometimes they get it all at once! However, youth has a habit of looking at older people and thinking "What do these people know of life? They've never lived as we live — they've missed most of the fun of life." Well, I'll ask any young person to look upon this charming couple and try to realize that in the course of fifty years of marriage they have experienced, many times over, more adventure, more excitement, more romance, as part of their daily lives than most young people can possibly conceive of.

And during all this they have held on to the most precious possessions they have — each other. Maybe on a number of occasions they might have doubted for a moment that the other person was so precious. They wouldn't be human if that hadn't happened once in a while, but down in their hearts they knew what they valued most.

A young person today is apt to say "For crying out loud! Married to the same person for fifty years? Well, that's what they get for being old-fashioned." Well, my friends, whether that's old-fashioned or not, I'm for it. I think that's what the Lord intended.

And these two people have shown us a perfect example of what the marriage service really means when it says: "For better, for worse — for richer, for poorer — in sickness and in health — I take thee for my wedded spouse." So let's give them our sincerest congratulations and our heartfelt best wishes for a long, happy future of more romance and adventure and enjoyment in the companionship they started fifty short years ago!

THE EMCEE AT A MEETING OF THE OLD - TIMERS

By Richard Drummond

Well, the Old-Timers meet again. So, gentlemen, lay your canes quietly beneath your chairs and adjust your hearing aids.

What is old age? It's hard to say. Some men are old at forty. Some are still young at ninety. Usually at ninety people say he has reached a ripe old age. Don't feel too flattered by such a remark. A ripe old age is nothing to brag about. Think of the tomato. A man is really old when he can pass an apple orchard and not remember a stomach-ache.

Some men grow old gracefully; others attempt the new dances. And, too, there's many an old rake that still has all his teeth.

Not long ago I was sitting on the front steps with Grandpa. A very beautiful girl came down the street. Grandpa got quite excited and grasped my arm. "Quick, son," he said. "Get my teeth. I want to whistle!" It sounded rather childish. I said to Grandpa, "You know, Grandpa, I think you are in your second childhood." He laughed, and said, "Well, if I am, I'm having a lot better time than I had in my first one."

Grandpa has a twin brother, and I've often wondered how both of them were able to live so long. I asked Grandpa to what he attributed their old age. He said, "Son, my brother has hit the bottle all his life. I've never touched a drop, so you can form your own conclusion." I asked him another question, "Science is working on ways to lengthen our lives. Do you think in time everybody will live to be a hundred?" He said the men might, but the women never. Did I ever see a woman that would admit she was over forty?

All right, gentlemen, you're on your own.

THE EMCEE AT A FAMILY REUNION

By Arthur L. Kaser

What is nicer than a family reunion? Answer: Two family reunions. Always lots of things to eat. Also, lots of food. Everything from soup to bicarbonate of soda.

Family reunions are all built around the same pattern. You meet relatives you haven't seen in years. You meet some you've never seen. You meet some you wish you'd never seen. Oh, it's wonderful! The old ones show off their new hearing aids, and the young ones show off their new babies. The old-agers talk about your ancestors, and the teen-agers talk about hotrods. It seems the younger generation are not so interested in their ancestors. Maybe they're right. We can't choose our ancestors. But that's okay. Probably our ancestors wouldn't have chosen us.

Family reunions with their ancestors and family trees! Some of us have big sturdy family trees. Some of us have nothing but scrub oak and underbrush. Yes, the family trees are funny things. They are not like they used to be. They are not like other trees. In regular trees the appearance of the sap is an indication of continued vigor. And there's another difference. It usually takes real trees five to six years to produce nuts. This isn't true of a family tree. On the other hand, many a family has a wonderful family tree, but the crop is a failure. My young son asked me one time, "Dad, what are ancestors?" I told him I was one of his ancestors, and that grandfather was another. The boy thought a moment, and then asked, "Then why do people brag about them?"

I recall the time a very proud and dignified lady remarked, "Oh, yes, indeed. We can trace our ancestors back to—to— Well, I don't know exactly who, but we've been descending for centuries."

A man by the name of Smith was explaining why there are so many Smiths in the world. He said, "The Smith family is very, very old. The line runs away back into antiquity. Nobody knows how far back it runs, but a long, long way back, and the history of the Smith family is recorded in five volumes. In about the middle of the third volume, in a marginal note, we read, 'About this time the world was created.' "

So on with the fun, my good ancestors, descendants and relatives. Let's make it a real family reunion.

THE EMCEE AT A STAG PARTY

By Arthur L. Kaser

They say this is a stag party. The dictionary says a stag is a social gathering of men only. I take it that means the stags come without their deers. In other words, each man left his doe at home. I didn't have any dough. My dear had already taken it. It has been said that a deer is very good at picking up a scent. Mine is good on picking up the higher denominations, too.

But it is good to see so many staggers here this evening. You know, when it comes right down to it, men aren't such a hot lot. Somebody said that a woman was nothing but a rag, a bone, and a hank of hair. But man—Man is nothing but a brag, a groan, and a tank of air.

Oh, yes, before I forget. I have an announcement to make. The local gun club will hold another shoot this coming Saturday at the usual place. The shooting will start about nine o'clock and will continue as long as there is any one left to shoot.

That reminds me of a woodsman in northern Michigan who went to the county seat and asked for a license. "You want a hunting license?" asked the clerk. "No, no," said the old codger. "I been huntin' all my life. I found what I was huntin'. I want a marriage license."

So on with the stag, men. Let each one of us be a real stagger this night, but not on the way home. Let's go.

THE EMCEE AT A HOUSEWARMING

By Vance Clifford

Tonight we are to have a housewarming. Now the right way to have a housewarming is to set the house on fire and not call the fire department. There is one drawback. It is against the law. Therefore, we must find other means.

I'll never forget our own housewarming. It was a brand new house that we had just purchased, so much down and so much a month indefinitely. Statisticians say that every fifth person in the United States owns his own home, but what they meant is, that every fifth person in the United States will own his own home if he ever gets it paid for. Why are we trying to lengthen the span of life? We are trying to get people to live long enough to get their homes paid for. There are many people who seem to be living on Easy Street when they are really living on Easy Payment Street. It is a little different with the furniture we buy to furnish the home. We have one consolation. By the time we get the furniture paid for we are the proud owners of some real antiques.

Anyway, we bought our first house. It was built on the sea shore. When the tide was out the house was in. When the tide was in the house was out. We had four kinds of water: hot, cold, clean and dirty. It was a two-story house with running stairways. When you were down they ran up and when you were up they ran down. We soon became run down from running up and down. The carpenter who hung the doors should have been hung, too. Every time you wanted to go from one room to another you had to take the door off the hinges. Everybody carried a screwdriver.

One time I got wedged in by a door and couldn't get through. I was surely in a jamb. My wife had to tear down the partition before I could get out. It wasn't much of a job for her, though. All she had to do was to tear the wallpaper off and it fell down. When I bought the house the agent said there wasn't a flaw in the house. He was wrong. There was a flaw but when you walked on it it sagged. There was only one good feature. The ceilings were made of sponge rubber. The builders knew that as soon as I discovered what a mess it was I'd hit the ceiling and they didn't want to be responsible for my death.

But, folks, here is a house that is a house. Make yourself comfy and have a good time.

THE EMCEE AT A HOUSEWARMING

By Louis J. Huber

Hold on and hold up, folks, this here celebration is about to begin. I do hope that you'll pardon my English and my grammar because my tongue and my mind are just a little twisted by the event that is before us.

As your master of ceremonies it is my job to take over the steering of this event. We are here to warm this house. Just how do we warm a house? Well, we could light a fire. We could? Yes, and that's just what we shall do.

Although Joe and Mary (owners of the house) invited us over here just to be friendly and have us with them we have other ideas. We are really going to warm this place and we have come prepared to do it.

Nothing is too good for Joe and Mary. Many people would have brought coal and coke or other materials to build a fire. Not us. We brought logs and we are going to burn them in tribute to the good folks who are going to inhabit this house. So what if the house burns down? Well, so what? They might be forced to build another but they can never say that their friends didn't have a warm spot for them.

Joe and Mary, we have brought us five logs. We would have brought more but we figured, if the fire does cool off a little, we can always throw on a small piece of furniture or a rug or a mattress. Anything, good friends, to keep you from forgetting us and the house warming that we have cooked up for you. Shall we proceed with the logs? We shall? Good.

The first log, please. (One log is brought to the center of the group.) This, Joe and Mary, is the log that is symbolic of happiness. We place it first on our fire-to-be because without it, without that happiness that you both have, there would be no necessity for a house warming. There would be no necessity for a house. So we place the log of happiness at your feet.

Our second log is now brought forward. (This is done.) This, Joe and Mary, is the log of friendship. We put it near happiness because one is necessary for the other. The two logs, as soon as we light the fire, will have their flames soaring skyward together.

Then comes the log of loyalty. This is the center log and it is an attribute that is so often overlooked when people get together. We feel that you two have this grand virtue and we place the log that is symbolic of it in the center of your room and the center of the group. For the flames from the log of loyalty will burn long and bright. (Log is placed.)

Now the log of sincerity. Any man would be forced to search far and wide for two folks with your sincerity. We know when Joe and Mary say something that they say it with an honesty and truthfulness that comes from their hearts. We know that anything done by Joe and Mary is done with a faith and frankness that doubles their sincere intentions. So we place the log of sincerity. (This is now done.)

Last but not least, the log denoting character. What is character? Character, according to a well-known authority on such matters, is one's moral strength. One's moral strength is their ability to keep from disagreeing with friends even when they think they are wrong. It is a strength that will keep you from interfering. You can prove you have it. So please do not interfere when we light the logs in the center of your living room. (Place another log.) Now! (Someone advances with paper and matches.) Hold it! I forgot something! This fire must be started by the folks who own the house! But if they feel that they should not do it they are very wise and we forgive them. Joe and Mary, with these logs of happiness, friendship, loyalty, sincerity and character we wish you everything that life can bring! (Continue with the program from here.)

THE EMCEE AT A STAG PARTY

By Louis J. Huber

Good evening, gentlemen. As your master of ceremonies I greet you and extend best wishes. I'm the type of fellow who would rather greet "ladies and gentlemen" but I can't always have things my way.

As this is a stag party there are certain things that must necessarily be explained. First, what is a stag party? It is one where there are no girls. It is a party where the "dears" have been left at home.

Oho, what am I saying? The ladies have been left at home? Well, we shall see. I now come to the part of the program, men, that has been prepared for you by the committee. They came to the conclusion that no stag party is complete without a little dancing exhibition.

So, as many of you remember the old by-word, she shakes, she shivers, she wiggles just like a bowl of jello — I now use that expression. There are some of you who are not permitted by your better halves to watch this kind of a performance. I would advise them to close their eyes and they can not be accused of any wrongdoing.

Let me continue. She shakes, she shivers, she wiggles just like a bowl of jello. Now, men, there are those of us who are willing to risk an eye on this kind of a performance. Let me assure you that the risk is well worth your while. Are you men ready for the show? Good.

Gentlemen, the committee searched far and wide for this type of entertainment. They wrote to a booking agency in New York and tried to get some of the most glamorous show girls in the world. Yes, they tried. But when they heard the price they didn't need any girls to do the shaking. They did it all by themselves.

Were they stopped? Were they hindered? Well, yes they

were. But they were not without their natural ability to come up with something just as good. They went west into Chicago and they again tried to get a beautiful show girl for your entertainment. Did they get her? Well, no, they didn't.

Now, men, please don't be impatient because we are coming to the highlight of this program. I promise you that and I always keep my promise. The main part of our menu is not quite ready so I'm forced to tell a few jokes. You've all heard about the terrible fight they had on a train yesterday. It seems that the conductor punched a ticket and —

All right, men, all right, I promise there will be no more of that. We come to the highlight of the program. And here it is, gentlemen. (Takes two searchlights.) Now this is the low light. (As he holds it low.) And this upper one is the high light. (As he holds this one high.)

Now, just one minute, men, we are making progress. Is the show ready back stage? It is? Fine. This is the hour for which we have been waiting, for which you have been enduring my terrible jokes, for which you have been holding your breath in anticipation. What's that, young man? You didn't hold your breath? How come you're blue in the face?

I continue, men. Here is the entertainment for which you have been waiting. Remember that she shakes, she shivers and she wiggles just like a bowl of jello. You've heard me saying that so you should know what to expect. Let me introduce to you, men, not the glamorous show girl that we couldn't get but the original object that shivers, shakes and wiggles just like a bowl of jello: Gentlemen, it is a bowl of jello! (Has the bowl brought to the table and shows it to the gathering.)

Please forgive me and I shall get into the real portion of our entertainment. **(Introduces the show.)**

THE EMCEE AT A SURPRISE PARTY

By Louis J. Huber

(Note: This stunt can best be promoted by doing it in the dark. If it is necessary to do it in the daylight, the party-to-be-surprised must be brought into the room blindfolded.)

As your emcee for this surprise party, folks, I must warn you to be very serious about the matter. Do not laugh at the wrong time and give away the theme of the thought that we are trying to leave with the victim. All right, now bring in the party. (Victim enters.)

Oho! (All this is deep tones.) So at last we have you in our clutches, my fine-feathered friend. Just in the event that you are thinking you have no feathers let me correct this thinking. Hand him a feather. (Someone does this.) There, you have your feather. We have more of them. There will be one slight difference between the one you just received and the ones that we have in reserve. Those we are holding back will be given to you at the time we are also applying the tar. It will be a real tar and feather party.

Perhaps, by this time, you have started to realize that you are in the power of a very strong organization. We who are gathered here belong to the Eye of the Turtle. The Eye of the Turtle sees everything! Right now we know that you are taking this matter lightly but you will change your tune. What is your favorite tune, sir? (Victim names one.) As we said: You will change your tune. From now on you will sing, each time you come to any street corner, the favorite song of all turtles. You will sing THE EYES OF TURTLES ARE UPON YOU. After this has been done four thousand times you will be permitted to change your tune again. You will then sing SLINK TO ME ONLY WITH THINE EYES.

We are about to prepare you for a long trip. We are going to send you around the world. As you know, the world is a globe. Hand this lowly victim a globe so he may know its shape. (Hand him an electric light bulb.)

Now that you have the globe you know that you will be traveling around and around. We must now blindfold you. (This is done if the party is in the dark.) Please remove your shoes and prepare for the trip. (This is done.)

Let me explain to you a few facts about a turtle. A turtle is a marine and fresh water species of the reptilian order Chelonia found in warm climates. Since this is the order of the day you must remove your shirt. (This is done.) Now that you have made bare your shoulders and your toes we can see that you have a shape just like a turtle and you will fit well into our organization. Now for further tests and the trip you are going to make.

Raise one foot, please. (This is done. When it is done a pan of water is placed on the floor.) Now lower the foot, please. (He does it and finds himself with one foot in the water.) You are in the ocean and there is room for both feet. Place the other foot into the sea. (Victim does this.)

Your daring as a turtle will lead you to many adventurous places in your cruise around the globe. You are about to be given a sample of a shipwreck. You are in the middle of the sea, a storm is at hand. Listen to the wind howl! (All make howling noise.) From out of the distant clouds comes a cry. You do not recognize it but it is your means of being saved.

The cry becomes clearer and near. It is the cry CALLING ALL TURTLES, CALLING ALL TURTLES, CALLING ALL TURTLES. I have just issued the call and the turtles have responded. They have come and they are here. And they are ready to greet you with their own favorite greeting. Listen to them as they scream at the top of their voices, SURPRISE! SURPRISE! SURPRISE! (At this point the stunt is ended and the victim's blindfold is removed.)

THE EMCEE AT A RETIREMENT PARTY

By Louis J. Huber

Ladies and gentlemen: To me has been handed the most pleasant task of the evening. I am to be your master of ceremonies at this evening's festivities. I say that the task has been "handed" to me but actually I put my foot in it by asking for it.

We call this gathering a retirement party because it is our means of saying farewell to a member of our group who is giving up his work for a life of ease. No more worrying about getting up in the morning, no more hustling to the bus line. No more wondering how soon there will be another collection toward which he will be asked to donate.

Yes, our friend is going to retire. Retire? Just what does that mean? There are many ways of doing it. You can re-tire by getting a new shoe for your car and having the garage man apply it. You can be re-tired by being tired and then by being tired again.

And you can retire as our Mr. (Name) is doing. Just think of it. Nothing to do but lay under the trees in the summer time and fight your way through a swarm of mosquitoes and ants. Packing a lunch and going out into the country and having some farmer chase you out of his field or having him send his dogs after you.

Ah, yes, blessed retirement. Taking your car and driving into the wide open spaces and having a flat tire eighteen miles from the nearest service station. Or taking a boat ride and losing the oars and finding yourself a few hundred miles down the river. Or taking a walk. Not a long walk, just five miles and ending the day putting salve on your sore feet and pulling yourself into bed with the help of your wife.

Ah, sweet retirement. Lying in bed in the morning while the rest of the world goes on its work-a-day way. Lying in bed being too tired to get out of it. Lying there so long that you get hungry and, by the time you do find the power to get out of it, you are too weak to make it to the kitchen. Then half-way between the bedroom and the refrigerator you starve to death.

Or sitting on the front porch and just letting the rest of the world go by. Sitting there and rocking. Rocking to and fro. Faster and faster, farther and farther. So far that you fall backward and—oh, I can't go into the horrible and terrible things that can happen to a man who falls backward in his rocking chair.

Yes, refreshing retirement. Doing nothing but eating and drinking and just waiting for the time when you are hungry again. Then, of course, going through the same eating and drinking routine again. Comes the awakening. Soon, very soon, it comes. When your clothes are too small for you, when your belt is too short, when your collar is too tight. You think the clothes are shrinking but that's not the answer. You're getting fat. You don't want to believe it and you step on a scale. What does it read? What?

It reads that nothing of the kind has happened. It tells you that this master of ceremonies is just a bit jealous that he isn't able to retire with you. It tells you that none of these horrible things will happen, that you are as fit as you were those many years ago when you were first hired.

And that, Mr. **(Name)** is really the way we all feel about you. Forget all my dire predictions; they are not so. Accept instead the good wishes of these folks who were your fellow employees. Let me read to you a few lines, written by our twentieth president, James A. Garfield: "If wrinkles must be written upon your brows, let them not be written upon your heart. The spirit should never grow old."

These were Mr. Garfield's words. He knew someone just like you when he wrote them. For we know that there are no wrinkles in your heart, none in your spirit. And with this thought we say good luck and goodbye, Mr. **(Name.)**

THE EMCEE AT A BIRTHDAY CELEBRATION

By Forbes Milliken

Birthdays are those things that come once a year—for some people. When a man has a birthday he usually takes a day off. When a woman has a birthday she invariably takes a year off. My birthday comes in the winter and on that day we let the furnace fire go out. We just light all the candles on my birthday cake.

Next week we are celebrating the fourteenth anniversary of my wife's twenty-ninth birthday. She said yesterday, "I hate to think of my twenty-ninth birthday." I said, "Why, what happened?" There will be twenty-nine candles on my wife's birthday cake, but we'll burn the candles at both ends.

Last year she baked her own birthday cake. She was very proud of it and said, "Don't you think my sense of design is wonderful?" I told her it was, but her arithmetic was terrible. She said to me, "Dear, what are you going to give me for my twenty-ninth birthday?" I said, "You've forgotten, my love, I gave it to you last year." I said to her, "Isn't it terrible to celebrate a birthday so close to your thirtieth one?" She said, "Oh, no. I'm getting used to it."

Speaking of birthdays, my little nephew spent too much time at the lake and acquired a real sunburn. In a day or so it began to peel badly. Junior saw himself in the mirror and murmured, "Only four years old, and wearing out already."

Our cleaning woman comes once a week. She came yesterday with a black eye. I asked what was wrong. She said, "Well, ye know me husband was in jail. Yesterday was his birthday and they let him out, and I wished him many happy returns."

Which is about enough preface to the opening of this birthday celebration.

THE EMCEE AT A CHRISTMAS PARTY FOR EMPLOYEES

By Jeff Branen

Christmas — a widely observed holiday of which the past nor the future is of so much interest as the present.

There are a good many employees here who have spent many Christmases with this company. For some, Christmas is the only day they got here on time. But that'll do for the present.

It's the wise person who does his Christmas hinting early. But don't do your Christmas shopping surly. Christmas for a woman means this and that, and this and this and this and—Christmas for a man is a couple of loud ties.

You will take note that of all the gifts given out here today no married man is receiving a billfold. To him no enlarging camera has ever been invented that will produce a picture of his post-Christmas bank account.

In some ways I feel sorry for the bachelors at Christmas time. On the other hand, I envy him. He knows when he receives a present that he won't have to pay for it later.

Ah, yes, Christmas time. Yuletide. Yuletide always reminds me of my banker. I always go to him around Christmas time and say, "Lend me fifty bucks. I know **you'll tide** me over." One can get along without holly, but one must have the berries.

MacDowell, a manufacturer on a small scale, called his employees together the day before Christmas and announced, "Men, we've had a splendid year, and I'm going to divide two thousand dollars among ye. I've written out the checks. I congratulate ye all on the way ye have worked, an' if ye do as well during the next twelve months I'll sign the checks."

Now with a ho, ho, ho!

Let's go, go, go!

AT A SALESMEN'S CONVENTION

By Arthur L. Kaser

One look at this gathering and there is no mistaking the fact that most of the salesmen here are traveling salesmen. You can tell by the bags under their eyes. And you salesmen out there—did you ever compare the difficulty of getting orders from some people with that of pulling teeth? You have to give them a lot of gas. Psychologists say a person who can withstand the high-pressure salesman illustrates the power of mind over patter. How's this one? It happens in a Sixth Avenue Fur Shop. "H'm, a boggain, lady, I'm telling you! Goes weet hitch seelver fox fur, a bottle genuwine seelver polish."

I notice so many ads in the newspapers—"Wanted: a live wire salesman." Now who in the world can sell live wires? It's shocking.

One salesman says to another salesman, "I made some very valuable contacts today." The other salesman says, "I didn't make any sales, either."

A salesman called on a prospect, but found the said prospect looking disconsolately out the window. "Well, well, what's wrong today?" asked the salesman.

"I'll tell you," said the gloomy one. "I promised my wife a Pomeranian, and the best price I can get is $150, and that's too much."

"It sure is," said the salesman. "Why, I can sell you one for $75."

The prospect brightened instantly. "You can? When can you make delivery?"

"Just a minute," said the salesman. "I'll find out." He rushed to the nearest public phone booth. Getting his firm on the phone, he said somewhat excitedly, "Listen! I've sold a man a Pomeranian for $75. Now tell me, what in heck is a Pomeranian?"

I hope I sold that one, Brother Salesmen.

THE EMCEE AT A ST. PATRICK'S DAY PARTY

By Vance Clifford

'Tis the wearin' of the green, and sure I'm hoping you're having a swell time, so I am. 'Tis a great party we're going to be having this St. Patrick's Day.

As I was coming here an old truck stopped and the driver motioned to me. I stepped out to the truck and the driver reached out and shook my hand. I was somewhat puzzled for I had never seen the man before. I said to him, "Now let me see—what is your name?" He said, "'Tis on the side of me truck." I tried to read the name but couldn't make it out. I said to him, "It's obliterated." The driver said, "You're wrong; it's O'Brien, Mr. Callahan." I said, "My name is not Callahan." "In that case," said the driver, "my name ain't O'Brien." Then we looked at each other real close, and sure enough it wasn't either one of us. "Just a minute," said the man as he pulled a paper from his pocket and handed it to me. "Maybe you can help me." It was an income tax blank. "Maybe," continued the man, "you can tell me. I been trying to figure out how much money I can save by not having any."

I could see that he was a real Irishman, so I took the liberty of inviting him here to the party, but he refused. He said he was going to see the mayor about changing all the traffic lights for St. Patrick's Day. He wants all the red lights taken out and replaced with green ones.

While on the subject I'd like to tell you about an Irishman and an Englishman who lived side by side on the seashore. Each one bought a beautiful boat. The Englishman christened his boat and painted in big letters on the stern: "Henry the Eighth." The next day the Irishman painted a name on his boat: "March the Seventeenth."

Now, me friends, leave your shillelaghs outside and have fun.

THE EMCEE AT A GARDENERS' CLUB

By Arthur L. Kaser

Once again the members of this gardening club get all enthused by the beautiful pictures in the seed catalogues. Pictures of tomatoes so large they hide the house. String beans that look like Indian canoes, and cornstalks that stick up in the air like television antennas.

Gardening fans cannot be blamed for becoming enthused. However, the one objection to gardening is that by the time your back gets used to it your enthusiasm is gone. In the last few years the Government has tried to develop a good relief program for the farmer, but about all the relief a mere gardener can expect is a back treatment from a chiropractor.

I ran across a few stunts about gardening that I'd like to pass along to you. For instance, if you turn your cucumber seeds inside out your cucumbers will have dimples instead of warts. Also, if you plant potatoes and then run a heavy tractor over the rows, when they mature you will have mashed potatoes. And again, to prevent your neighbor's chickens from digging out your new plantings before you are up in the morning, pull them up yourself before you go to bed. Do not try to get your garden rows straight. Remember, a crooked row is longer. Try crossing eggplant with milkweed to grow omelet. Last year I did some experimenting on my own. I crossed a potato with an onion. It wasn't much of a success. All I got was a potato with watery eyes.

My nearest neighbor is the man with the green thumb. He can raise anything from radishes to umbrellas. He is always boasting about the large potatoes he raises. Last fall when we ran short on potatoes I asked him to sell me a bushel. He refused. He said he wouldn't cut a potato for anybody.

So, garden club members, let's help one another. Let us dig into the earth and let the seeds fall where they will.

THE EMCEE AT AN IZAAK WALTON CONSERVATION CLUB MEETING

By Richard Drummond

We all know that it isn't necessary to attend a conservatory to be conservative. Also, a man who saves money nowadays isn't necessarily a conservative—he's a wizard. But money isn't the only thing you can save. You can save the fish you catch, but it isn't good policy to save them too long. If you save them too long, the health officer will get you. If you save them too short, the game warden will get you.

If all the fishermen would obey the laws and not take home more than the limit, there would be plenty of fish for everybody. Perhaps we can blame the over-the-limit type of fishermen on the doctors. Many doctors say that fish is good for the brains. So the greedy fishermen catch more fish so they can eat more fish so they can have more brains so they can catch more fish so—It's a **fishous** circle.

Many of the country's professional liars began their careers with nothing but a casting rod and a rowboat.

There is something about fishing that gets in your blood, and a kid doesn't have to be very old before it strikes him. Last summer my boy—he's seven—went fishing without my consent. When he returned home, I said to him, "If you wanted to go fishing, why didn't you come and ask me first?" "Because," he replied, "I wanted to go fishing."

I have an uncle who just loves to fish. He's like a magnifying glass. He can catch a three-inch minnow and make it look like a forty-pound musky. Fact of the matter is, he got such a reputation for stretching the truth that he bought a pair of scales and insisted on weighing every fish he caught, in the presence of a witness. One day a doctor borrowed this man's scales to weigh a new baby. The baby weighed forty-seven pounds. So there you have it, fishermen friends. It's time to wet your lines, and start angling, but don't go English and anglify your catch.

THE EMCEE AT A WRITERS' CLUB

By Forbes Milliken

It's good for all writers concerned to have these get-togethers. Not only are the social contacts invigorating, but the exchange of ideas, markets, et cetera, are valuable. The idea of poor struggling writers hunched over in an unheated attic is all right in fiction. If there are any in the attics it might be because they cannot live on the first or second story. However, literally speaking, I doubt if one will find many attics occupied by writers in real life.

I have heard writers complain that theirs is a thankless job. On the contrary, everything **I** write is returned **with** thanks. The last story I wrote was called, "Oatmeal, Bran and Whole Wheat." It was a serial. I started out by writing dime novels. When I had written ten I got a dollar. Only once did I write a play. I called it "The Broken Leg." But it was rejected because the cast was too large. The only real fiction I have ever written was my last income tax return.

I met a writer acquaintance yesterday. I asked him if he spent more time in the preparation of his material or in writing it. He said he has to do some traveling to get needed information, but he did most of his work sitting down. That is where he shines.

You have, no doubt, heard of Iron Mountain Mose, the well-known wrestler. He became so famous as a wrestler that he made money from every money-making endorsement scheme that he signed. Many autobiographies appeared in the papers. I met him one morning after one of these autobiographies appeared in a New York newspaper. I said to him: "Mose, your article in last night's paper was a knockout." "Yeah," said Mose, "that's what I heard. You know, there are times when I wish I knew how to read."

And so it goes. The secret of success in writing is in hitting the right keys on the typewriter.

Let's proceed with the meeting with this thought in mind: Don't ever write a story in the first person and call it "Adam."

THE EMCEE AT A BUSINESSMEN'S GET-TOGETHER

By Arthur L. Kaser

Business is nothing new. It began when the world started to become inhabited. The ancient Hebrews had a goat on which all the sins were placed. So you see, the holding company isn't a new idea.

Why do we hear: "Businessman—businessman—businessman?" You seldom hear businesswoman. Here is the lowdown on that: A businessman is always looking for the latest wrinkle in his trade paper. The woman looks in her mirror.

Successful concerns are always looking for some way to break their records. This does not apply to the phonograph companies. And what makes a successful businessman? Honesty. Most of them climb to considerable heights by remaining on the level. There is only one man I know who can succeed by letting things slide, and that's a trombone player. Most successful businessmen will tell you that the easiest way to get to the top is to go to the bottom of things. There is one other thing to remember—the key to success doesn't fit a night-latch.

If a business goes bad, a smart businessman will find a way to get out from under. Which reminds me of George Larson who opened a small store on Fairdale Street. His business went bankrupt within a few weeks. To put a humorous angle to it, he put a large sign on the front of the store which read: "Opened by mistake." Then he opened a filling station without a roof—no overhead.

The proprietor of a pet shop wanted to include a mongoose or two in his shop, so he wrote to the manager of a zoo about it. His letter started off; "Dear Sir: Could I purchase from you two mongeese—?" The wording didn't sound just right so he tore up the letter and began again. "Dear Sir: Could I purchase from you two mongooses—?" This didn't sound right, either. So he tried again: "Could I purchase from you a mongoose, and, by the way, could I purchase another one, too?"

Gentlemen, forget your parking meters and have a good time.

THE EMCEE AT A SCHOOL CENTENNIAL CELEBRATION

By Vance Clifford

One hundred years ago (or a shorter period) this ground was broken for the first little red schoolhouse in this vicinity. Since that time this ground has been trampled by many feet, for many, many children have here learned their three "R's" and passed on to higher learning, better fitted to cope with the world and its problems. That first school is a symbol of the truly American tradition that the three R's are, and always have been, the bloodstream of progress.

In those passing years there have been many changes in our schools. Back in those old days the school board was cut from a hickory sapling. This brings to mind the story of years gone by when a member of the school board walked unannounced into the school room as the lone teacher was about to dismiss the class. She had used up all her material for that day and was somewhat at a loss just what to demonstrate for the gentlemen. On the spur of the moment she called upon her star pupil with: "Who wrote **The Face on the Barroom Floor?**" Flustered by a question whose answer he did not know, the boy blurted: "I don't know. I didn't do it. Honest." The teacher told him to sit down, but immediately the board member said: "Don't let that boy get off so easy. He has a guilty look."

Even now, as in those days, education pays, unless you settle down to be an educator. In the old days the scholars absorbed the three R's and made use of that learning. Today there are many who attend school until they are eighteen years old and can't even read a traffic sign. The result is, an end to their career (car rear) as well as the rest of the car.

Learning is one thing that takes time. There is really no satisfactory short cut. Little David was just home from his first day at school. Mother met him at the door and asked: "Well, David, what did you learn today?" "Not much," said David, "I've got to go again."

Now, my friends, let us get on with the program.

THE EMCEE AT A BOOK-OF-THE-MONTH CLUB MEETING

By Sidney Steele

I have a number of books of the month. They are the books I take along when I pay all my monthly installments. They take more interest in them than I do.

I have found that the old-fashioned dime novel which is now selling for four dollars is printed on better paper. My favorite author is Oscar Wilde, and my favorite book from his pen is Salome. It seems that Salome is what made Oscar Wilde. When I first heard about Poe's Raven I asked the librarian what Poe was ravin' about.

You will find all kinds of people in a library. Low brows and high brows all browse in a library. I will confess that I rather like racy literature like "Ben Hur."

I was in a library when a very hoity-toity, over-dressed and over bejeweled lady entered and said to the librarian, "I want a couple of new murder stories committed by nice people."

In a more serious vein, there is a little story about S. S. McClure, pioneer magazine and book publisher. He had promised to read a manuscript left by a lady, but had failed to keep his promise. When she called he said he **had** read it and didn't want it. The lady suggested that probably the little verses at the beginning of each chapter detracted from the story itself, but Mr. McClure said on the contrary, the verses should be left in. "Mr. McClure," said the lady, "now I know you did not read the manuscript. There are no verses in the script." Mr. McClure, seeing himself trapped, immediately scanned through the pages, and decided to buy it. The lady happened to be Mrs. Ovid Butler. Mrs. Butler's brother was the author of the manuscript. Her brother's name? Booth Tarkington, and the manuscript—**Monsieur Beaucaire.**

Book friends, let's go on with the meeting of the Book of the Month Club.

FOR AN EMCEE AT A FATHER'S DAY PARTY

By George A. Posner

Ladies and gentlemen, tonight I want to talk about something no family should be without—a father.

The man who in the business of marriage is, shall we say, the silent partner?

Ah, those strong, silent men! The women love the silent men! Makes them think the man is **listening!** But do they consider it may be because he couldn't get a word in edgewise?

As for the female of the species—some put it "the female after the specie;" or "the female of the speeches"—what's it matter?—the saying goes they're more deadly when they're after the male. Or is it, "more deadly than the mule?" However it is, as far as silence goes, the last letter of female is silent—but it seems to be the only thing about her that is!

But to get back to those strong, silent men, the fathers. And why they are so silent. Why? Because it's also been said there are two kinds of husbands—those who fight with their wives, and those who have learned to say, "Yes, dear."

I remember Mother telling me how she got Dad to propose. They were at the beach and she says she just turned to him, that beautiful summer day, and said: "Willy, let's get married!" And he nodded.

I said: "He just nodded? Didn't he even say anything?"

She said: "How could he? I was holding his head under water."

And the next day there he was up before a judge, no, a minister, getting his instructions: "When the bell rings, come out of the corner, fighting"—no, that was another fight.

We had a large family. Nearly every year there would be

another addition to the family; a fresh heir. Pop was a regular fresh heir fiend.

There were so many kids we couldn't keep track of them all. I remember once one of the boys ran away from home, and it was a week before we missed him. We happened to take a roll call.

Even Ma got mixed up at times, keeping track of all those kids, what with the friends they brought into the house.

I remember one time Pa was working late in the evening. And when he came home he asked: "Well, Ma, I see you got all the kids bathed and to bed." Ma answered: "Yes, finally. But I sure had a lot of trouble with the red-head."

"Red-head?" shouted Dad. "We have no red-head! Well, it was that red-headed midget from across the street!"

"Gosh," said Ma, "no wonder he struggled and acted up so!"

Ma would get absent-minded, too, along with her other troubles.

Yeah, we had a mob. They said the stork was figuring on boarding with us, to save commuting time!

Then there was the time Dad took all us kids on a picnic. And as we were following him down a road, a sheriff suddenly grabbed my dad by the coat collar, and shouted: "What have you been up to?"

"I've done nothing!" stammered my father.

And the cop hissed: "Oh, ain't ye? Well, you sure must have done somethin', or why is this crowd following ye?"

Poor Dad! Father brought me up to go straight. But I wanted to be a comedian.

Pa warned me to stay away from the theaters—especially the burlesque theaters. He said I might see something there I shouldn't see.

One day I played hookey and did go to a burlesque show, and sure enough I saw something I shouldn't see there—Dad!

Yeah, we were pretty poor those days. We were so poor, the mice were eating out. Later it got so we even had to borrow a mouse from next door, just to keep up appearances.

Yes, we tried to keep up with the Joneses in the only way we could. But we were too late. The Joneses were already six kids ahead.

We had period furniture. You know, here for a short period, then the installment company takes it away.

In fact, the rooms were so small, a lot of the furniture had to be painted on the wall.

One of my kid brothers went around with a girl who was a chocolate dipper in a candy factory. People thought he had such beautiful European manners—always kissing and licking her hands.

I was born in an adobe house, with a cement patio—the only child I know born with a cement patio. Also had a solid concrete back porch.

Anyway, dear old Dad really had his work cut out for him. He had no money, but what good is money? Will it get you happiness? Will it get you comfort? Will it get you love? . . . Of course I'm speaking of Confederate money.

Mom and Dad got along all right—they got to realize there are two sides to every question. Her side—and her mother's.

But enough of my dad. Let's get to the father we are honoring today, ————.

ADDITIONAL MATERIAL

There was a little boy who had a dog named Pat of which he was very fond. One day he came home from school, whistling merrily, and asked his mother, "Where's Pat?"

His mother knew how much he loved that little dog, and now it was up to her to break the sad news to him that the dog had been killed by an automobile that afternoon. So she took him aside, talked of other things for a while; and then, after a deep breath, she said gently: "Darling, I'm afraid I have bad news for you. You must brace yourself, dear, and not take it too hard, will you promise?" And when he nodded, she said: "Pat was killed by a car this afternoon."

"Oh," said the boy. Then whistling again, he went out into the street to play.

The mother was astonished, of course, and then finally convinced herself it might be all for the best.

A while later the boy came back and asked: "Where's Pat?"

"But, darling," said his mother, softly. "I told you Pat was killed by an automobile this afternoon."

The little boy burst into tears. His surprised mother said, "But darling, when I told you this afternoon, it didn't seem to bother you!"

"No," sniffed the boy. "But I thought you said Dad!"

* * *

The other day I brought my wife and little daughter to one of these affairs, these talking bouts. A day or so later, when we had visitors at my home, my little girl spoke up, told about the affair, and said: "My daddy was mastoid of ceremonies."

Of course I laughed merrily, right out merrily, and said:

"Ha! Ha! Isn't that funny? No, dear, mastoid means a pain in the ear."

So my wife had to speak up and say: "Must you humiliate her, dear? So, instead of master of ceremonies, she said **mastoid**—was she so far wrong? And maybe you **were**! . . .

You'll notice I came alone today.

Well, here it's Father's Day. The day fathers all over the country are being presented with beautiful blank check books. Or a tie. Works like a dog all year long, and then on Father's Day he gets it in the neck.

* * *

My dad and mother got along beautifully. They made an agreement, right after the wedding, that he was to take care of all the big problems which came up and she was to take care of all the little problems. Wasn't it odd? It seems there never was a big problem that came up!

* * *

When Dad stayed out late, came home in the wee small hours, took off his shoes, and crept up the stairs, she didn't say a word. She had put thumb tacks all over the steps.

* * *

But Dad's biggest embarrassment, I think, was one day when he was traveling on a streetcar. The woman sitting opposite him, it seems, was a schoolteacher. She thought Dad's face looked familiar, and after a while, she smiled and said: "How are you, Mr. Smith?" As Dad's name is not Mr. Smith, of course, he didn't make any sign of recognition, or reply. And after a while she said: "Oh, pardon me, sir, I thought you were the father of two of my children."

THE EMCEE AT A WRITERS' GUILD MEETING

By Richard Drummond

Well, my writer friends, I'm sorry to bring this up, but have you ever noticed how many good books are written in our penitentiaries? These writers usually write under pen names. They do not submit their manuscripts directly to the publishers. They dispose of their work through the sell blocks. However, there are a few good writers outside our penitentiaries. One writer in one of these penal institutions has written such books as "The Wonderful Outdoors," "Free to Fish and Hunt," and "The Wide Open Spaces." Someday he hopes to write some travel stories.

But let's get out of prison. There are too many bars, and I'm not a drinking man.

When I first started to write a friendly critic said to me: "Your work seems a little raw." I said: "It shouldn't be. It's been roasted enough." It was right after that I wrote something that was accepted by a magazine. It was a check for a year's subscription.

I was convinced along about that time that the publishers had a conspiracy against me. Ten of them refused the same story. But, now, brother and sister writers, I am beginning to be recognized. A lady said to me yesterday: "It was just the other day I saw something of yours, about something or other, in some magazine."

I will never forget the struggle I had when I started writing. There was one time when my landlady said: "Just when are you going to pay your room rent?" I said: "As soon as I receive the check which the publisher will send me if he accepts the novel I am about to commence when I have found a suitable subject and the necessary inspiration." That same day I went back to my folks to live. So, my friends, that is Chapter One. Chapter Two is up to you. If you have any questions to submit, please enclose return postage.

THE EMCEE AT A READERS' AND WRITERS' CLUB MEETING

By Arthur L. Kaser

Welcome, members of the literary club. I want to take this opportunity to prove that I am a bona fide victim of the literary virus. In writing verse, I have endeavored to follow the style of the English poet laureate, Alfred Tennyson. Like this:

From behind the steering wheel
There came an angry roar.
He was trying to fold his road map
The way it was before.

I have also tried to copy the style of our own American philosophical poet, Walt Whitman. In this way:

When a hen lays a nice fresh egg
She makes a speech in cackling tones,
Similar to some officials when
They lay their cornerstones.

So you see, my friends, poetry is where you find it—if you can find it. On the other hand, prose has its place, and no matter how bad prose may be, it might be verse.

It has never been my desire to make money writing poetry. About a month ago I submitted a poem to a magazine with this note attached: "Dear Editor: I expect no renumeration for this poem. I merely submit it as a compliment." A few days later I received a reply from the editor. It read: "Dear sir: Allow me to return the compliment."

I see where they have unearthed a cornerstone of an ancient library in Greece, on which is inscribed "4000 B.C." Meaning, I take it, "Before Carnegie."

Before I married I called on a girl one evening, and she said: "Daddy is so pleased to hear that you are a poet." "Oh," I said, "he likes poetry?" "Not at all," she said, "but the last friend of mine he tried to throw out was a professional boxer." And then came the punch line.

And now, friends, let's get our heads together and think up a plot.

THE EMCEE AT AN OFFICE WORKERS' PARTY

By Forbes Milliken

Welcome to our picnic, you poor, tired office help who never know what your bosses don't know what they want you never to do next. Welcome to our picnic, you poor, tired businessmen who can never get your help to understand that they are not supposed to make mistakes according to your orders. I'm tired, too.

Sometimes the bosses are wrong; sometimes it's the help. I presume you heard about the stunning, but absent-minded stenographer who left her coat in the office and took her boss to the cleaners. But it works both ways. A secretary I know says her boss is the best businessman in the whole world. He buys all his goods from Armenians and sells it to Scotchmen at a profit.

He was a new clerk in the office. A very good-looking lady entered, and asked: "Could I see the manager?" "Certainly," said the new clerk, "the manager always has time to see pretty ladies." "Well," said the lady, "tell him his wife is here." See what I mean? Right here, both the help and the boss are going to get in trouble.

Even the office boys have burdens to bear. However, you find some that are smart and diplomatic. A man entered the office and said to the office boy: "Boss in?" The boy asked: "Are you a salesman, a bill collector, or a friend of his?" The caller said he was all three. "Well," said the boy, "the boss is in conference. He is out of town. Step in and see."

I still say that businessmen have a hard time of it. I was on my way home the other evening on the train. A portly man sat down beside me. "Whew!" he puffed. "Been a hard day." "In what way?" I asked. "Well, for one thing," he confided, "my office boy asked the afternoon off to attend his grandmother's funeral. I knew right away he was playing me for a goof, so I said I'd go along." "And he headed right for the ball park?" I said. "I wish he had," he said sadly. "I had to follow him to his grandmother's funeral."

THE EMCEE AT A BARBERS' CONVENTION

By Arthur L. Kaser

I like to hang around a barber shop just to hear the remarks and comments. You can hear funny ones, sad ones, boastful ones. I was in a barber shop yesterday when the barber applied the clippers to the back of the neck of a very small boy. The boy said to the barber: "Is my neck so dirty you have to use a vacuum cleaner?"

They say that the cutting of Samson's hair caused him to lose his strength. It wasn't that. He was weakened from protesting that he didn't want a shampoo and massage.

Joe, the barber, has a mongrel dog that spends all his time sitting beside the barber chair. I remarked to Joe: "Joe, your dog seems very fond of watching you cut hair." Joe said: "It ain't that. Sometimes I snip off a bit of a customer's ear." I asked Joe where was the helper he used to have. The one that told so many funny stories. Joe said: "I had to let him go. He got too ambitious. He started to illustrate his funny stories with cuts." Joe said that he was losing money on him. He could only charge his helper's customers cut prices.

While I was there a young fellow came in with a rather badly cut-up face. Joe asked him: "What happened?" The other said: "I went to a barber college for a free shave and one of the students failed in his examination on me."

The barber always thinks that two heads are better than one if it means cutting hair.

I see where an author is taking legal action against a publisher because he received only $1.50 for 8,000 words. This is the very thing that's always burned up the barbers.

All right, Royal Barbers, get out your razors and let's cut loose.

THE EMCEE AT A HOUSEWARMING

By George A. Posner

So our lodge finally has its new home. Confidentially, fellers, it was about time!

Do you know, I heard the building was so old the termites were having their meals outside? In fact the walls were so shaky the termites had already got to wearing parachutes. That's what they tell me.

I'll let you in on another secret. The place was getting so small, do you know they were going to pass a rule that members give up smoking king-size cigarets, and go back to the regular ones?

And why do you suppose some of the fellows got to wearing crew haircuts? **Loyalty!** They realized we needed the room. Bless their little hearts! Forget the bald heads, though —extremists!

Why do you suppose the president, the treasurer, and a few others—including myself—went on a **diet**? I had a definite **end** in view. Also a front, **very** definitely. My front, in simple words, was an affront to our lodge, considering our space needs.

We were even going to ask the ladies to get themselves together to help us in our crowded situation, as well as get the wherewithal for a larger place. They were to help us squeeze pennies, as well as other things, until we could get larger quarters. Squeezing **pennies** to get larger **quarters**—hm! A joke!

Yes, sir, those old quarters of ours were so tight, a woman without a girdle we called a **traitor!** She was letting us down, besides letting herself out. We got so we just weren't going to let them **in!** If they protested, we'd say: "Now don't go to pieces, lady; pull yourself together!"

You never heard these stories before? Well, they didn't **spread.** No room!

Why, even the kids were having a terrible time. Do you know they weren't even allowed to have growing pains? One day one kid cut his finger in the lodge, and couldn't even bleed. No room!

I think these conditions went on so long because most of the time we weren't sure if the rooms were really so small, or if it just seemed so because the mice were so big.

Somebody said the real reason this continued so long was because there wasn't room for complaint!

And that landlord! How could we ever stand him? That curiosity of his! Always curious to know when we were going to pay the rent.

Then one day he comes around and says: "I'm going to raise your rent." "That's wonderful," we answered. "We were wondering how **we** were going to raise it."

So finally we told the gentleman—and I'm using the word gentleman loosely—that we were leaving. We wanted a better neighborhood. So he answered: "It will be a better neighborhood when you leave!" Can you tie that? After all we did to— I mean, for—him? . . . I'm just kidding, of course.

When we planned for our new place it was really surprising how everyone rallied to the cause. And some of the schemes some of those well-meaning souls suggested to help with our plans!

Some of them actually reminded us of that classic of the Irishmen who planned to build a new jail out of the materials of the old one, and use the old one until the new one was completed. But bless their hearts, they meant well.

And so finally here we are in our new quarters, having a housewarming. I hope it doesn't end up like the housewarming of a Methodist church out my way. They had just paid the last lien and there they were at the church having a ceremony of burning the mortgage—when the building caught fire, and burned to the ground!

Let's be careful with those matches, eh?

In all seriousness, I am sure the officers deeply appreciate the efforts of the lodge members in working together to realize the attaining of our goal—a better place in which to carry on the work and play of our organization. And I am certain the members appreciate the work of our officers in this accomplishment. It was a big job, and a well-done job; and due credit and appreciation belongs to all.

There's a little story I would like to tell in conclusion which seems to fit in here.

It seems there were two skeletons that had been imprisoned for many days in a dark and dismal closet. And finally one skeleton said to the other: "What are we doing here?"

And the other skeleton said: "I don't know. If we had any **guts** we'd get out of here!"

And so I say: "We did have the guts to get out of a bad place, into a better situation."

And because we had the guts to do something about it is reason for thankfulness and rejoicing.

THE EMCEE AT A SURPRISE PARTY

By George A. Posner

My father told the story of a farmer who brought some products to the city and sold them, then thought: "I'll surprise the wife."

So he bought a suit, a hat, a pair of shoes, underwear—just everything from top to toes—and put it all under the seat of his buckboard.

On his way home he stopped at the river. There he took off his old clothes—everything, top to toes—and threw them in. Then he looked under the seat for his new clothes—and everything he had put there was gone.

Finally he got back up into the seat of the buckboard and said to the horse: "Giddap, Maud, we'll surprise her anyway!"

Yeah, some of the surprises we plan just don't turn out the way we planned them. Especially these days. It's getting pretty hard to surprise anyone.

In the old days, to hear my father talk, there were lots of surprises. The young bloods standing on the street corners, in front of the barber shop, on a windy day, watching the girls go by. And if they saw an **ankle**—wow! That was a thrilling surprise.

The gals in those long dresses, with long trains besides. Oh, the boys didn't mind the trains, as long as they were well-crowded! But those long dresses sweeping the ground, how the mothers complained. They said they were picking up dirt and disease germs. Now the girls wear shorter dresses, and look what they pick up!

When a man married a woman in those days, at least she had a few surprises to show him. But nowadays? After he has taken her down to the beach, and seen her in one of those Bikini bathing suits? No more surprises.

Want to know how to surprise a girl these days, young fellow? Get her alone in the parlor, or some secluded spot. Then suddenly speak up to her masterfully: "C'mere, kid! I'm going to **kiss** you!" Of course she'll say, "No! No, Hubert, don't!" (But that's just camouflage, feller, just some of that playing at hard-to-get). So then, when you've blurted out you were going to kiss her, and she's said "no!"—then just drop it and **don't** kiss her. **Then** notice the **big surprise** on her face!

Yes, that seems about the **only** way to surprise her, these days . . . the suave darlings. But we love them, don't we?

Now take the married men. Every once in a while, maybe, you get an idea you haven't been showing the little woman enough attention, and **love.** You've just read an editorial, or maybe it's a song: "She may be weary, just a little weary, wearing that old shabby dress"—ta, de, da, dum—"so try a little tenderness!"—ta, de, da, dum!

So you buy a box of candy (the kind **you** like) and a big bunch of flowers, and take them home as a surprise for her. So how does she take that? "You bum!" says she. "What have you been doing now? . . . C'mon! What is it?"

Oh, you can't win! . . . Well, finally she comes over and kisses you. But what was that for? Just to smell your breath; to see if you haven't been drinking! You know that.

I was over at Sears Roebuck's the other day. A fellow was there looking over some household appliances. It seems he was trying to decide between a washing machine and a cook stove. He said to the clerk: "I'm buying this for my wife, for her birthday."

"Oh," said the clerk, "A surprise?"

"I'll say," said the customer. "She's expecting a fur coat."

Well, I guess there was one way to surprise her.

Never mind. We love them, don't we, fellers?

"Here's to the ladies, God bless 'em,

"No matter how they dress 'em!"

They've had quite a tug-of-war of it, anyway, as regards the size of the ladies' dresses. For a long time—when they raised the hems, making the dresses shorter, the material manufacturers raised heck. And when they lowered the hem to the shoe tops again, the silk stocking manufacturers raised holy ned. So what were the style makers to do? If the darlings would only realize that we would look at them no matter what they wore. Or if they wore nothing at all! Honestly!

But we're getting off the subject of surprises. And getting back to that subject, I recall a good one my dad told along that line. My father was what you might call the John Gunther of his generation. He seemed to know the "inside" of more things than you could shake a stick at. Where he got those facts I do not know. He certainly could deliver them in an authoritative and convincing manner. Although sometimes I thought I caught a twinkle in his eye.

Anyway, here is an "inside" story out of the Bible, which he dug up somewhere; and which I feel would fit in with the occasion we're celebrating today. It does concern a "surprise," at least.

It seems, said my dad, that when the Ark pushed off, Noah assembled all the animals in the social hall and made quite a serious speech. He said: "You know we're not overly supplied with space, and we have probably a long trip ahead. So I want you to know we can't have any population increases at all until the emergency is over, and we've landed again. I'm appointing Mr. Giraffe here, being the tallest, as overseer; and he will see that my orders in this respect are carried out."

So, in due time the rains stop, and the waters recede. Finally they land the Ark on dry land again. And the animals begin coming out of the Ark by two and two, as they went in—with no more of any species, until the two cats come along. And lo, and behold, these two cats are followed by a litter of kittens! The tom cat, as he passed the surprised giraffe, winked an eye and said: "Ha, I'll bet you thought we were wrestling."

Speaking of the Ark, my father said he had a few more facts he had dug up regarding that trip.

He said that while the Ark was several days out, Noah found a small leak in the hull of the boat. And he asked a dog to stick his nose in the hole to stop it.

And later Noah found a still larger leak, and asked his wife to put her hands over the hole. Still later there was a still larger hole, and Noah sat down on the spot.

And that is why, said my dad, a dog's nose is always cold; a woman's hands are always cold; and why, on a chilly day, a man always stands with his back to the fire . . .

I suppose these "statistics" related by my father will surprise you. They're different, anyway, and surprising—no?

And so, let's proceed to the surprise party.

THE EMCEE AT AN ANNIVERSARY PARTY

By Louis J. Huber

Ladies and gentlemen, as your emcee I now take the floor and move this party into high gear. You know how that works at times — in one gear and out the other. I'm very sorry but all emcees have corny jokes.

I need not tell you that this is the fiftieth anniversary. (Or any year.) Fifty years in one building denotes one thing: We didn't have the money to pay for a moving van.

Fifty years is a long time for anyone or anything to be in one place. I would like to be here fifty years and, at the rate I'm traveling, I'll be that long getting this celebration under way.

A half century. Multiply that by ten and you have five hundred years. Subtract that from today and you would be back near the time when Columbus discovered our grand and glorious land. You might think that I'm trying to impress you with my knowledge of history but that is not true. I'm just trying to show my old arithmetic teacher, who might be listening, that I still know how to add and subtract.

Since I do this, and take the time to brag about it, I'd better be adding the minutes that have been allotted to me and do something with them. So, getting down to the serious aspect of the celebration, let me start by stating that only a wonderful concern, headed by a grand management, could ever hope to attain the goal reached by us today.

It has been said that time and tide await no man. Let me change that just a bit and say that time and trade await no man. Not unless the merchant with whom you are trading has an outstanding record for fairness. This, I believe sincerely, can be said of our company.

If it were not true time and trade would have passed us in the struggle for existence. For time is a harsh dictator. It lets you start in a race and then, if you are not fit and worthy, it sends you to the sidelines and lets a better man run in your place.

The same thing could be said of trade. If you are to stay in the business world and do it by unfair means you might make a few extra cents. But the years will add the total and in a short while your competition, if it has been fair and worthy, will engulf you and you drown in the lack of business.

There is no need to tell you that our company has withstood the tests of time and trade. Or else we would not be here today. The Roman philosopher, Seneca, once said that it takes an age to build a city but only an hour to destroy it.

We think that some thought could be applied to a business concern. Only one that is founded by honest people with a desire to do the right and proper thing can succeed. Only one that is furthered by the same type of folks can stay successful.

So we look upon our company as a tradition. And what is a tradition? Simply this: The handing down of knowledge, beliefs, customs from one generation to another. It is something handed down from one age to another, something so strongly rooted that it is as inviolable as a law.

What can I add to that belief? Nothing. So I move that we enjoy this party given to us by time and trade and tradition. Let's eat, drink and be merry. And if you can't be Mary because you are a boy then just eat, drink and be Joe. Let's celebrate!

THE EMCEE AT AN OPEN HOUSE

By Louis J. Huber

Friends, let me take a bit of your time as I ask you to gather around this platform and hear my few words. As the master of ceremonies it is my pleasant duty to bid you welcome to this open house celebration.

The Acme Company (name of firm holding the open house) wants me to bid you welcome and I do this in my name. However, I do not wish to usurp the task that has been given to someone more worthy of it. In a short while you will hear from Mr. Brown, the president of the company.

I would like to tell you the story of how this open house party came into focus. Truly, it is the work of Mrs. Brown. You will notice that she is — oh, I'm ahead of my story — wearing a new piece of apparel. I am not going to point it out to you, you can see for yourself that she is wearing last year's hat and some of the other clothing is not so new either.

When Mr. Brown finally consented to buy for her this new you-know-what, she was so astonished that she couldn't speak. Mr. Brown was highly pleased with this condition. He told her, since she was tongue-tied, that she could have anything she wanted. He thought she would be unable to ask for anything. Ah, the power of a woman! She gathered her strength and she asked. She wanted the Acme Company to hold open house. Know why? She wanted a chance to show off this new dress and here is her chance to do it. Ladies and gentlemen, Mrs. Brown, who is a good sport and who does not mind the small fib that I just told about her. (Mrs. Brown takes a bow.)

Mrs. Brown is also responsible, in a direct way, for this beautiful building. Let me tell you the story and you will agree with me in every detail. Even if you don't agree, please let me tell the story. Thank you.

You see, folks, Mr. Brown wanted this building but he did not want to put out the money to build it. He hired a bricklayer to start things. One day he watched the man getting some of the bricks ready for the building. The man, being a master of his trade, made it look very simple. So simple that Mr. Brown fired him and decided to take over the job himself.

It didn't look hard. You just took one brick and put it on another, then you took another brick and put it on top of that. Like the old adage: One stone upon another and the highest wall is laid.

Mr. Brown was getting along quite well. He had about twenty bricks, one upon the other. Then came the tragedy. The whole thing collapsed. It shouldn't have happened to anyone and it should never have happened to the boss. But it did. He re-hired the bricklayer and then he learned something. Why didn't someone tell Mr. Brown that you must put mortar between those bricks to keep them from falling over?

It's true, folks, he just didn't use any cement. But he did use cement in joining together this fine organization known as the Acme Company. He welded it into a concern that has become famous locally and nationally. And he is also famous.

We don't know how far his personal fame has gone over the nation. We do know that here, among his friends and co-workers, he has become a gear in the machinery. More than that, he is the big gear that drives the big wheel. Without him there would be no Acme, without Acme we would not be here. Let me present to you the man who has made all this possible, Mr. Brown, president of the Acme Company.

FOR THE EMCEE AT A BIRTHDAY PARTY

By George A. Posner

Say, how did I get into this? . . . It reminds me of the story of the nervous bridegroom at his wedding reception. They had coaxed him into making a speech, and the fellow was shy, as well as unprepared. But he finally got up on his feet, so flustered that he didn't notice his hand was resting on his bride's shoulder as he stammered: "Ladies and gentlemen, this thing has been unexpectedly forced upon me!"

I've been asked to emcee at this birthday party in honor of our esteemed friend, neighbor, lodge player, kibitzer, and what have you?

You know a birthday party is something celebrated almost entirely by children and men. I was really surprised recently when I was invited to a **woman's** birthday party. Some relative of mine. I **guess** it was a birthday party. As near as I could figure it was the sixth or seventh anniversary of her 29th birthday. Well, they do say the ten happiest years of a woman's life are those between 29 and 30.

Yes, women **do** live longer than men. Statistics say so. I guess maybe it's because paint is a great preservative. I don't know. Looking over the Hollywood divorce figures, it seems the women, seeing they can't get more life in their men, are getting more men in their lives. Maybe that can be taken in more ways than one.

But to get back to the honoree of our birthday party, Mr. ————. I'll give you a few facts and figures. He was born. Yes, he was born and at an early age. His birth seemed to come as a surprise to him. In fact, it seemed to strike him speechless, so he couldn't talk intelligently for more than a year afterward. Da, da, da, da! Like a punch-drunk prize-fighter.

Well, he came from a bashful family. His mother told me

confidentially that if his father hadn't been so bashful he would have been three years older.

He was an original st—thinker. Had a good sense of citizenship practically from the start. Although he was born during the prohibition era, and both his parents were ardent Drys, whenever he expressed himself it was as a Wet.

You know, an astrologer once asked his mother, "Under what sign was your baby born?" She told him, "Under the one saying, 'Visiting hours from 2 to 5.' "

The truth of the matter is (I'll whisper it), he was born under the stop sign. His mother was late reaching the hospital.

It was some years later that I saw him again. He was going to school. He asked me, "Have you noticed the way I've growed?"

His mother said, "Grown, darling, **grown.**" And he says to her, "Why should I groan?"

He said, "I got 100 in the school exams today." I told him, "Why, that's wonderful! What were the subjects?" So he says, "50 in arithmetic and 50 in spelling."

Always, it seems, his teacher wanted him to stay after school. But he said she wasn't his type.

One day I found him crying, and I asked, "What's wrong?" He cried, "I—I lost the quarter the teacher g-gave for b-being the best boy of the class."

"Oh, well, never mind," I told him, "here's another one to take its place. But tell me how you lost it?"

"'Cause I wasn't the best boy in the class," he answered.

That boy was in hot water so often he felt like a teabag.

It was his father who gave him his musical background. He used to spank him with a base drum stick. He went to the woodshed so often he had to be inspected weekly for termites.

It's sure different in my family. My wife and I never struck our kids except in self-defense.

He sure was a skinny kid. He was so thin you had to look at him twice to see him once. A backache hit him in the same place as a bellyache. And if he sat on a dime, eight cents of it showed.

He joined the Boy Scouts, but when the old ladies looked at him, it was **they** who helped **him** across the street.

He was a boy scout until about sixteen, and then like all boys, he became a girl scout.

I asked him when was it he first became interested in girls. He said, "When I found out they weren't boys."

And boy, has that guy a way with women! He has them alphabetically listed in his address book, and they say the twentieth name is Alice Adams!

I've put in my bid for that little black book; I want to get there first before the rest of you fellows. Because I've heard he's decided he wants to live dangerously—in other words, he plans to get married.

All this, of course, has been just in fun; and now, seriously, I wish to present as fine a fellow as it's ever been my pleasure to know—a hail fellow, well met and all-around good sport, ————. Come up here!

THE EMCEE AT A POLICEMEN'S BALL

By Sidney Steele

First, gentlemen, a warning. I understand that last week five cars were recovered, although only two were stolen. We may hear a protest from the thieves about these unfair tactics.

There has just come out of Washington a bulletin on safety. One chapter deals with burglars. An excerpt from the chapter reads: "How to get a cop when you need one. Write your representative in Congress. He will forward your letter to the district assemblyman. If he is on good terms with the commissioner he will have the commissioner appoint a member of your family as a cop, and you will have protection in the family all the time."

Which one of you men pulled this funny one yesterday? You said you couldn't seize the thief when you found him because you had a club in one hand and your gun in the other.

Perhaps you heard about this one that happened locally last week. A certain Irishman had a stranglehold on a lamppost because he didn't want to fall and hurt somebody when one of our kind-hearted officers said to him, "I've known you for a long time, Tim, but for two cents I'd run you in." Tim blinked his eyes. "Sure, an' I'm glad you said two cents. Because it would take more than one copper to run **me** in."

I have one from Japan that might interest you boys. It seems that in Tokyo a police inspector retired after thirty-five years as Japan's Number One foe of pickpockets. He was so expert at picking pockets that to save time when he saw a pickpocket pick a pocket he picked the pickpocket's pocket and repocketed the pickings in the pocket of the man whose pockets the pickpocket had picked, and went on about his business without saying a word.

If I am not under arrest, I would like to join in the festivities of the evening. What say?

THE EMCEE AT A GOLDEN WEDDING ANNIVERSARY CELEBRATION

By Louis J. Huber

Folks, there comes a time to everyone when he or she does not feel that they have the right to fill the capacity to which they have been appointed. I have that feeling right now. When I was asked to guide this golden wedding celebration I accepted it immediately.

And then I started to think about what I had done. What could I say when the people you are honoring are so far above you? When your tribute to them would be much greater if you just stood and admired them? What could I say? Well, many things. Not because I am capable of saying them without feeling a certain humility but because an emcee must have his mouth open or people will wonder what is keeping it shut.

Let me tell you about some of the things that have been learned about our honored couple since I have delved into their past. It seems that their wedding day was like most wedding days. The neighbors gasped when they saw the bride. She was so excited that she had forgotten to wear shoes. This caused all of them to ask: I wonder what he saw in her? Those who did not ask this time-honored question asked another almost like it. They asked: I wonder what did she see in him?

In answer to both of those questions all one needs to do is look at their happiness this day. What did they see in each other? They know. And it matters little if the neighbors never found the answer to the question.

Fifty years of married bliss! I like to say that over and over and over just to hear how it sounds. To me it sounds good. To them it must sound so much better because they drank of it.

Don't let all this sweet talk of mine let you be fooled into thinking that each day was peaceful. It was not. There was the time when her mother wanted to come and live with them. The head of the house was annoyed. Mrs. **(Name)**, thinking she could win her husband's consent, suggested that they build a new house so Mother could drop in at any time. He agreed to that and all seemed well. But when the new house turned out to be a houseboat, and he even invited her mother to drop in, there were sounds of war.

There was another reason why this happy couple were that way fifty years ago and remained that way through the years that followed. She never missed him very much. No, she had an accuracy that would have done justice to a big league ball player. However, he learned to duck and they settled down to a peaceful existence.

None of this is true, ladies and gentlemen, and you know it. We are here because we are honoring two people who have walked before us and who have made a path that we would all like to follow. We are here because they have been a source of inspiration that has helped us over many of our own domestic problems.

Little do they know that they have been looked upon as leaders in that great institution called marriage. Little do they know that many of us, who came later and were married, did so because their example had been a grand and glorious light that also showed us the way to happiness.

Let the cynic scoff and let the quipsters make jokes about married life. Their efforts will fall on so much barren ground that they will give it up. Especially when we have such shining examples of golden happiness as Mr. and Mrs. **(Name)**. Let them stand and be honored!

FOR THE EMCEE AT A BACHELOR DINNER

By George A. Posner

Fellow bachelors and fellow mourners. We have met here in the sight of God and the presence of this goodly company for a sad occasion. We have come to pay our final respects to one whom God in His infinite wisdom has seen fit to take from among us.

What is man after all? Here today and gone tomorrow. A frail creature. Along comes another frail, and pffft! As the proverb says, man is made of dust; along comes a woman with the hose, and his name is mud! Or again, what is man but a worm? He comes out of his hole, wiggles around a little, and is picked up by a chicken.

Well, we all have to go sometime. And when you gotta go, you gotta go! It is our part as good neighbors to help ease our dear brother into this valley of the shadow.

Look at him! Doesn't he look natural? Look at that smile on his face. So young to go. So young and innocent. You know, I asked him, "Do you want a big wedding or a little one?" He answered, "Can't I have both? A big wedding, and then a little one—nine months later?" Bless his heart!

It sure was a fast courtship. I listened in when he proposed. She said, "I think we'll be very happy together, stranger."

Yes, he spoke fast. I guess maybe he realized it was his last chance to do any talking. You know, marriage is like a railroad crossing. You see a pretty girl. You stop—you look—and, after you're married, you listen.

Very soon you'll be walking down the aisle—she with a bouquet of roses over her arm, and you with four roses, on your breath. With the organ pealing out that beautiful war song, The Wedding March.

It reminds me of the story of the Hebrew father who was giving his daughter his benediction at her wedding. He said:

"We do three things in this world. We are born—we marry—and we die. My daughter, you've been born, you are now married—there is nothing left for you to do but to die."

But don't let that depress you. Remember, after you're married there will be times—many times—when you would be **glad** to die!

And now a few words of advice to you—it probably won't do a bit of good, but here they are, anyway:

Remember, a girl doesn't always marry a man because she thinks he's good for her. She often marries him because she thinks he's too good for the other girls.

Remember that after you're married your wife still enjoys candy and flowers—speak of them occasionally.

Be like a king to her—well, at least like Henry the 8th.

Don't be afraid to tell her you'll grant her smallest desires. Don't worry—you'll find she has no small desires.

Tell her she should decide on the little things, while you take care of the big things. You'll find **few** big things come up! There may be a lot of little ones come along, though, but of course she'll take care of those.

Marriage is a fifty-fifty partnership—unless you watch out. She gets the $50 dresses; you get the 50-cent shirt. It's a give-and-take proposition—you give and she takes.

You know why they call the wife the better half? Because when she asks you for money, you better have some.

So don't forget, cooperation is the thing. If the wife wants to wash the dishes, wash the dishes with her; if she wants to clean the windows, clean the windows with her. And if she wants to mop the floor, mop the floor with her.

Don't criticise the bread she bakes. If you compare it unfavorably with your mother's, she may compare your roll with her father's.

If she wants to drive the car, don't stand in her way.

If she wants the world, **let her have it!**

But above all, don't criticise her taste — remember, she picked you for a husband!

ADDITIONAL MATERIAL

Speaking of bachelors, I have a friend who is a confirmed bachelor, and not a bad speaker. Anyway, he had been persuaded to talk at a benefit affair given by a Woman's Club—said he would do so if they furnished the subject.

The ladies knew he was a hardened "reprobate" bachelor, and you know how women subconsciously are a little resentful of such a man. Maybe they figure it's a sort of slur on their charm and man-baiting abilities. Anyway, they decided to have a little fun with him, and so they gave him as his subject: "Woman. Without Her, Man Would Be a Savage."

He seemed a little non-plussed for a while; then when the time came for him to speak, he arose and said, blandly:

"My subject, which I consider is a very fine one, is nevertheless not of my own choosing, but was furnished me by the ladies. It is: 'Woman, Without Her Man, Would Be a Savage'."

* * *

Someone has said: "Bachelors are men with nobody to share the cares they would have if they were married men."

* * *

Another certain bachelor friend of mine thought the time had arrived to end his aloofness and enter into the double harness—he had found the girl of his dreams.

He was a pretty bashful sort of fellow; and the father of the girl was a rather crusty-natured gentleman. So he thought he'd take a pal along in the hope it would help out.

He said to his pal: "The old man, I'm afraid, doesn't think so much of me. He'll ask all kinds of questions. It'll look better if I answer modestly, then you sort of come out each time and build me up better. Eh?"

The friend agreed, and soon they were at the girl's house. And soon after the boy had popped the question, the pop was questioning the boy. Said he:

"What kind of work do you do, young man?"

"Oh, I'm a minor executive," he answered.

Then the friend chimed in: "A minor executive, will you listen to him! He's vice-president, that's what he is!"

"Have you saved any money?"

"Oh, I have a little at First National Bank."

"Huh! A **little,**" broke in the friend. "Why don't you tell him that besides First National Bank, there's Second, Third and Fourth National and only four or five more! And what of your U.S. Steel stocks? And A.T. & T. and duPont?"

At this point this modest bachelor was afraid his friend was stretching it too far, so he coughed warningly.

"Have you a cold?" asked the father.

"No, just a slight cough."

"A slight cough! Listen to him!" chimed in the friend. "He's in the last stages of galloping tuberculosis!"

THE EMCEE AT A BABY SHOWER

By George A. Posner

I have just been reading some automobile statistics. It is said that men have most of the big accidents, but the women have the little ones. Of course, they're speaking of two different things in one breath there. Accidents, and babies—or are they?

The excitement—most of it—is over. Father and child are doing well. I say father and child, because he was the one we were most worried about.

I know that when it was about over, the mother was saying to the doctors: "I'm all right—just see how my husband is holding up!"

How does the poem go?

> "The stork is a bird with a great big bill;
> "He brings the babies, whenever he will;
> "Then comes the doctor, and when he is through,
> "We find that **he** has a big bill, too."

Yes, the father they say is recovering, but he isn't strong enough to be shown the bill yet.

Was he in a **condition!** This baby business is mighty tough on us fathers! I'll never forget the way he looked, shouting: "Tell me, quick! Is it a boy or girl?"

"Certainly, it is," said the nurse. "What else could it be?"

"Don't tease me!" he shouted excitedly, "but tell me quick! Am I a father, or am I a mother?"

He was so upset he got the doctor confused, too. The doc began to stutter: "T-t-t-t- - - -"

And the father shouted: "My heavens! T-twins?"

So the doc continued: "Tr—tr—tr—"

And the father, turning white as a sheet, shrieked: "Tr—triplets!"

"No, no!" said the doc. "I'm t-t-t—tr—tr—tr—trying to say—qu—qu—qu—"

And the father moaned: "Quadruplets!"

Then—when they had revived the father—the doc told him: "What I was t—tr—trying to say was **QUIET!** Take it easy. It's a boy."

And then the father said: "Thank heaven, it's over! But I was hoping it would be a **girl.** I didn't want a son of mine to ever have to go through what I've gone through!" How we fathers suffer!

You know, one of their other daughters said she knew definitely it was going to be a boy. Here's how she had it figured, when I asked her, this little girl of five.

"Well, last year, mother was sick and she got a baby girl. But this time it was **father** who really looked sick!"

Kids have a right to their own little logic, and superstitions, along with their elders who surely have many ideas of their own.

I remember how a relative of mine, a mother, was weeping during the wedding of a daughter—her third daughter, it seemed.

The bride said to her: "Oh, you mustn't cry so, Mother. You really mustn't."

"Boo, hoo!" said the mother. "Oh, darling, you don't know just what it is I'm crying about. Dear, when your oldest sister married, she went on a honeymoon to the Twin Cities in Minnesota and the next year she had twins.

"And when the next daughter married, her husband took her to Three Rivers, Ontario, and she got triplets. Now **you** tell me you are going to live in the Thousand Islands!!!"

From what I hear, they had quite a rhubarb among the family and relatives as to what to name the child. I understand some thought they ought to name the boy Bob after his mother's hair, while others wanted to name him after his father's chest—Harry.

Well, it doesn't matter, so long as the boy's healthy. And I understand he's in the **pink.** That's swell. Mine's a robust **yeller.**

I saw a cute announcement of a blessed event the other day. It was written by an engineer who lives on our block. It read this way:

"The Scott Family, Inc., proudly announces the latest addition to their lines of nifties, the Scott Baby Girl. . . . Carol Elizabeth. . . . Dr. K. M. Scott, sole designer and chief engineer. . . . Genevieve S. Smith, production manager. . . . Dr. H. A. Scalpel, technical adviser and assistant. . . . Model Number 3, released Tuesday, Dec. 8. . . . Outstanding features of this new model include the predominant color of red . . . a high speed motor of two-lung power . . . economical feed; screamline body; well-upholstered; free squealing; bawl bearing; water cooled exhaust; changeable seat covers; automatic clutch. A free demonstration of this model is to be given any time, subject, of course, to conditions which cannot be foreseen, or over which we have no control. The management assures friends and relatives there will be no new models."

Now isn't that cute? Well, it seemed so to me, anyway!

And so we're going to give the baby a **shower.** That is fine. It will make him nice and clean for his folks.

Well, I've been reading a book of instructions regarding babies, so I've come all prepared for this. I'll let you have the benefit of it. Let's see now.

You put him in the bath (him or her, whichever it is). If he turns blue, the water's too cold! If he turns red, it was too hot! And if he turns white—why, he was too dirty. It's all quite simple.

At night, before you retire, feed him some garlic. Then you can find him in the dark. That's good, strong advice, I think.

I know a friend who got an extra high crib for his kid. So they could hear him when he fell out. I don't advise that, though. It's unfair to the people living below you.

Here's some more advice I copied: "If the baby doesn't like fresh milk, it should be boiled." . . . Huh? Boil the baby? Sounds a little drastic to me, somehow.

Boiled babies? I used to add a little whiskey, but that used to get the baby **stewed.** When I was a baby, and they had any trouble with me, they **basted** me.

Well, here's some more advice. "If the baby cries, it's usually due to one of three things. He's hungry, a pin's sticking him, or . . ." Let's get on with the doings. What's first?

ADDITIONAL MATERIAL

There was an Italian on our block who was having his baby baptized. He took the minister aside, and said earnestly:

"Mr. Minister, pleasa excuse me, but dis boy of mine—you promise me you will name-a heem exactly like I tell you, and no different, **please?"**

"Why, certainly, Tony," answered the minister. "But this is very strange. Can you tell me why you are so particular and anxious in making this request?"

"Well, I tella you," answered Tony. "Lasta year I have a son, and I aska you please, I want to name him Tom—and you name-a him Thomas. Now disa one I want to name Jack."

They married early in life because they wanted to have their children young, they said. I can't blame them. I don't like old children myself.

A little boy had been sent to the department store to get some diapers. After the girl clerk had attended to this purchase, and wrapped it up, she said:

"There you are, little boy. That will be sixty cents for the diapers, and five cents for the tax."

"Never mind the tacks, lady," said the boy. "My mother uses **pins!**"

Have you heard of the little girl, daughter of a building contractor, who when asked what she would like best for Christmas said: "I'd like to have a baby brother."

"But, darling," said her mother. "Christmas is only a month away—that's too short a time!"

She said stubbornly: "But can't we put some more men on the job?"

"Well, little boy, I understand you have a new baby over at your house. Is she going to stay?"

"I suppose so. She's got her clothes off."

Little Boy: "Where did our new baby come from?"

Mother: "From Heaven, darling."

Little Boy: "Dressed like that? No wonder they threw her out."

Hear about the little boy who was taken in to see his newly-arrived baby brother? He looked the infant over critically, then said: "He hasn't much hair, has he, Dad?"

"No, he hasn't," answered the father.

"And he hasn't any teeth at all."

"Looks like you're right," said dad.

The boy thought a minute and then said, confidentially:

"You know what, Dad? I think you've been swindled—he's an old one."

My little boy looked at his new baby sister lying there, squealing and wailing away lustily in her crib.

"Did you say she came down from Heaven?" he finally asked.

"Yes, Johnny, she did," I told him.

"They like it quiet up there, huh?" says he.

"Did you hear about Mrs. Jones? She had triplets, and two weeks later she had twins."

"That's impossible. How'd it happen?"

"One of the triplets got lost."

Do you know, with our present national debt, every baby who comes into the world owes the government $16,000? No wonder those babies are crying their heads off!

There were twins—a boy and a girl—born to a couple on our block.

The females sure have an advantage over us men! Just think. They're twins—but when he's getting close to forty, she'll still be only 29.

In a child nursery, one of the infants had been howling its head off, and the nursery teacher, finally, driven almost to complete distraction, left one of the older boys in charge while she rushed off to phone the child's mother.

Returning a short time later, the teacher was surprised to find an atmosphere of complete and most surprising tranquility. There was not a single note of crying from the baby to disturb the heavenly stillness.

"Johnny," she asked, "how on earth did you manage to get that baby quiet—and so soon?"

"Aw, it was nothing at all—it was easy," bragged the boy. "I let her suck on a bottle of glue."

During a Parent-Teacher Association meeting, the following amusing story was pieced together by the accidental meeting and exchange of confidences by one parent and a teacher.

It seems a certain small boy had come home with the assignment of writing a composition regarding his family's background and origin. So he asked his mother:

"Mother, where did I come from?"

"The stork brought you, dear," was her answer.

"And where did you come from, Mother?"

"Why, the stork brought me, too, honey," said she.

"And Mom," he went on, "where did grandmother come from?"

"The stork brought grandma," said the mother.

And the composition the boy turned in next day began: "There have been no natural births in our family for three generations."

When one of Samuel Goldwyn's stars became a father, and proudly conveyed the news to the big boss, Goldwyn asked:

"And what are you going to name him, may I ask?"

"John," answered the proud papa, grinning happily from ear to ear.

"John!" exclaimed Goldwyn, in a voice that was almost a scream. "Man alive! Every Tom, Dick and Harry is named John!"

THE EMCEE AT A CHRISTMAS PARTY FOR EMPLOYEES

By Louis J. Huber

Good day there, merry gentlemen, and a hearty welcome to this Christmas party for the employees of Standard. You will notice that I greeted only the merry gentlemen and you know why. On this day, and on all days, the good ladies are always merry.

As your master of ceremonies I take the rein from the hands of Santa Claus and guide his reindeer through this party. I do this because Santa has been so busy that his voice is failing him. I do it also to keep the good reindeer from stepping on any of you as they make their way through the crowd. Imagine going into a hospital and telling them that you were run down by Blitzen. No one would believe it.

So, without any further delay, I give you the man who is better known than anyone in the world today, especially at this time of the year. I want you to meet that great custodian of the deer, that peerless driver whose only interference comes from TV antennas, none other than Santa Claus. (Santa appears on the platform.)

Now, Santa, I just want you to lean back and give with that merry twinkle in your eye. You might also give a few presents but I'll tell you who these people are and what you should give them because I got the gifts from Mrs. Santa Claus and I know what they ordered. Okay with you? (It is okay with Santa.) And even if it isn't okay, you'd better say it is because I'll tell Mrs. Santa and you know what that would mean, don't you? (Santa nods.) She'd send him out in the cold without his heavy underwear, that's what she'd do. (Santa nods that this is true.)

Now, of course, Santa has many useful gifts for you folks but there are some minor matters that must be handled. In looking over the records of the company we find that one certain employee was late a number of times. In fact, she was late so many times that they started calling her the late Mrs. Jones. Oho, I've given the name so I must also give the gift. Mrs. Jones, through the courtesy of your employer and Santa Claus we want you to have this alarm clock. It has a special device on it. It rings like a regular alarm and then, when you do not get out of bed it will yell "hey, you" at you. (Santa gives this gift to an employee who is late at times.)

We have with us another employee who thinks he is quite a hot number. Someone, a fellow employee, wrote to Santa and accused him of this crime. We do not know who it is but we think that Santa does. Santa, who in this group considers himself a pretty hot number? Whisper it to me. (This is done.) Oh, yes, I thought it might be John Smith. John, come forward and let Santa present you with a number of other hot numbers. This telephone directory is filled with them. Take it home and be happy with those of your kind. (John Smith is presented with a telephone directory.)

And a gift for the boss, Santa? I thought you had something in the bag for him. This gift, folks, was suggested by one of the employees who was caught in the act of taking too much time at the water cooler. (Or some other place where employees tend to stop and chat.) It seems that the boss came up from behind and caught him flat-footed and bare-handed. This must not happen again, Mr. Boss, and Santa is doing something about it. From now on, when you walk around the shop or office you must wear this small bell. (Small bell is presented by Santa Claus.) If, when wearing this bell, you still catch the employee loitering then you may rush up to him and ring it in his ear. This will give the employee enough time to think of a good excuse and you will be happy at the thought that not one of your employees is caught without a good alibi for it.

Also in our group is a gentleman who is quite a follower of the ponies. This, folks, is just a long way of saying that he likes to bet on the horses. He got this trait honestly. His great grandfather also followed the horses and he inherited the idea.

Of course, his forebear followed them in his wagon while selling fish to the neighbors. He made much more money than the lad we have in our group.

Enough of this nonsense and past history. Our boy needs help. He must be given something that will enable him to clean up at the races. They say there is no sure way of beating them but we have one sure way of cleaning up. So, with great pleasure, Santa presents to you, Mr. Horseman, the one certain way of cleaning up at the races. We present you with a wash cloth. All you need is soap and water and a small amount of energy. (Santa gives this present.)

Enough of this levity, good people. The management has other things in store for you and we will get to them. Without detracting from the mighty man who sits here close to me I'd like to say a few words about Christmas. Without it we would have no New Year. At least we would never know when New Year arrives because it comes a week after Christmas and if there were no Christmas how could we know?

But we must think of Christmas in a more serious vein. We must think of it as a time when it is much better to give than to receive. Without this kind of feeling in our heart it will not be Christmas. We must think of Christmas as a time when we are the kind of folk that God intended us to be in relation to our fellowmen and to Him.

Just think, good people, what a world this would be if we were every day as good and kind as we are on this Holy Day. We could be mentioned in the same breath as the angels; we could be put on the same pedestal. Would that be nice? It would. And this Child, whose birthday we are celebrating, would be very happy with us. It's worth our effort and I urge you to try it. I turn the party back to the man who has more gifts for each of you. (Turns it back to Santa or employer who has other presents.)

THE EMCEE AT A CONVENTION

By Louis J. Huber

Oh, ho, all you delegates! Let me have your attention, please. Come on over to my place of business and hear what I have to say. I am just a poor downtrodden married man and I have so little to say at home that they elected me to be master of ceremonies for this opening. They knew that I would have a lot of unused words and that I would be happy to find a place for them. So come on over and hear me, please.

All you delegates, hear this! Are there any of you who have not registered at the desk? It is of the utmost importance that you do this because you are not a delegate until we have your credentials and your name and number. What's my number? Everybody has my number, folks, so there is no use in my giving it to anyone. Everyone knows that I'm just a big blabber-guy and they gave me this position so they could keep an eye on me. You insist on knowing my number? Very well, here it is: 131234. Oh, what am I saying? That's the number I had before they let me out. It's changed since then and they have it at the desk. Now let's see all of you get over to the same place and they will see to it that you also get a number. We have some nice numbers over there, men. Some of them are blonde and some are brunettes and some — hold it, men! There is no sense in getting hurt. Take it easy and get your identification badges and we can soon proceed with the business of this convention.

And, speaking of identification badges, let me remind you that they are very necessary. Without them you might have difficulty in getting into the sessions of the convention. Please wear them and let your neighbor know who you are. Who am I? I can show you in one fleeting second, I can show you with a twist of the wrist. You see this badge? Read it. Never mind, I'll read it for you. It says: Stolen from the sheriff's office — hold it, men. They have no right to mark their badges with that kind of writing. I'd better put that one away and bring out my real badge. (Does this.) Now this is the one that I use for identification purposes. Read this one. No, I'd better do it. See, right here. It reads: Chicken Inspector!

If I don't soon find the right badge the convention will be over and no one will know me. There, now I have the right badge. It so happens that I am Joe Smith (his name) and that I've been asked to move things along. I'm the kind of boy who knows a lot about moving things along. It's happened to me many times. Every time the cop passes me on the street he gives me that old greeting: Move along, bud, or I'll run you in.

That's why I've been asked to move things along. My wife knows quite a bit about moving along. She learned it from me. We've used the thought many times and it always works. We wait until the landlord asks us for the rent and then she looks at me and she says: Joe, it's time that we move along. And so we move along before the landlord gets back to us the second time.

Now let's move the convention along. At ten o'clock we have the opening business session. And then (He reads some of the order of business of the convention.) Here are some other items of interest that I've been asked to read to you. Will the person who took the bond by mistake please return her immediately? Took the bond — wow, that's wrong. Will the person who took the blonde by mistake return her immediately? I certainly will do it, men. I didn't know she belonged to someone else. I'll find her. In the meantime, don't forget the opening session at ten o'clock. 'Bye now!

THE EMCEE AT A SILVER WEDDING ANNIVERSARY

By Earl Jay Gilbert

Ladies and gentlemen, I'd like to take this opportunity to say a few words about a deadly germ which has been infecting unsuspecting people for many years. It's called the love-bug.

While I called it a deadly germ, its effects are not necessarily fatal, although in most cases it's incurable. Once it bites you, the effects usually remain for a long time. It strikes most people when they least expect it. Many people never know they've been infected until it's too late to do anything about it and then they don't care.

In most cases this germ can be acquired by an apparently harmless glance of the eye from one of the opposite sex or perhaps a touch of the hand, and the bug gets in its vicious bite. The victims suddenly become conscious of a strange, peculiar sensation. The heart starts beating more rapidly. Sometimes they break out in a cold perspiration.

Then, sometimes immediately, or it may take longer, as the malady progresses, they feel drawn toward each other as if by some irresistible force they can't control. They embrace—they kiss! And with that first kiss—wham! The victims get a jolt similar to a powerful electric shock. Now they're doomed. No hope for them. The bug has started its deadly work.

Now the next symptoms appear. They begin to lose interest in anything but each other. They can't concentrate on anything else. Half the time they don't know where they are or what they're doing. They lose their appetites. They toy with their food.

The girl's mother will say: "Why aren't you eating? You used to like fried eggs so much," and the girl will reply: "My Georgie-Porgie-Pet doesn't like them, so I despise them." And Georgie-Porgie-Pet will say to his boss: "Yes, Mr. Sweetie-pie, you have the most wonderful eyes!"

They can't sleep. They roll and toss from side to side, murmuring the other party's name, coupled with romantic phrases and endearing words, such as "Darling, Sweetheart, Precious Baby." Their minds are filled with glorious images of each other. When they're apart they pine and languish, and go around in a daze, wondering what the other party is doing, and if "Precious" is thinking of them.

Sometimes the horrible thought strikes them that maybe "Precious" is thinking of someone else, and they fall into deep spells of dire despair, and gloomily consider thoughts of self-destruction.

When they meet again the symptoms change. Their blood pressure suddenly rises to the danger point. They ascend from dismal depths of dark despair to lofty heights of exalted romance and glorious nonsense. They fall into a clinch and start to smooch, whispering sweet nothings into each other's ears, such as "Whose sweet darling precious lamb baby are you?" —"I'm your sweet darling precious lamb baby"—"Who do you love, my enchanting angel?" —"I love you, my adorable pet. Do you love me?"—"Uh-huh—do you love me?"—"Uh-huh—do you really, really, really love me?"—"Uh-huh—do you?"— This goes on for hours. It doesn't make much sense, but it's part of the illness.

Now, my friends, that's only part of it. There's lots more to come. By this time they've become kissing addicts. That's worse than taking drugs or drinking strong liquor—smack-smack, smack-smack! It's no use suggesting medical attention, or dieting, or taking long, brisk walks. It wouldn't do any good. It's too late, anyway. These people are really sunk.

By this time they're trapped and snared in the toils of this insidious malady. So here we have two nice people, who probably have never wilfully harmed anybody in their entire lives, decide that the only way they can be happy is to spend the rest of their lives together. So the first thing there's a marriage—and they actually gloat over their happiness!

Frequently this disease not only stays with them after they're married, but it grows on them with each passing year. Now, my friends, I'd like to show you what I mean. We have with us, as guests of honor, a charming couple I'd like to hold up as an example of what can happen if you let that love-bug bite you.

This couple was bitten many years ago with the result that today they are celebrating their Silver Wedding Anniversary —twenty-five years of marriage and they're more in love than ever, and they don't seem to be any the worse for it. We know that in the years to come their love for each other will continue to grow as it has in the past, and we all hope to be present at their Golden Wedding Anniversary.

Now one more word of caution to all unmarried persons here. Beware of the love-bug, or you're liable to find yourselves some day celebrating twenty-five years of love and contentment like our dear friends here, Mr. and Mrs. ————.

THE EMCEE AT A FOREMEN'S BANQUET

By Arthur L. Kaser

Pity the poor foreman. He works and strives to better himself. Finally he is made foreman, and what happens? All the troubles imagineable are dumped on his shoulders. Then he wishes he was right back where he started. Why didn't they promote him to janitor or something?

I was a foreman once. I was the big boss. I ran things, including my legs. My feet were worn off up the ankles. That first day was a dinger. In the first place, when I entered the shop all the men were sitting down doing nothing. I said: "How come when I come in here I find you all loafing?" "Maybe," said one of them, "it's because you wear soft rubber heels."

At another time I got so utterly disgusted with one of my men I blew my top. During the whole day I didn't see him do one lick of work. I got the office to make out his time and mark it "final." I took his pay to the shop and gave it to him, saying: "Here is your pay for loafing seven hours." He said: "Excuse me, boss. It was eight hours." Nothing but trouble. That same day I caught an employee smoking. I said to him: "You know it's against the rules to smoke while you're working." He said: "Who says I'm working?"

Most of the men got to be steady workers. They got so steady they were motionless.

One day the census taker asked me how many men worked at our place, and I told him about one out of every ten.

I hadn't seen Bill Travis for some time. When I did meet him I was surprised. He certainly looked seedy. I said to him, "Bill, what's wrong? Been sick?" "No," he sort of sighed, "I ain't been sick. It's the work that's doin' it. Work from midnight till eight in the morning, and just an hour off. Man, it's tough." I said: "How long have you been on the job?" He said: "I ain't been on it yet. Begin tomorrow."

Well, boys, I've told my troubles. Now you tell yours.

THE EMCEE AT A BIRTHDAY CELEBRATION

By Louis J. Huber

Ladies and gentlemen, I have been assigned a most pleasant duty at this gathering. I have been asked to act as master of ceremonies and to see that all is done in order and perfection.

We are here to celebrate a birthday. It is that of a famous American. Now is not the time to have your thoughts wander and wonder who it might be. Don't bother trying to figure Lincoln and Washington into this gathering. Although they were famous in their own right, and they still are, the recipient of our good wishes is equally famous.

Not for some great and outstanding deed as you might think when the word fame is mentioned. No, rather it is because of his (or her) daily dignity in his walk of life. That is why our guest is famous. Because his contacts with his fellow human beings have been so sincere he has cornered our good wishes.

For what is fame? A great athlete may be famous. He may run a hundred yards with a football tucked under his arm and the newspapers will herald his name across the front pages of the nation. And two years after this happens to him? Only a few will remember the deed.

Benjamin Franklin has a very good definition of fame. He advised: "If you would not be forgotten as soon as you are dead, either write things worth reading or do things worth writing."

We have taken the time to contact the wife (or husband) of our honored guest. We have learned that the only worthwhile writing that he has ever done were, according to his wife, the love letters that he wrote to her. That, of course, is her opinion.

So, coming from someone very close to him, his writings have been limited. It must be his deeds that he has acquired the honor that we, in our humble effort, seek to bestow upon him. Do I need to mention them? No, most of you know them and any repetition would be onerous and distasteful. I would like to say this: It is the manner in which he has acquired his fame that must be lime-lighted.

The great French writer, La Rochefoucauld, had a word for fame. He, like Benjamin Franklin, must have met folks like our guest. He said that the fame of men should only be estimated by the means used to acquire it.

Our guest used no means to acquire his and that's why we consider him famous in our eyes. He just stood still and let the word and the world catch up with him. A kind word when it was needed, a pat on the back when the daily burdens were making it ache, a whisper of encouragement when the worldly routine was making it seem very hopeless and useless.

There was no shouting to the skies for personal acclaim for a deed well done. There was no self-elevation for the personal favors bestowed upon his friends and acquaintances. There was only that smile of satisfaction when he was able to lend a hand to a friend.

All these things have made our guest famous in our eyes. And what if he isn't famous to those who do not know him? It is only because they have never met him. Had they done this, he would also be deep in their hearts and minds just as he is with us. So would you like to meet this guest who needs no introduction? You would? I present him to you, Mr. ——————.

THE EMCEE AT A CHRISTMAS PARTY

By George A. Posner

Gosh, here it's Christmas, again! Just about when I've started to recover from last Christmas. Time marches on. Marches? It runs! September runs into October; October runs into November; November runs into Christmas—and Christmas runs into **money!**

(Hmm.) "I'm dreaming of a White Christmas!" Ta-de-da-da — You know what they mean by a "White Christmas"? It's when you see all those bills, and your face turns pale. . . .

Especially us fathers and heads of families, eh? It's the time when you stop worrying about the wolf at the door and begin to worry about the mink in the window. That is, when you've got a wife like mine. Our neighbor bought his wife a mink coat to keep her warm, last Christmas. And this Christmas I've got to buy my wife one to keep her **quiet.** That's the kind of wife that I've got.

I went into a store, and asked the clerk: "I want to buy a Christmas present for a lady."

He asked: "Something expensive, or is it for your wife?" That's how much he knows about my wife. Something expensive, or is it for my wife? I said, "Listen, my wife and expensive are synonyms."

Never mind. They're priceless; my wife, and my kid. Every Christmas it's a race between them as to who will give me the best surprise for Christmas. It always ends in a tie. And when I say tie, I mean **tie** — just that.

The little tyke. He's cute. These modern kids! Know what he said he wanted for Christmas? A pair of ice skates! That's nothing so unusual? No. But he wanted Sonia Henie on them.

A tie for Christmas! But maybe it's supposed to be symbolical. Meaning it's the time I'm just about fit to be tied.

The annual Christmas drive for the heathen, down at my church, comes coincidentally at my church — just about this time. And it's fortunate. Soon I'll hear my wife proudly telling the neighbors: "My husband is so unselfish. He gave his best tie to the heathen — the one I gave him for Christmas. I'm so proud of him!" She should have heard what I told the clerk who sold her that tie! She might have changed her mind. Well, what she doesn't know won't hurt her.

There's such a thing as doing your Christmas shopping **too** early, too! A gent in my neighborhood was **arrested** for doing his Christmas shopping too early — no fooling. They caught him in the store several hours before it opened.

Down at my office I can always tell when Christmas is approaching — the Yuletide spirit. A certain fellow begins going around with his usual Yuletide greetings. "If Yule lend me five bucks Yuletide me over, pal." I won't say who he is — but there's one in every office.

And there's another certain party at my office I hear has already bought a present for the one he loves best — **himself.** This guy is so conceited they say he walks down Lovers' Lane all by himself. Well, when he came out of the store, he accidentally dropped the present and it fell to the sidewalk. There was a sound of breaking glass and the smell of Four Roses — and not the kind that grows on a bush. They heard him moaning: "Oh, look! Christmas has come and gone already!" . . . There's one in every office.

And there's a certain shy little thing at the office whom I asked: "Do you think your little stocking will hold everything you want for Christmas?" She sighed, and said: "No, but a pair of short socks would!" . . . There's one in every office.

Every year I take my kid to a certain Department Store and he sits on Santa's lap and tells him what he wants for Christmas. And the little beggar always says: "Now you won't forget, will ya, Santa? You'll remember?"

Well, this year the wife had to louse up the deal. The day after I took the kid, what does she do but take him to the same place, same Santa. And so, of course, Santa asked him: "What'll you have for Christmas, sonny?" And my kid gave him such a kick in the ankle that Santa fell flat on his fat-pillow, as the kid yelled: "You numbskull!!! Already you've forgotten!"

That kid's a dinger. Last year I bought him one of those unbreakable toys. Well, it was unbreakable, maybe. The morning after Christmas, the wife met me in the hall and said: "You know that unbreakable toy you bought for Johnny?"

"Sure," I said. "And I suppose it wasn't unbreakable?"

"No," she said. "It wasn't unbreakable. But he used it to break all his other toys — and those of the neighbors' boys, too."

What a kid! Precocious. I wonder what he'll be when he grows up — if the neighbors let him.

I asked him if he was saving his money to buy Christmas seals. He said: "Christmas seals? Shucks! I wouldn't know what to feed them!"

Last Christmas the neighbors asked him: "Did you come out well on Christmas?"

"Oh, yes, I got more than anybody in the house!"

"My," they said, "what a good little boy you must have been! How did it happen?"

"I got up before they did."

In a couple of days he had that new suit we bought him for Christmas all muddy and torn.

"How did that happen, Johnny?" his angry mother wanted to know.

"I was trying to keep a bad little boy from hurting a good little boy," said he.

"Oh, that was noble," said his mother. "Who was the good little boy?"

"Me."

The other day he found a box of moth balls. Ate them all up. Now we're thinking of renting him out to warehouses — to breathe on clothing.

Well, they say children are a great comfort to you in your old age. They sure help you to get there fast, too.

He brought a cute story home from school, apropos of the Christmas season. I'll tell it to you.

It seems the teacher was speaking to the kids about the spirit of Yuletide, and how it is more blessed to give than to receive.

One kid raised his hand, then spoke up and said: "Please, ma'am, my daddy says he always uses that motto in his business, that it's 'more blessed to give than to receive.' "

"Well, isn't that nice!" said the teacher. "And what business is your father in?"

The kid answered: "He's a prize fighter!"

I thought that was kind of cute. No? . . .

Well, the foregoing, fellows, of course was mostly in fun. Aside from the gayety of the season — which has its rightful place, of course — there are other things, more serious things which we ought not forget. The fact is, in reality, we can't help being mindful of them — almost subconsciously — they come creeping into the hearts of all of us at this time of the year, as naturally and inexorably as the pure air seeps into our lungs. It is the spirit of good will.

Business may be more brisk than ever, traffic heavier than ever, the weather perhaps more trying — people in a bigger hurry, carrying bigger loads, maybe, both mental and material. But about you, you can't help noticing and seeing — it's so tangible, so inevitable; — that spirit — of better neighborliness, of kindness, understanding, tolerance, OF BROTHERLINESS! Have you noticed it? Of course you have. You couldn't help it.

The smile on the face of the tired department store clerk; the busy but cheery traffic cop on the corner, the extra courteous bus driver. And the rank and file — the people about you — there's a **graciousness** there.

And what an inspiration it all is, what an uplift to the heart and to the soul! Wouldn't we love to have this beautiful spirit with us for a longer time, perhaps throughout the year!

But we're grateful that at least for a season we are privileged to drink in its warmth. And meditate on its promise.

It might be described as something like the mists rolling away from in front of the sun, on a murky day, showing that it is still there — in the words of a beloved poet:

"God's in His heaven,
All's right with the world."

And that we are really brothers under the skin, one big family, forever encompassed by His love. . . .

Now go ahead — have fun. And God bless you!

ADDITIONAL MATERIAL

"And what did you find under your tree on Christmas morning?" a little boy was asked.

"Pop," was his answer. " He came home late, and Mother hit him over the head with it."

A Hollywood couple had as their house guest a relative from New York who had intended to stay "just a few days" originally, so he said. But the stay had lengthened into a week, then several weeks, and finally, months later there he still remained, happily rooted, sopping up and enjoying his hosts' hospitality, with seemingly all thought of leaving having been blotted from consciousness.

And when the weeks had lengthened into months, and month after month trailed by, the couple finally felt quite fed up with their guest, but they wondered how they might suggest that it was time for him to leave without hurting his feelings.

Finally, with the Christmas season coming on, the host had an idea. He called his guest aside, and with a preliminary depreciative cough, said: "Ahem! You know the holiday season is approaching. And I know what a fond husband and father you are. Undoubtedly you would want to be with your family, don't you think? . . ."

His guest thought a minute, and then his eyes brimmed with tears. He seized his host's hand, and with a voice choked with emotion, said: "How thoughtful of you! And, do you know, I had never thought of that? I'll send for them at once!"

THE EMCEE AT A HOUSEWARMING

By Earl Jay Gilbert

Mr. Jones and Mrs. Jones, we're here to greet you as our new neighbors and to wish you a long and comfortable and contented existence in your new home. Now, according to the way we understand the word, to be neighborly means to be friendly — and that's what we try to be, as you'll find out when we become better acquainted.

I've been asked to introduce the members of this gathering, so I'll start with this contented-looking couple, Mr. and Mrs. George Smith. You'll find Mrs. Smith to be a real good neighbor, in addition to being a good housewife, an excellent cook —and she has many other virtues—which helps to explain why George always looks like the cat that has just swallowed the canary. He's a nice guy to know, and we all think a lot of them both.

This is Mr. and Mrs. Fred Brown—two more real neighbors, as you'll discover if you ever want to borrow a cupful of sugar or a lawn mower. Mrs. Brown would be insulted if you needed something and didn't ask her, and George is the kind of a guy that would not only willingly loan you his lawn mower, but would probably insist on cutting your grass himself.

This is Mr. and Mrs. Tom Curtis—more nice people. You'll notice Mrs. Curtis has a rather resigned expression. I don't know whether this has anything to do with it, but Tom, in his spare moments away from business, is an amateur inventor. He's always fooling around with some gadget that's going to revolutionize everything. One of these days he's liable to succeed, we hope. Anyway, it must be wearing on his wife's nerves. I've heard it said that sometimes when he's working on some doodad he gets so interested that she's had to rewarm his supper six times before he even realizes she's calling him. However, she seems to bear up under it nobly, and it hasn't prevented them from being very good neighbors.

This is Mr. and Mrs. Art Ford—more good people. Mrs. Ford is another real friendly neighbor. When anyone is sick or needs help of any kind, they're among the first to respond. They're real folks and you'll be happy to know them.

This is Mr. and Mrs. Bill Johnson. Mrs. Johnson is another wonderful woman to know. She's a great asset to our neighborhood, and Bill is a great guy. But watch yourself if you get in a poker game with him. He plays a pair of deuces as if he was holding four aces, and he'll bluff you out of your shirt if you're not careful. But we like him just the same. He's a regular guy with a regular wife.

This charming couple is Mr. and Mrs. Lester Bryan, two more members of our good neighbor community. Mrs. Bryan is a nice person to be around. She's a great listener. She seldom has much to say, but she likes to hear people talk—and I don't mean gossipy talk—I mean general conversation—which makes it nice for Les, because he enjoys talking. His specialty is political conversation. Get him wound up and he'll keep on until he runs out of words. He's a pretty interesting talker, though. He never has anything unkind to say about anyone—unless certain politicians are mentioned. Then he really explodes. Who doesn't? We all have a great deal of admiration for them both.

And this is Herbert Wallace and Mrs. Wallace. They haven't been in our neighborhood very long, but they seem like old-timers. As you can see by looking at this lady, she is a very sweet, likeable person. And although she has never been known to lose her temper, I'd hate to have her get mad at me. Herb knows all the dirt in the neighborhood. He's a real estate salesman. But don't hold it against him. He's another regular guy with a charming wife.

And this is Mr. and Mrs. Henry Barnes—more good people. Believe me, we've got plenty of them in this community. Mrs. Barnes is a former schoolteacher, but don't let that fact frighten you. She won't go into hysterics or faint if you split an infinitive or use bad grammar. She pays no attention to it—

but just takes it in her stride—which is a good thing, because Henry has been known at times to slightly murder the English language in spite of the good example his wife sets him. Henry is a good guy and a lucky guy. One look at his wife proves that. But he's the kind of fellow who really deserves a lovely wife.

And here are Mr. and Mrs. Alfred Mason. You'd probably never guess from the way they hold hands and look at each other, but they're practically a bridal couple. They haven't been married very long. They can still tell you how many days, hours and minutes have passed since they were married. We all regard them with a great deal of affection, Lord bless them!

I'm reminded of the newlywed couple who registered in a small Southern hotel the first night of their honeymoon. The young husband tipped the old Negro bellhop not to let anyone know they had just been married. The following morning, in the lobby, they noticed other guests looking at them and grinning and whispering to each other. The bridegroom got nervous and he called the old bellhop over and said, "Did you tell anyone we were just married?" "Naw, suh," said the old Negro indignantly. "When they asked me I told 'em you wasn't married at all. I said you was jes' a couple of chums, travelling around together!" Which proves that sometimes things can be carried too far. Anyhow, in this community I think we've shown that people can be married and still be chums. Married life would be very unpleasant otherwise.

Well, my friends, I don't want to monopolize all the conversation. While I haven't introduced everybody here, I'll suggest, now that the ice has been broken, that those whose names I haven't mentioned introduce yourselves to our hosts. I can assure our new neighbors that if I had introduced those who were omitted, I could have nothing but good things to say about them. I'll repeat that we'll try to be friendly neighbors, willing to lend a helping hand when it's needed. If we can do anything to help you get settled comfortably in your new home, don't hesitate to call upon any of us. You have our best wishes for peace and happiness here. We're happy to include you in our group of nice people and good neighbors.

THE EMCEE AT A SALESMEN'S CONVENTION

By Arthur L. Kaser

Gentlemen, may I warn you that this is a salesmen's convention? So don't keep telling the man next to you that you made some valuable contacts this week. Maybe he didn't make any sales, either.

It was during the depression that I entered the ranks of the salesmen. Everybody said I was crazy to become a salesman during a depression—that I would never make a sale. But I did make sales, and I cleaned up. I never had as many sales even after we had boom times. What did I sell? Red ink.

A salesman must be aggressive. An acquaintance of mine was just that type of salesman. For example, he called on the manager of a certain large concern. The manager's office was separated from the waiting room by a glass partition. When the receptionist handed the salesman's card to the manager the salesman saw him tear the card in half and throw it in the waste-basket. The receptionist came out and told the salesman the manager could not see him. The salesman requested his card back. A moment later the girl returned and gave the salesman a nickel, informing him that the card had been torn. The salesman produced another card and sent the girl back to the manager, saying, "Tell your boss I sell **two** cards for a nickel." He got the interview.

I met a salesman friend last week in a restaurant. I said to him, "Bill, what's the matter? You are eating only crackers and milk. Are you on a diet?" He said, "No, on commission."

I'll wager we'll all hear some new stories before this convention is over. What say?

THE EMCEE AT A FAREWELL BACHELOR PARTY

By Earl Jay Gilbert

My friends, we are gathered here to bid farewell to a dear comrade who is about to start on a dangerous journey. It's a hazardous voyage on the Good Ship Love, which will carry him into the storm-tossed waters of the Sea of Matrimony where he will encounter many unforeseen and unpredictable situations.

He will discover that at times the ship will have smooth sailing and then it will be a glorious and beautiful journey. At other times unexpected squalls and fierce storms will arise. The craft will often be in danger of floundering and sinking. But by judicious maneuvering it can ride out the heavy weather and find smooth sailing again.

No accurate maps have ever been drawn to guide the traveler through the perilous reefs and shoals that will arise to confront him. However, I might add that many have survived this pilgrimage by charting their own courses as they went along.

The object of this voyage is an attempt to reach a destination frequently mentioned, but seldom found. It is called Happiness, a romantic land where all is sublime—where nothing disturbing or upsetting exists—where only peace and contentment reign—where the sun always shines and the air is filled with the sweet fragrance of lovely flowers. Some individuals claim that this miracle land is an illusion, to be found only in dreams. Frustrated pilgrims, no doubt. However, I might add that many have not only survived this journey, but have reached their goal.

We hope that our friend, although he might be thought misguided in leaving the safety and security of his bachelorhood, will come through safely on his journey to this land of the Mental Mirage. To try to help him, we offer a few words of advice and caution.

First, remember that you are the Captain of the Ship. When you are confronted by unexpected mutinies, be firm. Put your foot down and say nothing. However, if silence does not end the controversy, oftentimes a judiciously placed "Yes, dear, you're absolutely right" will suffice. If it doesn't, try this: "Honey, take this dough and buy yourself a new hat, or suit, or coat." Maybe it'll be expensive at times, but it should quickly nip any uprising. If it doesn't, Bud, you're really sunk. Just crawl under the bed and stay there until the skies are clear.

But whatever you do, don't attempt any logic in dealing with your mutinous crew—or expect any logic in return. If you attempt sensible discussion, you will wind up a bewildered and confused man. You will meet with tears and cries of "You don't love me any more." Perhaps even flying dishes. That's where the term "flying saucers" originated. But remember you're the Captain—be firm—give in. You're going to lose anyway because, brother, you'll be wrong from the beginning.

And if she calls you an old tightwad or a sourpuss, don't lose your temper. Be fair; she might be right at that. I'm reminded of Henry Jones, the colored man, who said to a friend of his, "That wife of mine is drivin' me crazy. Every time I turn around she yells and hollers at me. She says all kinds of mean things to me. She's got me so nervous I'm scared to go in the house." His friend said, "Son, the next time she yells at you and says mean things, you say them right back. You do that two or three times and first thing that woman's going to lay off you."

They met again the next day. Henry was all bandaged up. He was using two boards for crutches. His friend said: "Man, what happened to you?" Henry glared at him and said: "You're a fine kind of friend—tellin' me to talk back to my wife!" "But, **boy,**" said his friend, "You didn't talk out **loud,** did you?" That story is offered as a suggestion. If you talk back to your crew, don't talk out loud!

And as an example of what not to say, a certain lady said to her husband: "Our new neighbors, next door, are a very affectionate couple. Every time he leaves the house he hugs and kisses his wife. Why don't you do that?" "Well," said her husband, "I will if you want me to, but I hardly know the lady." Now, if you are ever in a similar position, keep your thoughts to yourself, and use your own judgment about following her advice.

Now, Bill, on those nights when you're sitting comfortably before your fireplace enjoying a quiet game of Casino with your better half, now and then give a thought to those of us remaining free and unredeemed, who are ruining our health by staying up late, indulging in liquid refreshments, ruining our eyes and our pocketbooks playing poker, and turning our lungs black by too much smoking, and say to yourself, "There, but for the Grace of God, go I."

Bill, we all secretly envy you. You've got a wonderful girl, and she's going to get a wonderful guy. So farewell, my friend. We all wish you from the bottom of our hearts a wonderful and happy voyage—and Godspeed.

THE EMCEE AT A G.I. HOMECOMING

By Richard Drummond

Attention! All right, now you rookies, listen. Right after this meeting we're gonna police up these barracks. And wipe that opinion off your faces. At ease! Rest! Or something.

Good to get together again, isn't it? A meeting like this brings back a lot of old memories, some pleasant, some not so pleasant. Not so pleasant when you remember some of the tough sergeants you had, especially when you first go in the army.

We had a sergeant that was tougher than a range bull, and just about as bright. One day he lined us all up for inspection. We were new and didn't line up very good. Finally he yelled: "Okay, okay! Everybody fall out and look at the crooked line you've made." The sergeant yanked the man next to me out of line, and bawled: "You for the guardhouse!" Some time later I said to the lad: "What did he stick you in the guardhouse for?" The kid said: "I didn't do anything. While he was looking in my direction I got a bad itch on the tip of my nose. All I did was scratch it with my thumb nail."

Yep! It was a great life if you didn't waken.

When I left home to enter the service, my mother said to me: "Remember, my boy, when you get to camp try to be punctual in the mornings so as not to keep breakfast waiting." I never kept breakfast waiting. It was in the mess hall I did a lot of waiting. When I first went in the army it didn't make sense. There was too much drilling and fussing around between meals. And you can't stop me till I tell this one. We were on maneuvers way down in Mississippi. We filed past an old ramshackle cabin. A very aged colored man was standing out front watching us pass. He called out in sort of a cackle: "Doggone, you all gonna git dem Yankees dis time, ain't you?"

THE EMCEE AT A LIARS' CLUB MEETING

By Arthur L. Kaser

Some white lies are funny. Some white lies are yellow. Times are surely changing. In the old days only the professionals would tell smooth and convincing lies. Nowadays millions of amateurs are in on the act.

I was under the impression that this was a meeting of the Liars' Club. I find there is no truth to it.

My second cousin, once removed by remote control, was very careless about telling the truth. In fact, the only thing that keeps him from being a bare-faced liar is his mustache. One time his minister said to him, "Nothing that is false ever does anybody any good." My cousin said, "You are wrong, Revvy. I have false teeth and they do me a lot of good."

As I said, times are changing. We are progressing, so to speak. Remember George Washington? Washington couldn't tell a lie. Now there are a good many lies that come from Washington. Wordsworth once said, "Heaven lies about us in our infancy." Now everybody lies about us in our maturity.

Today there is so much lying we have to use lie detectors. However, lie detectors are not new. The first one was made thousands and thousands of years ago. It was made out of the rib of man.

Not long ago my brother caught his little boy in a lie. He said to him sternly, "Do you know what happens to liars when they die?" "Yes, Dad," said Junior, "they lie still."

But tall tales—Wow! My grandfather told me one of the tallest when I was quite young. He was in the Spanish-American war. He said when he was stationed in Florida the mosquitoes were so big the people living up North wouldn't believe it if you told them. He said one night the mosquitoes were exceptionally bad, so he took a candle and went around in his tent burning them. He got all but one big one, the largest in the group. He finally got this very big mosquito cornered and was just ready to burn him when the mosquito blew out his candle. He finally got the mosquito, had it stuffed and presented it to a museum where it stands in the entrance, and is used for a hatrack.

All right, boys, you may not be contortionists, but I'll bet you can stand up and lie at the same time.

THE EMCEE AT A GOLFERS' BANQUET

By Forbes Milliken

We are sorry to announce that our speaker, Woody Niblick, couldn't show up because he had putt too many irons in the fire, and to get here was too long a drive. He hopes you won't be teed off about it. I'm sorry; I thought it was all in the bag.

For those of you who are not familiar with golf, I might say that a golf ball is that small indented object which remains on the tee while a perspiring citizen fans it vigorously with a large club. If you get the club too near the ball, you might hit it. If you don't hit it low enough, you'll top it. You can prevent topping the ball by turning it bottom up. If you are just learning the game, do not become discouraged. The course of true golf never did run smooth. The only difference between learning to drive a car and learning to play golf is that when you learn to play golf you don't hit anything. So take it easy. Be nonchalant — light a skyrocket. You will find that lifting the elbow is the cause of erratic drives and wild swings. This is particularly true when the elbow lifting starts in the clubhouse.

Don't blame anybody but yourself if you play a bum game. I know one golfer who, when he missed his drive, would express himself to a tee. Keep your eye always on the ball. The stress laid on keeping one's eye on one's ball is probably the best proof of the Scotch origin of golf. Always carry a compass when playing near a woods. You might lose your ball. The best golfers are found in the nudists' colonies. They usually go around the whole course in nothing.

Let's on with the banquet, fellow putters, and remember, no matter how you slice it, it's still a golf ball.

THE EMCEE AT A LADIES' DAY MEETING

By George A. Posner

(At the Lodge, Athletic Club, Social Club, or Other Meetings)

Well, this is Ladies Day. And to fit the occasion we're having a lady speaker. That's because we want you to feel at home. And what could be more like home, you married men, than having a woman talking, and you sitting there listening?

The ladies, God dress—I mean, bless them. What would we do without them? Where would we **be** without them? Mighty scarce, I think. Some fellow—a darn cynic, of course—has said that if you took away women, half the troubles in this world would disappear. Take away men, and the other half would disappear. So what?

Ah, the female of the speeches—I mean, species. More deadly than the mule—I mean male. So they say. But I'm for them. I've traced my ancestry back and find that half of my ancestors were women. Takes all kinds of people to make this world, doesn't it?

God made the world, and then made man, says the Bible, and then He rested. Then He made woman, and neither God nor man has rested since!

He made man first. That was to give him a chance to say something. Then He made woman and called her Eve because she brought the end to Adam's perfect day.

There are all sorts of theories as to why the Lord made man first. I overheard a girl and a fellow talking this over the other day. Said the girl: "Woman is the superior sex. She was made last, wasn't she, when the Creator had more experience, and could profit by His previous mistakes?"

And the fellow answered: "Oh, no. The Lord made man first, and then He made woman to please man, and she did. And it surely was the only way. Because if He had made woman first and then tried to make man to please woman He would be tinkering away on Adam yet!"

I think he had something there. Eh? Anyway, we can't get away from it—it's right there in the Bible, that when a woman was made out of a man's rib, someone pulled a bone! Anyway, it's the first time she was ever on his side.

God bless their little hearts, anyway. I used to have a bachelor friend—never married—but his favorite toast was: "To the Ladies. God bless you and keep you. Wish I could afford to do so."

Looks like **he** had something there, too. With present-day prices, looks like about all a man can afford to keep these days is a secret.

But why should keeping the little darlings be any problem? They wear almost nothing. You have to look twice to see their dress once, it seems. As far as clothing goes, the female seems to dress on the theory that nothing succeeds like nothing. What a howl they'd raise, wouldn't they, if it was **poverty** made them wear so few clothes? They used to ask for equality with the men—but that isn't enough any more. Now they're outstripping us! Those are the bare facts, men.

You know, in the Garden of Eden Eve ate an apple and discovered she was naked. The way they're dressing now, I think it's high time we passed the apples again!

How in Sam Hill does it take them so long to dress when they put so little on? **That** will forever remain a mystery. Someone has said it was because they have to slow up when going around the curves. I don't know. Maybe Dior **did** have an idea. He was certainly reversing things. It is usually the **women** who leave us **men** flat.

How did they ever get those curves in the first place? Every woman you meet, it seems, says she is on a diet. But once you get them inside a restaurant and they get that menu into their little lily paws, oh, brother! Little gold-diggers!

I heard a couple of cute definitions of gold diggers. What's a gold digger but a cute little girl, usually, after all? After all you've got! A gold digger is just a little girl who wants to meet one of the filthy rich, and take him to the cleaners. That's all.

There's a difference between men and women, and it's interesting: If a man says yes, it means maybe. If he says maybe, it means no. And if he says no, he's no gentleman. If a woman says no, she means maybe. When she says maybe, she means yes. And if she says yes, she's no lady.

Ah, women, they're the conundrum of the ages. But we men just hate to give them up!

And so enough of this tomfoolery. I was just fooling of course. I will now bring on what you have been waiting for so impatiently, I know. The speaker of the evening, that charming and delightful young lady, ———, who will address you on the subject of ———. Ladies and gentlemen, give her a hand!

ADDITIONAL MATERIAL FOR LADIES' DAY

By George A. Posner

Georgie Jessel was telling me the other day: "Ah, Spring. That's when my wife starts her spring cleaning. This year she started six shopping accounts at different stores. She had me cleaned in no time."

These modern girls! She is one who can meet the wolf at the door, and come out with a new fur coat.

You know, the fashion editor of a Paris newspaper received a letter in the mail one morning. It read:

"I'm so sorry to bother you, but I would like very much to know exactly where the pockets will be on the new dresses and coats the coming season. You will greatly oblige me." And it was signed: "A Pickpocket."

"Women are all right," says my next door neighbor. "Me and my wife have a quarrel once in a while, true, but we soon patch things up—my nose, my jaw, my skull."

You know the women were mighty particular about their fashions and always wearing the correct dress. When they would go out walking, it used to be they'd wear walking clothes; when they went out riding, it was a riding outfit; when they went out in the evening, it was evening clothes. But judging by what they are wearing nowadays, it looks almost like most of them must think they're on their way to birthday parties!

We used to say a girl was a little dear, nowadays it would be better to say a little bare.

A man thinks he can read a woman like a book, until he tries to shut her up.

If you're proposing to a woman, I would quote a little poem which goes something like this:

"Say it with flowers
"Say it with eats,
"Say it with kisses,
"Say it with sweets,
"Say it with jewelry,
"Say it with drink,
"But always be careful
"Not to say it with ink."

A man finds his ideal woman is one who possesses virtue, beauty, amiability, loyalty, affection, domesticity, comradeship and patience.

A woman finds her ideal man is one who possesses mazuma, kale, cash, dough, coin, currency and money.

THE EMCEE AT A GOLDEN WEDDING CELEBRATION

By Bob Royce

Well, folks, this is it. A golden wedding—fifty years married. That's a long time to sit and look at each other. On the other hand, a person never tires of looking at a beautiful flower, and that is what real love is. Perhaps to some people the golden wedding is the day on which the couple celebrate that fifty years of married life is over.

Remember the old-fashioned woman who saved her wedding dress for her daughter who now has a daughter who is saving her wedding dress for her next wedding. Men have changed, too. They are not like the old timers. Today many a man lives by the sweat of his frau. I had a cousin like that. Finally his wife got tired of it and ran away. She ran away while he was taking a bath. She'd waited months and months for that very opportunity. The following day my cousin stopped me on the street and asked what he should do. I told him to wait a few days before celebrating.

An elderly couple was sitting on the porch, saying nothing. Finally the old man said, "What were you thinking of, Marthy?" She shook her head slowly. "I was just thinking how long we lived together and that it couldn't go on forever like this, and the time will soon come when one of us will have to go." "Yep," said her husband, "that's right, but there ain't no use to worry about that now." "Maybe not," said the old lady, "but I was just thinking that when it does happen I would like to go and live in California"

Let us hope that the things here that are gold will be like this marriage and never tarnish.

THE EMCEE AT A LETTER CARRIERS' CLUB MEETING

By Arthur L. Kaser

Members of the Mail Carriers' Club, welcome. I think the best way to open this meeting is with a letter opener. Our speaker, Mr. **(name)**, will address you. I don't think you will have any difficulty understanding him as you have had considerable experience figuring out addresses.

I am well aware of some of the difficulties experienced by the street-treading man of letters. I was one of these unappreciated individuals with a bag on my shoulder and one under each eye. However, this house-to-house flea-hopper job was better than my first postal experience. I was placed in a room where the atmosphere was absolutely putrid. It was the dead-letter office. And you can imagine how any male can smell if he is dead. It was a smell of a job. I had to hold an autopsy over each letter by partial dissection. It was a postal-mortem examination. After I completed my internship I was transferred to the out-of-doors for fresh air and was assigned to a route.

You know as well as I that when you are delivering mail from house to house and wondering whose goes to whose, you meet a lot of the queerest people. One lady asked me where she could buy a round mail box. She was receiving so many circular letters.

Then one morning a man stopped me and said he had been receiving some very threatening letters. I said: "Who from?" He said, "the finance company." At another time a lady hailed me and said: "Maybe you can help me. My husband mailed me fifty dollars and now I find I can't spend it." "Why can't you spend it?" I asked. "Because," she said, "it says on the envelope to return it in five days."

And there are the gripes. A lot of people say the postal service isn't efficient. Most of them who yell for first class service receive nothing but fourth class mail. Our boss was rather difficult to work for. "Nothing," he ruled, "goes out of this office without stamps. Every morning before we left we had to stamp our feet. Now, ladies and gentlemen, our first class male speaker, Mr. **(name.)**

THE EMCEE AT A BACHELORS' CLUB MEETING

By Jeff Gannett

Members of this bachelors' club, I greet you. I don't believe there is a single man in this gathering that is married. So if you brought one of your own socks along to darn, darn it. I forgot to bring mine. Darn it!

I was just thinking of the three stages of married men—First, there is love. Love is like getting drunk. Then marriage, which is like the headache the next morning, and then divorce, which is the aspirin tablet.

And then look at these poor birds—No, it's worms. Look at these poor worms that do marry. The only reason they marry is because some chicken picked them up. Have you ever noticed that it isn't the girls they flirt with that they marry? They usually marry the girls that wouldn't flirt with **them.**

Woman! Did you ever analyze that word? It is made up of two words: Woe and man. It is a warning that so many men fail to heed. But, oh, the woe after they're married.

God first created the universe, and then rested. Then He created man and rested. Then He created woman, and since then neither God or man has rested.

However, we must be fair. We must admit that we men aren't so hot, either. We're like a new car. We cruise along perfectly when—boom! We have a blowout, and are thrown for a curve. We can go so far, but if we don't have our valves ground occasionally we're out of the running.

Men are not good or bad—they are good **and** bad.

Any other bachelor present who has anything nice to say?

THE EMCEE AT A BACHELORS' CLUB ANNIVERSARY

By Franklin Phelps

I think a definition of a bachelor would make a good slogan for this organization. The definition of a bachelor is: "A selfish, callous, undeserving man who has cheated some worthy woman out of a divorce."

I have another suggestion, Brother Bachelors. If we want to increase our membership, let's go after the milkmen. Most of these milkmen are bachelors because they see women too early in the morning.

I was approached just yesterday by one of those nosey sort of women, who demanded: "And what excuse have you for not being married?" I told her I really didn't have any excuse. I was just born that way.

There is one thing in our favor, gentlemen. The colleges and universities are all behind us. Look how many bachelor degrees they give.

A young man asked me recently: "What'll I do? I've got enough money to either buy a car or marry a girl I like." I told him to buy the car. It had something under the hood.

It is true a bachelor has nobody to share his troubles. On the other hand, a bachelor shouldn't have any troubles.

Perhaps some of you fellows know Herb Ketchum, alias Charlie the Chaser. I met Herb not long ago. Just the way he talked I'll bet a bachelor button he wishes he never married. He said things weren't going so good in a marital way. I asked him if he had many arguments with his wife, and he said: "Oh, some, but whenever we argue I always make sure the children don't hear them. I always send them out for a walk." I didn't tell him, but he sure has healthy-looking children.

Most any man has a good many chances to get married. But, my gosh, why take chances?

Yes, where singleness is bliss 'tis folly to be married. After all, the oyster is not the only one who has a crab for a mate. Are you a man or a mouse? Be a man, for if you're a mouse some cat will get you. Always be on the alert. Watch your step at every turn. A young lady acquaintance of mine recently got a divorce. I said to her: "Well, now that you have your divorce, how do you feel?" She said: "I feel like a new man." See what I mean? Remember, brothers: Marriage is a play in three acts. Act I: "Oh, boy!" Act 2: "Obey!" Act 3: "Oh, baby!"

So enjoy yourselves now while you may,
You may be hooked most any day.

THE EMCEE AT A NEIGHBORHOOD MEETING

By Vance Clifford

Welcome to this meeting, all you new home owners. I think it is a wonderful idea, organizing this group. Together we can accomplish things that wouldn't be possible if we went about it individually. Together we can make this new addition one of the beauty spots of our beloved city.

I'm sorry I couldn't get a certain friend of mine to buy a house here. Instead, he bought one on the other side of town. He phoned me to come out and see it. He said it overlooked the water. I did drive out there but I couldn't find any water. Afterward he told me I should have looked in the basement.

It's such a little compact affair. The front door leads right into the kitchen. He says it's nice that way. His wife's relatives don't have to waste any time. It's what you might call a bungaloette with a dinette and a kitchenette. His wife says she's nothing but a housekeeperette. Perhaps we should be happy that we are where we are.

THE EMCEE AT A NEWLY-WEDS' PARTY

By Arthur L. Kaser

Time and bride waits for no man—except on payday.

Well, folks, post office, as a party game, is not very apropos at this time, so we'll skip it. Wedding bells are still ringing in your ears. Just on the side, men, it won't be long until the rings are in your nose. A few more like that and I won't even have a nose.

My sister hasn't been married so very long. A short time after she was married I said to her: "Well, sis, what do you think of married life?" "Oh," she said, "there isn't much difference. I used to wait up half the night for George to go home. Now I wait up half the night for him to come home."

When she got married she didn't know any more about keeping house than she did about going over Niagara Falls in a basket. The first time she ordered groceries by phone she told the butcher to send her some nice steaks with the gravy. He said he couldn't accommodate her. So she asked him to send a nice fresh shoulder of smoked ham. He said he didn't have that, either. Would she like a nice fresh leg of spare ribs instead? She settled for a pound of ground beef sliced thin.

When her husband got home all he found on the table were cheese sandwiches. He said: "Do you mean this is our meal?" She sobbed a little. "Yes, dear. You see, I was making hamburger soup. The meat caught on fire and fell in the dessert and I had to use the soup to put out the fire." Her husband said kindly: "I'll wait, sweetheart. You go ahead and prepare something else." A half hour later he went to the kitchen to see how dinner was progressing. He accidentally knocked her cookbook off the ledge. "Oh, George," she exclaimed, "now see what you've done, knocked my cookbook to the floor and lost my page. Now I haven't the slightest idea what I was cooking." And was she a poor coffee maker! Hubby asked her at dinner: "Is this tea or coffee?" She said: "What does it taste like?" He said: "I don't know." "Then," she snapped, "what difference does it make?"

Okay, newly-weds, we can't do a single thing. We're married.

THE EMCEE AT LINCOLN DAY EXERCISES

By Sidney Steele

Ladies and gentlemen, we are fortunate indeed to have with us this evening, **(name)**, who is an authority on the life of Abraham Lincoln. I am going to leave this part of the program to Mr. **(name.)** However, I would like to demonstrate with a story or two how witty Lincoln really was.

There is the story of Lincoln when he was practicing law in Illinois. A competitor lawyer in the same town hadn't been having much success in a financial way. For one thing, he wasn't liked by so many people. As a joke some of Lincoln's friends handed Lincoln a petition for money to buy the other lawyer a pair of trousers to replace the worn-out trouser seat pair he was wearing. Lincoln wrote on the subscription paper: "I refuse to subscribe to the end in view."

Someone once asked Lincoln whether he did not find the ceremonies of the President irksome. "Yes, sometimes," said Lincoln. "In fact, I feel sometimes like a man who was ridden out of town on a rail. He said: 'If it wasn't for the honor of the thing, I'd rather walk.' "

Everybody knew, including Lincoln himself, that he was a homely man. He was in a crowd once when he overheard someone say: "Lincoln is such a common-looking person." Lincoln turned and said to the man: "My friend, the Lord prefers common-looking people. That's the reason he made so many of them."

Now, my friends, allow me to introduce our speaker, Mr. **(name.)**

THE EMCEE AT A SILVER WEDDING ANNIVERSARY

By A. Guy Visk

Twenty-five years ago two of the nicest people I know signed a mutual agreement. Today I am happy to say they are celebrating their final payment on the ice box. This you can believe, because I am one of their closest friends—I'm the fellow who's been collecting on that ice box for the past twenty-five years.

There's only one other person closer than I to those two delinquents, er, delightful people—the ice man! For twenty-five summers, he's been carrying ice across their kitchen floor. And for twenty-five winters, their kitchen floor has been the best place in town for ice skating.

Things haven't always been easy for this couple. The first year of their marriage found them in a small flat over a jewelry store. The next five years were spent in the big house, er, a bigger house.

Like the rest of us, they were victims of the depression. When the big crash came, they were forced to start all over again. They moved back to that small flat over the jewelry store. It was here that they reached the top of the ladder together. There was no stairway to that upper flat.

I will say though, that they have a lot to show for their marriage. Most of it is under a swamp, but it's a **lot.** They intend to build on it. They're planning on putting land on it.

Actually, the lot was sort of a wedding present. Instead of throwing rice, one of the guests presented them with an entire rice paddy.

They're a wonderful couple, and they've been through thick and thin. He was always the thin one. Nevertheless, for twenty-five years, she has worked her fingers to the bone for him. And with her fingers, it would take twenty-five years.

Earlier today I asked the happy couple what advice they could give for a happy marriage. They both told me, "the secret for a happy marriage is doing little things." It's a fact. For twenty-five years, he did very little for her, and she did very little for him.

Of course, it wasn't always like that. When they were first married, she would go so far as to press his shoelaces for him. After a week, she decided to give up the idea. He was getting blisters on his feet! Every night when he came home from work, she would run to him, grab his clothes and hang them in the hall closet. He wanted to put his foot down, but it was impossible. He was still wearing the clothes.

During their twenty-five years together, there was only one blemish to mar their wedded bliss. It happened right after their first anniversary. He was working late at the cesspool. It was raining hard that evening, and he walked all the way home. He was wet and tired, and when he arrived at his house, he tripped over a man's raincoat, rubbers, and umbrella in his hallway. He became so furious, he threw them into the incinerator. He had a perfect right to do this. They were his!

Another wonderful thing about this couple is, they never disagree. They always compromise. A few months after they were married, they felt that something was missing. Like all newlyweds, he wanted a boy, and she wanted a girl. Well, that's exactly what happened. Her mother and father came to live with them.

THE EMCEE AT AN ATHLETIC BANQUET

By Franklin Phelps

It certainly is gratifying to see so many game sports here this evening. What would we do without our colleges? There'd be no football teams, no basketball, baseball, highbaw—I mean—We should feel proud of our colleges. You know, there are two kinds of colleges—those that wish they had fired their coach last fall, and those that wish they hadn't.

At first I attended a very small college. It was so backward in many ways. For instance, instead of "Rah, rah, rah!" it was "Har, har, har!" We had only one football and the coach used that for a pillow. We never won many games. We were good losers, though. I might say, we were perfect losers. So consistent. But how we did root. At the pep meetings we all drank root beer. Every time a game started our coach would tell the quarterback: "Get out there and run the team. It's entirely up to you, but don't forget to watch the bench for signals." It got so we called the quarterback "Guided Missile."

The reason I went to this little college was because I couldn't get into the college I wanted to get into—Vassar. After I left college my father looked me over, and said: "Son, I've come to the conclusion that there isn't much difference between a college and a laundry. You get out of it just what you put in—but you'd never recognize it." Maybe so.

I know there is a similarity between western cattle and college boys. You can always tell a college boy, too, by the brand on his hip. That is the reason college courses seem to include, not only Latin and Greek, but a little Scotch. Maybe so. Webster's dictionary says that taut means tight. Some of us have been taut quite a bit in college. Maybe so.

Now for our speaker, gentlemen, **(name of the speaker.)**

THE EMCEE AT A BUS DRIVERS' PARTY

By Vance Clifford

Gentlemen, I'm not going to ask you to stand and give your seats to the ladies. If you do give your seats to the ladies, what will **you** sit on?

This morning I was on a bus when a passenger got on and asked: "Does this bus stop at the Skyline Hotel? (Localize.) "No," said the driver, "we leave it in the barn at night."

Anything can happen on a bus. No wonder bus drivers go nuts before their time.

> There was a fellow named Gus,—
> For years he's been driving a bus,—
> Said, "I'll bet eleven to seven
> I'll not get to heaven,
> For I can't drive a bus and not cuss.

When I was on this bus I mentioned, a little boy got up and gave his seat to a lady that was standing. I said to the boy: "That was nice of you to give the lady your seat." He said: "I wasn't trying to be nice. I'm half-scared of any woman with a strap in her hand."

A very stout lady was trying to board the bus. Finally she turned to the man behind her, and snapped: "If you were half a man, you'd help me on this bus." "Madam," said the man, "if you were half a lady you wouldn't need any help." The driver suggested: "Why not try it sideways, lady?" "Humph!" she snorted, "I don't have a sideways." She finally got on, all of her. She said to a passenger: "I'm a stranger. Does this bus stop at Eleventh Street?" The man replied: "Yes, it stops at Eleventh Street. Just watch me and get off one stop before I do."

This one happened in New York. A passenger, a little wobbly from too much tinting the town red, pestered the bus driver with too much talking and hiccuping. The bus driver, annoyed by the flow of gin-flavored conversation, suggested that the passenger go up on the second deck of the bus and enjoy the view and the fresh air. The passenger staggered up to the top. A few minutes later he was down again breathing in the driver's ear. "What's the matter?" asked the driver. "Didn't you like it up there?" "No," said the stew. "Between me and you, 'tain't safe. There ain't no driver up there."

Well, boys, you're here for a good time, so I'll drive on.

THE EMCEE AT A PRE-GAME RALLY

By Arthur L. Kaser

Horse racing and bullfights are fine sports, but they can't hold a scandal to football.

We can't win every game, that's for sure, but we can always hope to. Look at the number of times Sir Thomas Lipton tried to win the America Cup, and didn't, but he kept right on hoping. There always seemed to be many a slip 'twixt the cup and the Lip-ton.

Our boys are always hoping they'll win just like I always was hoping to get on the team. I got on the scrub team. We had to scrub the mud off the regular team. The only time I ever played a real game was when I was under eight. I was a wreck when that eight got off of me. But I did make a touchdown in that game. I ran sixty yards and crossed the goal line. Then I discovered I didn't have the ball. It was somebody's helmet. Football is a great sport. I remember our coach. He was a good coach but he didn't have all his wheels. He'd tell his men, "And remember, fellows—football developes individuality, initiative, and leadership. Now get in there and do exactly as I tell you." He was coach at Sing Sing when they played the army, but they failed to prove that the pen was mightier than the sword.

It was Joe and Henry who went to a football game. Joe had a bottle with him. Henry had a terrible thirst, but no bottle. Joe was hitting said bottle quite often. Henry just licked his lips. Joe knew all about the game. Henry didn't know football from basketball. As Henry watched Joe taking so many nips without offering him any, he said, "Joe, you're a wonderful dribbler, but you're no good at passing."

THE EMCEE AT A BEAUTY CONTEST

By Sidney Steele

Which is the prettiest?
Which is the wittiest?
Which one will take the prize?
Maybe the smallest;
Maybe the tallest.
What is a prize-winning size?
Will thinness discredit?
Is plumpness a debit?
Just what are we seeking to find?
Is it right, in our hunt
To judge from the front,
Or better to sneak up behind?

A girl cousin of mine won a beauty contest once. The other girl didn't show up. If she had shown up, it would have been a tie. Neither one could have been any homelier. What one didn't have the other did, only more of it. Where one curved out the other curved in. Where one would stop, the other'd begin.

But these girls we have tonight! Wow! They're gorgeous. Beautiful, every one of them. If somebody told me I could take my pick, I'd refuse. I wouldn't take a pick. I'd take a scoop and get all of them.

When the rib was taken from man to make woman, Adam sure got a good ribbing. He lost the only good-looking rib he had. Of course, that operation was just a side issue, but beautiful women have been a side issue ever since. That is what inspired that wonderful appealing verse: "He sighed and she sighed, then they both sighed side by side.

They say that beauty is only skin deep. That's enough for me; I'm no cannibal.

I met a friend of mine this morning and we were talking about this beauty contest. This man has a very beautiful wife and I said to him: "You should feel mighty proud to have such a beautiful wife." He said: "Do you know, I've put a fortune into my wife's face." I suggested that he shouldn't let her go to the beauty parlors so often. He said: "Oh, it isn't that. I'm talking about the food that goes into that face."

A physical instructor once told my wife if she wanted to keep her slim figure she should do a lot of swimming. He said swimming would improve any figure. My wife said: "Not for me. Did you ever pay particular attention to a duck?"

Anyway, girls, I don't agree with my wife on that. I really think swimming is beneficial. Did you ever see a fish with skinny legs and big hips? Fish are very particular about their weight. They always take along their scales.

The only time I ever did any judging was out west one time. I was appointed to judge some cows. When I had made my selection I was told I had picked the best horse in the corral.

Beauty is as beauty does—

That's a phrase I like because — Finish this jingle in twenty-five words or less and win a jar of Glamour Goo, the famous facial smear-on.

THE EMCEE AT A BANQUET

By Sidney Steele

A banquet without food is like a slipcover with nothing under it. Whenever I think of food I recall the plight of Joe Vacanto. The first day he went to work on his new job in the factory he eagerly opened his lunch box at noon, took out a sandwich, lifted the edge a fraction of an inch. "Darn it!" he exclaimed. "Cream cheese." He turned up his nose and tossed the sandwich back into the box. The second day the same thing happened. "Phooey!" he said. "Cream cheese again." When the same thing happened for the third day a workman sitting near him asked, "If you hate cream cheese so much, why don't you ask your wife to fix another kind of sandwich?" "Wife?" said the new man. "I'm not married. I make these sandwiches myself."

A minister went to a banquet and a careless waiter dropped a plate of hot soup in his lap. The minister looked around the room with agony in his face, and finally whispered: "Will some layman kindly say something appropriate?"

This one has nothing to do with a banquet, but it does with food. Mrs. Frucci was so very fond of spaghetti. One day she was spooning it up happily when a committee of three of her husband's friends came slowly in. "Mrs. Frucci," the spokesman of the group said sadly, "we are here to tell you that your husband has been badly hurt in an auto accident." Mrs. Frucci went right on eating spaghetti. Again she was told of the accident, but there was no reaction. "Look," said the puzzled speaker, "we are telling you that your husband is badly hurt." She went right on with the spaghetti. "Men," she said between mouthsful, "just as soon as I get through with this spaghetti, are you going to hear a scream!"

Now, ladies and gentlemen, I take pleasure in introducing the banquet speaker, **(name.)**

SECTION FOUR

NOVELTY TREATMENTS

On certain rare occasions the emcee may discover that he is in an unusual situation that requires a special treatment of some novelty approach if for no other purpose but to entertain an audience. In this section we have assembled some unusual material that can be used for this purpose. It may suggest other original treatments to the wide-awake emcee that will brighten the meeting or party.

THE DEAF EMCEE

By Louis J. Huber

My good people, I would like to start off this part of the program by yelling you all (Does this in a loud voice.) or rather, by telling you all that it is about to begin.

Now if I am not talking loud enough—what's that? I'm talking too loud? I'm sorry, friend, I can't do anything about that. It so happens that I'm a bit deaf and I've got to yell.

So if I sound boisterous I hope you will forgive me. Most people have the full use of their ears. I don't have that. However, I do have some use for them. When I was a small boy my dad used them. Not as a hearing aid. He used them as kind of a steering wheel when he wanted to lead me into the woodshed.

As most of you people know—am I talking loud enough? —good. As I was saying, most of you people know that ears are good for many things. Take a man whose ears are big; like the fellow in the first row. If he could learn to wiggle them, he would be the first man to fly without wings.

Some of you might possibly think that I am standing here trying to be an ear specialist. A friend of mine—one Dr. Boucher—(Or any doctor.) is an ear specialist. He doesn't know what he's doing from ear to ear. Take my ears; that's what the teacher did when he wanted me to pay attention. They have other uses even if they are no good for listening. They keep my hat from falling down over my eyes. They can also be used as a temperature gauge. As soon as they get cold you know it's time to put on your long underwear. But now it's time to put on the show and we bring you the first act.

HIS HONOR, THE EMCEE

By Louis J. Huber

Court will now come to order, ladies and gentlemen, as we go on with the proceedings of the evening. I come to you as a judge of the Inferior Court. There was a time I was in the Superior Court but I was demoted and here I am.

I've had several cases in front of me in the past few weeks and I'd like to tell you about them. Would you like to hear about them? You wouldn't. Shame on you. I'm going to tell them to you anyhow.

We had a case the other day that really made me outdo myself. And when I outdo myself I'm better than usual. This case had to do with a matter of identity. The criminal had a scar under his left arm. He was brought to me and I demanded that he remove his shirt. The man refused.

He said that we would not be able to pin anything on him and he had a point right there. I thought of an easy way out of the situation. I asked him to be honest with me and tell me if he had a scar under his left arm. He said that he did not have any scars but he could offer me a cigarette. And right then and there I burned him with a ten-year sentence.

Then we had another case that made me reach into the depths of my wisdom. I'm a regular Solomon. We had already empanelled the jury when this prisoner was brought into the court room. I told him that it was his right to challenge any member of the jury. He challenged the smallest member because he figured he had a good chance of licking him. If the fight was fair, of course.

I knew it was bound to be a good fight. Just as I know that we have a good show for you. And here is the first act ———.

TIME OUT FOR THE SPONSOR

(A Fill-in for the Emcee)

By Arthur L. Kaser

And now an important message from our sponsor. Are you ill, run down, or not up to par? If so, listen! Are you deficient in alphabetical vitamins? Are you getting enough B12, 13, 14, 14 plus, or 15 minus? No coaching from the audience, please. Is your blood red? Or is it purple, green, or beige? Does it lack the necessary minerals—iron, zinc, copper, chrome or platinum? If so, you should not despair. You are not beyond repair, but you're a mess right now.

Don't you have any more ambition than a worm? Or don't you have worms? Do you throw yourself into your work? I am not referring to well diggers. Do you lack the ambition of a go-getter like a man who runs out of gas ten miles from a filling station? Do you have a false ambition? Do you work your fool head off because you're too nervous to steal? Do you have some chronic evil which has deprived you of health and happiness, or are you still unmarried?

My friends, you are in a bad way. A very bad way! You either weigh too much or too little. Are you so fat when you sit on a kitchen stool you have a hang-over? Or are you thinner than all your friends put together? If you have any of these symptoms, or some original ones, take heed. Then take Nag-Lag. Don't let lag nag you. Take Nag-Lag for lag nag. Nag-Lag comes in handy tablet form, in capsules for slippery throats, liquid, and the familiar stick candy form for those who know they are born suckers. Nag-Lag is fully guaranteed. If you are not cured within two weeks, any surviving relative may return the empty bottle and have the money refunded. Remember for fag or sag or lag, take Nag-Lag.

INTRODUCTORY REMARKS OF AN EMCEE TO OPEN A SHOW

By George A. Posner

I was supposed to be on a vacation this week. The fact is, I could only afford a Scotsman's vacation—stay at home, and let my mind wander. It couldn't go very far!

So I finally took the notion to take a walk; and I was just passing by here, when your vice-president dragged me in. Asked me to give "just a little speech to open the show." And how about it?

I said: "Hey, feller, I'm on a **vacation!** You know what that is, when you don't do any work?" He said: "What's this about work? All you do is say a few words to the mob."

He reminds me of the time I was in the army. My commanding officer and the colonel were arguing about **love.**

My commanding officer—a captain—claimed that love was 50 per cent work, and 50 per cent fun. The colonel said it was 25 per cent work and 75 per cent fun.

And I was just passing the place—on K.P.—while they were arguing, and they seemed unable to decide the argument one way or the other. So they came to the door and dragged me into it. They thought they would get my opinion.

So I listened carefully while they asked me: is love 50 per cent work and 50 per cent fun, or is it 75 per cent fun and only 25 per cent work? And then, after thinking just a minute, I said: "It's 100 per cent fun and no work at all."

"That so?" said the officers. "And why are you so sure of it?"

"Because," I said, "if there was any work in it at all, I am sure you would have had **me** doing it!"

And so I'm saying to the vice-president: "Being a vice-president must be all fun and no work, or he would certainly have had **me** doing it—instead of speech making."

No, I'm just kidding, of course.

You know a brilliant speaker once said that he really made four speeches every time he delivered a formal address:

First Speech—The one he prepared (pretty good).

Second Speech—The one he delivered actually (only fair).

Third Speech—The one he could have made afterwards (marvelous).

Fourth Speech—The one reported in the newspapers (any resemblance purely coincidental and accidental).

And incidentally, did you ever wonder why the statues of politicians and speakers look so unnatural? Well, it's because the statues keep their mouths shut continuously.

The curriculum for us speakers seems to teach: If you have nothing to say, keep talking—eventually an idea may come. So please bear with me for a few minutes while I fulfill my destiny.

From my inspection of the program here, we seem to have a pretty good show ahead. First I see we have a "Novelty Act." What can that be? Must be a man in love with his own wife.

Or can it be the costumes or make-up? I was out with a girl the other night and she said that was a Novelty Lipstick she had on. But the novelty soon wore off.

There was a good-looking girl. Just one little blemish, between her ears—her face.

And the clothes the girls wear when they're dressed for the evening! This formal gown of hers—well, I couldn't tell if she was coming or going. If she was on her way into the gown, or on her way out—and if it was a case of arrested locomotion.

They wear less on the street today than their grandmothers did in bed.

But the girl I was with was as nothing compared to some of the others we came across. Women trying to dress like men. Those toreador pants. The lastest thing in men's clothes these days is women. Isn't that so?

I turned to someone sitting next to me in the cafe and said: "Look at that gal. Isn't it terrible the way the girls try to ape the men?"

"Pardon me," said the person I was addressing, "but you are talking about my daughter there."

"I'm sorry," I said, "I didn't know you were her father."

"I'm not," came the answer, "I'm her mother."

So under what gender would you classify women? I guess the only safe bet is to classify them under the **Nuder** Gender. And why worry over what they wear? It amounts to so very little. Their hearts are in the right place. You can see that—at least almost. They aren't as bad as they are painted, but some of them are certainly badly painted! They don't call them Bobby Soxers any more. They call them Easter Eggs, because they are hand painted on the outside and hard-boiled on the inside.

But enough of these comments. Let's go on with the show. Let me introduce, first ——————.

TWISTED NEWS

By A. Guy Visk

(To be delivered by an emcee at bachelor parties, bridal parties, or wedding receptions)

Years ago, a famous American humorist said, "All I know is what I read in the papers." If he were with us today, this elegant gentleman of the past would probably quote something to this effect, "All I know is what I read between the lines in the papers." There are times when I find the blank spaces more reassuring.

Whether we like it, or not, we are reading twisted news. If the editor slips up, the carrier makes certain of it by stuffing it into the mail box.

I have come prepared to prove my accusations are true. (Produce a newspaper clipping.) Here is a simple news item concerning a wedding announcement. A pack of lies! I attended this particular wedding, and believe me, I could read between the lines. Listen, "Couple Married in Double Ring Ceremony." Some ceremony. It was more of a boxing event. That's why they used two rings.

"The Love Nest Hotel was the setting for the marriage of . . ." Setting, nothing! It was an arena! "Escorted by her father, the bride's . . ." What an escort! Everything was swell until he left her at the altar. Then the old boy fell flat on his face. "The bride's embroidered Swiss organdy gown, fashioned with a tiered hoop skirt, was complemented by a miniature blossom tiara with fingertip veil." Ha! At first glance I could tell her gown was Swiss. It was full of holes. And that hoop skirt! The way she walked down the aisle I could swear she was wearing hoops from beer barrels. She sort of rolled when she walked. And no wonder, the hoops were still around the barrel. Her fingertip veil reached down to the floor. That's where her father was, and of course, it touched his fingers.

"The bride's attendants wore white . . ." (Looks up and smiles.) Oh, "The bride's attendants wore white organdy over taffeta." Later in the day they wore food over taffeta.

"Following the ceremony, a reception for four hundred people was held on the lawn . . . " Following the reception, a collection was taken for grass seed. "To receive her guests, the bride's mother chose a street-length red lace gown with matching accessories . . . " It was splattered with blood! "The bridegroom's mother wore a white costume with navy blue accents." She was a Chief Petty Officer.

"The couple left for a wedding trip to Chicago and El Paso with the bride traveling in a black-accented white suit." There's no question about it, the groom will arrive first. He traveled by car.

INTRODUCING A TIMID SOUL

By Louis J. Huber

Ladies and gentlemen, it is my proud privilege to bring to you, as our speaker, a man about whom you've heard much. I won't mention any of his well-known accomplishments. I would like to tell you about some of his personal matters.

You would never suspect, as he sits before you, that he is a timid man. But he is. There was the time he was asked for his middle initial. He answered that it was the letter E. His questioner then asked for the name it represented. Our man told him that it stood for "echo," because he only spoke when he was spoken to.

The neighbors love our speaker because of his timidity. But there was a time when he was more forceful. He had been playing the radio a bit too loudly and one of the neighbors called his attention to it. He kept right on. He never changed the dials or the tone control. He did not touch that radio. But he did pull the lead-in plug out of the wall receptacle.

There was another time he declared himself. He walked right up to the telephone, dialed the number and started shouting. It's too bad he didn't take the receiver off the hook.

Yes, he is a timid soul. Not always. Tonight you'll hear from him and his messages are always vigorous and important. You'll see what I mean. I proudly present Mr. ——————.

ABSENT ENTERTAINER

(To Be Used When an Entertainer Fails to Appear)

By Bob Royce

Ladies and gentlemen, I am sorry to announce that Miss Bessy Buzberry, who was scheduled to appear on this program to recite some of her original poetry is unable to be with us because of technical difficulties beyond her control. It just happened that Miss Buzberry **blew a fuse** when her **current** boy friend couldn't **meter** because he took a **short circuit** to another girl's house. Miss Buzberry was so **shocked** and under such a **high tension** she could not possibly get here for a number of hours and she didn't want to come **insulate.** However, she was kind enough to send her latest poem which I will endeavor to read to you. It is titled "Tippy, the Toper." **(He clears throat and reads with forced dramatics.)**

Tippy, the toper, from Tippecanoe
Took a trip in his Skippy,
A tippy canoe.
Mister Tippy was tipsy
To take such a trip.
Too, he carried some extra
On the place called his hip.
Tippy claimed that his Skippy
Was as safe as a ship,
As it glided away with nary a dip.
At the end of ten minutes
Tippy took from his hip
A receptacle fragile
He called his equip,
And pulling the cork
He took a small sip.
Then a big wave came rolling—

'Twas really a pip—
And it frightened him so
That he took a big nip.
Another big wave—
A sip and a nip!
Then another! Another!
He was losing his grip!
His balance was waning;
He felt himself slip.
Then he floundered around
Like a chick with the pip.
He grabbed the canoe
And floated to shore.
His head was clearing—he was tipsy no more.
On the shore he just pondered,
What a fool he had been.
Would he do it ag'in?
No, never ag'in!
He was going back home
In Tippecanoe—
As a tipsy sailor
He surely was through.
He'd walk, so he would,
Back to Tippecanoe,
Walking straight, and a-totin'
His tipsy canoe!

NO BUTTS ABOUT IT

"A Silly TV Commercial"

By A. Guy Visk

(Close-up of a man's hand rubbing out a cigarette butt in an ash tray. Camera moves back for full view of the announcer seated behind the desk.)

Announcer: Hello there. Impressive, wasn't it? Of course, the really unusual thing about what you've just seen is, I don't smoke! That's right. You see, I've given up smoking one hundred percent, and I like the idea.

It's easy if you know how, and the know how is as simple as this. You can give up smoking without giving up cigarettes. Change to the newest cigarette sensation in the world—Change to "Butts!" **(Hold up a miniature pack of cigarettes. Camera moves in for a close-up. The word, "Butts" appears on the wrapper.)** They're not regular size; they're not king size. They're butt size!

(Camera moves back for a full view.) It's the easy way to break the tobacco habit. Whenever you get the urge, simply remove a Butt from the pack, then crush it in the nearest ash tray. **(Perform the same while speaking.)** They not only save you time, they enable you to travel in the smartest circles, without blowing a single smoke ring.

Now the entire family can enjoy cigarettes. What could be cuter than baby brother running about with his little Butt in front? A little difficult, but cute.

The tobacco used in Butts cigarettes comes from a vintage crop. Every two, or three hundred years, tobacco growers produce a vintage crop. Brother, this is it! Don't put it off until the next crop. Rush down to your nearest jewelry store and get yourself a carton of Butts. Only forty-two fifty a carton.

And here's good news! For people who like the taste of fine

tobacco, Butts has come out with a tobacco-flavored lozenge called, T.B.—Tobacco Breath! Tobacco Breath lozenges stop normal breath almost immediately. It leaves you with the taste of tobacco all day long. Take the T.B. test. Let a tobacco lozenge dissolve in your mouth, then turn to the nearest person and breathe directly into his face. His reaction will be definite proof that you have tobacco breath.

Here's the most exciting news of all! For people who want cigarettes, and only cigarettes, you can now buy king size Butts. King size Butts leave no unpleasant after-taste. They burn your tongue right out of your head. And, king size Butts do not discolor your teeth. Smoke without fear of tar stains on your teeth. One puff and they disintegrate.

King size Butts are made only for the daring. We defy you to smoke them. And remember, king size Butts are the only cigarettes made covered by Blue Cross. **(Fade out.)**

THE RURAL EMCEE

By Louis J. Huber

Hi there, neighbors, and all the other people who do not live next door to you. You'll have to pardon me if I don't speak too good but I'm having trouble with this weed I got in my mouth. (Is chewing grass.)

Now the reason I got it there is to kind of slow up my speech. I was told to take it slow because we're running ahead of time and there is no one who can slow up a show like yours truly. Now settle back.

I would have got here earlier but I had to stay home and do some of the milking before I could get out. Actually, I wasn't doing the milking but someone stole Pa's milking stool and the poor fellow couldn't stand so I just bent over and he used me for a stool.

At the start I did put up a little protest and I assured Pa that I wasn't made of wood. But he reached over, put his hand on my head, got himself a dandy splinter right from out of here (Indicates.) and I just couldn't convince him that I wasn't a wooden stool.

Almost didn't get here on account of the health officer. He came to the farm this morning and he just kept nosing around. Then he saw that the pigs were living in with us. He told us that he thought it was unhealthy. Pa assured him that our pigs was healthier than any others and he didn't worry about it any longer. We'd sure hate to lose a pig on account of ill health. Pa would much rather lose me. And that's understandable. He gets a good price for hog bristles and I know I couldn't produce any of them. Or could I?

But I can produce a show for you and that's what I'm going to do right now. So ho-de-ho and hi-de-hi, here we go with the first act. Introducing to you the **(Name of the act.)**

THE FIGHT ANNOUNCER

By A. Guy Visk

(Announcer enters the "ring," reaches up for a boom mike. Mike comes off in hand. He tries to replace it, but fails. Places it in his back pocket. Motions to the ringside. Bell rings twice, then falls apart.)

Announcer: Lay-dees and gentlemen. Tonight's fixed, er, feature bout is a ten and a half round match between "Hurricane" Smith and "Tornado" Jackson. Hurricane and Tornado? **(Glances at the paper in hand.)** For a minute, there, I thought I was reading the weather report.

I'd like to give you a brief history of each of these boys. "Hurricane" Smith, to date, has a very colorful ring career. Very colorful! Whenever he fights, he leaves blood—His! Smith fought his first amateur fight while a member of the second grade class in Public School No. 18. He fought a lad from the eighth grade class. The fair thing about the match was, both boys were the same age.

Smith is a natural-born fighter. He has seven brothers at home, and only two beds. Smith never sleeps on the floor. He fought with Golden Gloves for two and a half years. Before that, he stuffed them with horseshoes. Smith has forty-two knockouts to his record. Of course, he has wonderful recuperative powers. His real name is Gaylord Gigglegay. He received the name "Hurricane" when a small electric fan kept blowing him across the room.

Next, we turn to "Tornado" Jackson. In order to do this, we'd have to be in a horizontal position. Jackson is the only fighter in the business who can boast of leaving the rings the same way he enters it. On a stretcher!

Jackson's fighting career dates back to a small boy in knee pants. Lucky for him the small boy's mother happened along. He had Jackson down and was all set to bash his head in.

Jackson is the only fighter in ring history who fought eighty-seven amateur fights (Pause), all in one night. They were all members of the "Tornado" Jackson Fan Club. Every fan came at him with a club.

Jackson is a firm believer in that old adage, "early to bed and early to rise." Except, of course, on fight nights. Then, he never rises before ten.

Before each fight, Jackson spends a very active day. Three hours of road work; two hours in the gym; and four hours of calisthenics. After the fight, he spends a very busy night. Three hours of cold packs; two hours of blood transfusions; and three nurses around the clock. It was a Grandfather's clock, and after the fifth time around, he caught up to them.

Unless there is a knockout tonight, the winner will be chosen by points. The fighter with the most points on his head wins. Before the fight, both fighters will receive instructions from the referee. Some instructions! No rabbit punches; no kidney punches; break clean. In case of a knock-down, apologize. Some of these instructions sound like the third lesson at Arthur Murray's. As a matter of fact, tonight's winner is going to challenge Marge and Gower Champion.

(Bell rings twice.)

There goes the bell.

THE EMCEE INTRODUCING HIMSELF

By Louis J. Huber

My good kind people! My very good, kind and gracious people! Well, that should do it. I would like to repeat those first two lines but I am afraid that I might be overdoing a good thing.

You folks will please note that I called you good people and kind people and gracious people. I did this to prepare you for the shock that I am about to give you. Simply this: I am to be your master of ceremonies for the entertainment that has been planned for you tonight.

I take this opportunity to introduce myself. I know that there are some of you who know me; some of you other folks might be more fortunate. Perhaps you have never heard of me.

It isn't every day that a master of ceremonies is bold enough to introduce himself. Usually he does it only when he runs out of material. I have another purpose. Too many times the folks who hear the voice of the emcee, and do not know his identity, wonder about him. They keep looking at each other and asking "who is he?"

My method avoids this question. I want to tell you right now that you will not need to ask each other who I am. Before the evening is over you will know and you will probably wish you had remained in blissful ignorance.

There are other reasons why a master of ceremonies should let his hearers know about him. I could come up here unidentified and let some poor fellow who was not here share the consequences for my mistakes. People would place on an innocent man's shoulders the errors which should be placed on my doorstep.

I would also like to demonstrate, before I actually go into the show, that I am fully qualified to be the emcee. An emcee must have poise. That is one thing that I have. You can't tell it by looking at me but I've been given poise with the letter N added. That made it poison and it is something that was suggested to me many times but I never took the suggestion. A fellow could get awfully sick following those kind of ideas.

A master of ceremonies must also be witty and I think that I am more than that. You would like to hear a joke? I have one. It ties in with the fact that I am a family man. Of this I am very proud. By this time you are learning all about me and I still haven't told you my name but names are so unimportant.

The little humor that I inject at this time has to do with my daughter. One day I was using a nail and hammer. I held the nail in my right hand and used the striking instrument with the other. I hit the nail, I hit the nail, I missed the nail. I wasn't happy about it. My daughter, who was watching me, had a brilliant idea to prevent this in the future. And I pass this on to anyone who wishes to use it, anyone who might miss the steel nail and hit the finger nail. She suggested that I hold the hammer with both hands and that would make it impossible to hit myself. And, ladies and gentlemen, I followed her idea. Since that time I have never hit my hand with a hammer. Of course, I've never driven any nails because I haven't figured out a way to hold one when I have both hands on the hammer handle.

Enough of this and on with my original purpose. I know that those of you who can't hide their emotions will be very unhappy to hear that I am (Name.) I am—and I repeat—your master of ceremonies. If anyone would like to sue me for saying that again, let me warn you that I have no money. But I do have a show that you will enjoy and, without any further syllables from me, we go into it. Our first act is ——————.

THE HANDSOME EMCEE

By Louis J. Huber

Good evening, ladies. You will notice that I did not greet the gentlemen in the audience. I have a reason for this omission. I am not going to address any of my remarks to those creatures called men.

I take this attitude because I have a feeling that the ladies will be pleased with a man as handsome and charming as I happen to be right now. If any of you men would care to leave, it will be all right but don't take your wife with you. If you do, she will miss the greatest treat of her life.

There was a time when men resented me as I took this attitude. Not any more. Now they just ignore me and that's what any man should do if he had any thought of leaving. I recall when one of my closest friends began calling me auger. Auger? It mystified me until I looked in the dictionary. I discovered that an auger is a bore and I knew what he meant.

Another of my friends thought he could stop my blowing about myself by buying me a French horn. It worked. Now I blow about myself in French. That also helps. None of my friends understand French so they are no longer annoyed. Most of the people I meet do not realize that I know a lot. But I do. I do know a lot. And I'm going to buy it and build a house on it.

Let me assure you that this handsome face of mine wasn't always this way. There was a time when I was ugly. I had my face lifted five times. That helped my face and it also made me two inches taller. It was no ordinary lifting process. Let me tell you about something else that is handsome and wonderful. It is the show we have for you tonight. Without any more words from handsome me here is the very first act. Presenting to you, **(Name of the act).**

THE SCHOOLBOY EMCEE

By Louis J. Huber

Hello, people. I am here on my way home from school. The teacher told me that it would be a good idea if I wasted a little of my nonsense at other places so I just thought I'd stop here.

I love my teacher very much but I don't think that she feels the same way about me. It's too bad. Because I can be a very lovable chap after you get to know me. However, I think you will be much better off if you don't get to know me too well.

The teacher was angry with me today. I asked her if the second day of the week was spelled T-u-e-s-d-a-y or T-o-o-s-d-a-y? She blinked at me with her beady little eyes and she told me it is spelled T-u-e-s-d-a-y. I told her that she was wrong. The second day of the week is spelled W-e-d-n-e-s-d-a-y. She got very annoyed with me. I thought she was going to send me back to M-o-n-d-a-y.

We also had a little trouble in arithmetic class. My, but she gets fussy about those answers. I don't want her to get fussy. I don't like those kind of folks. I'll tell you what happened and you'll see what I mean. She asked me how much is three and four. I told her it was eight. She asked me again. I told her it was nine. She informed me that three and four are seven. I told her it didn't matter to me. I didn't want to start an argument over a couple of numbers. I was satisfied with eight but she wanted to be exact about it.

Which shows that I don't know much about arithmetic. I do know something about the show we have for you at this time. I want to tell you that it is one of the finest you will ever see. I'll prove that to you by introducing the first number. A big hand, please, for **(Name of the act).**

THE FORGETFUL EMCEE

By Louis J. Huber

Ladies and—what's the name of the fellow who brought you? Oh, yes, I remember now so I'll start over. Ladies and gentlemen, I came here tonight—I think I did anyhow—to be the emcee of this show. Or was I supposed to do that last night? Or is it tomorrow night?

Let me assure you of one thing, folks. I am here. Of that I am certain even if I am too forgetful to remember anything else. Yes, I am here. Why am I here? Oh, yes, to act as your emcee. I must write that down on paper so I won't forget it.

I want to tell you that I prepared a long time for tonight because I wanted to be a real good—what am I? Oh, the emcee. I wanted to be a real good emcee. I wanted to be funny too. Do you know what I did last night to prepare myself for the comedy? I ate nothing but whole wit bread. Since I was a half-wit I bought two loaves and—no, that's not right.

Here is a funny one that I dreamed up just for you folks. Let me see if I can remember it. Like this: I call my girl potato because she is sweet. Does that sound right? No, that isn't it. I call my girl potato because she is half-baked. Is that funny? It is? Then it must be right.

Despite my failing memory I am a good driver. I've had a car for seven years and never had a wreck. I think that's right. Or did I have a wreck for seven years and never have a car? I could just cry because I can't remember things. And I'm going to do it if I can find a dance floor. That will give me more bawl room. No, I don't need to cry. I remember everything. Especially that grand act with which we open our show and here they are. I give you the—**(Name of the act.)**

THE LITTLE GIRL EMCEE

By Louis J. Huber

Dear people, I am here tonight to act as the emcee because my daddy, who was supposed to do this work, is sick. He has a sitting headache. No, he does not have a splitting headache. His is a sitting headache. When he gets it he can't walk or he can't lie down. All he can do is sit.

I did not go to school today because I wanted to get ready for this show. I did do a little reading and I learned things that I never knew. I learned that the word FISH has an E in it. Yes, after much research I discovered that FISH is spelled with an E. It's very simple and I'll do it for you. Like this: H-e-r-r-i-n-g. There, that has an E in it.

Most of the time I am a good girl but there are times when I slip. Like when I get out of the bathtub, when I step on a banana skin and when I run across an icy sidewalk. Wow, what a slip! It was real red and pink. I mean the place where I stopped when I slipped.

At Christmas time I am always very good. I always write a letter to Santa Claus even though he never writes back. I wrote one last year and I'm wondering if he got it. This is what I wrote:

Dear Santa, please bring me a sled, bring my brother a sled, bring my sister a sled. If you have any left, dear Santa, why don't you try it yourself? Sledding is great fun, Santa. My daddy says that my mother and I are the most biased girls in the world. He says that all we know is buy-us this and buy-us that. Don't believe it, Santa. But do believe this. I am going to emcee a show here tonight and I am going to introduce some very wonderful talent. And here is the first of these acts———.

THE UNDERTAKER EMCEE

By Louis J. Huber

Ladies and fellow mourners, I am here at this time to bring to you good people tidings of great joy. It is always a great day of happiness when I can bring you something that does not involve a burial. It is a great day for you but not for me. For an undertaker without a funeral is like a rainy day with nothing but sunshine.

Since I do not have the opportunity to bring you a sample of my profession on this day I would like to tell you about some of the things that could happen to you and bring you nearer to me. I had a very sad case just the other day. A man came to me and told me he wanted to arrange a funeral for his mother-in-law.

Strange to say he wasn't happy about it. I am the type who likes to make that kind of a funeral a jolly event. I asked this poor man what happened to his dear relative. He broke down and cried. Now I was in my glory. When I can get people to cry I know I am doing a good job.

I suggested that the good lady might have had an accident. He told me that I was wrong. She did not meet with an accident. And when an accident did try to meet her the accident met with an accident. Seems like the old girl was quite a sturdy character.

After some further delving into the topic he finally confessed that the poor departed had died of lint on the lung. It was something of which I had never heard. Then he explained. The dear soul had got a dose of lint on the lung because she couldn't stop chewing the rag. And that is what I'm going to get if I don't stop so I'll go right into the show with the first act. **(All this in a very sober and somber tone.)**

THE SOLDIER EMCEE

By Louis J. Huber

All right, folks, attention! If any of you don't give me your full time, you will end up in the guard house. That's the place they put you on bread and water. No matter how well-bred you are you still get water.

As an old sergeant in a man's army I want to tell you that I don't stand for any silly stuff. Most of the time I sit down for it. Which reminds me of an incident that happened just the other day.

We were out on the parade grounds and we were doing a bit of drilling. Which is a nice way of saying we were going on a ten-mile hike. I wanted my men in condition for this ordeal so I had them running around the outside of a field. This was to get them a running start for the hike.

I called them to attention. I told them that we were going on this hike. It was to be a hard hike; it was a man's game. One wise guy in a back row thought he should say something. When I told him that we were going on this march he whispered that a little child would lead them. Meaning me.

My ears caught his words. I again told them that we were going. Again the voice piped that a little child would lead them. So we went. And a little child did lead. It was yours truly. I led them. Riding on the nicest jeep you ever saw. This just gives you an idea of how tough I really am at the right time.

This army life is hard. My girl told me I was handsome and I told her to tell it to the marines. She did. And one of them married her. So you can see why I don't like people. But I do like the show we have for you and I feel sure that you will also like it. Introducing the first act . . .

THE ANIMAL-LOVING EMCEE

By Louis J. Huber

Ah, my good and gentle people. Allow me to introduce myself. I am Phineas P. Phineas, the great lover of animals. The middle initial also stands for Phineas. Actually that is not my real name but I never heard anything else when I was a boy so I kind of adopted it. All my mother would ever yell was Phineas, Phineas, Phineas, get home! So I've used that name ever since.

What have I done that I should be bold enough to call myself a lover of animals? What have I done? Well, to tell the truth—nothing. But I call myself that because I can't think of anything better at this time. My friends call me other things but you wouldn't like to hear those kind of names.

To get back to animals. I love them. Ever since the days of my youth when I could skin-the-cat on the gymnasium bars I loved cats. I have a cat that purrs "thank you" and I have learned to purr a "you're welcome" in return. Of course, no one but the cat and I understand this language.

I am also good to birds. Tell me if you've ever heard of anyone who put bath salts in the bird bath? You've heard of someone? And where is he now? The same place where I should be? Thank you.

Let me tell you about my dog. I call him Rover because his name is Fido. In this manner I can confuse him. I've taught him to learn, by smell, the difference in the people who come to our door. He will allow the delivery boy and the milkman to come on the porch. He chases all the tramps and bums away. I haven't been home for three days because he thinks I'm also an undesirable character. But I'll get back one of these days. Until I do I might as well carry on here with the first act on our program. Presenting to you the **(Name of the act.)**

THE FAMILY MAN EMCEE

By Louis J. Huber

Ladies and gentlemen, I'm thrilled beyond words to be the emcee of this show because it puts me in front of a crowd of my own people. Let me explain that. I consider you my people because most of you are parents and family folks and that's what I am.

Yes, I'm a family man. Isn't it terrible the things that we must go through to gain this honor? First, you must be born and then you must grow up. And then you get married and then the trouble begins. Take a friend of mine. Let me tell you about the trouble he had to find a home for himself.

He went house hunting. Unless you've had this experience you can't fully appreciate the predicament. Imagine yourself on the street with nothing but your kitchen table and that gives you an idea.

My friend went to one landlord. Everything was fine. The price was right, the house was good, the conditions were excellent. Then he was asked how many children he had and he confessed that he was the father of five. The landlord drew back and was about to cancel everything.

My friend started to look very sad and sober. The landlord queried about this. He got his answer. Yes, he was the father of five but they were all in the cemetery. No, he didn't want to talk about it. The landlord agreed to sign the lease under these conditions. The deed was done. Then my friend drove around to the cemetery where the children were attending a memorial service and brought them to their new home. Now I would like to render a service to you, folks. I take my place as your emcee and introduce the first number. Here it is, the **(Name of the act.)**

THE RINGMASTER EMCEE

By Louis J. Huber

All right, folks, let me have your attention, please. (Blows a whistle.) At this time it is my pleasure to bring to your attention the entertainment for the evening. (May wear a ringmaster's costume.)

As the ringmaster of this presentation I want to assure you that you will be enthralled by the wonderful things we have in store for you. We have gone to the far corners of the earth, and to the near corners, and we have gathered for your pleasure a tent full of surprises.

Ladies and gentlemen, I would like to present to you one of the most spectacular aerial acts in the circus world today. Let me tell you what this act, the one I would like to present to you, would do and will do. They are the Flying Floogies. There are three in the family; the father, the mother and the son.

The Flying Floogies will enter the tent, not by climbing up a ladder like many artists do, but by coming into the tent through an opening. They will be flown over the building (or tent) by helicopter and they will descend. Then you will see them at their very best. The father, who is the weakling of the act, will have propellers attached to each ear. Mind you, folks, not one but two and they will be turning at a speed of 17,000 revolutions per minute. The son will then descend and catch these whirling blades, pick them off with his teeth, hand them to his mother who will be doing handsprings as she gets them. Yes, I would like to present the Flying Floogies. Unfortunately, we do not have them here so I won't be able to present them even if I would like to do so. In their place we have an even greater act. I bring them out now, the **(Name of the act.)**

THE FRIGHTENED EMCEE

By Louis J. Huber

Gaydees and lentlemen—I mean, madies and dentlemen—I mean, ladies and gentlemen, I have been asked to act as your emcee for tonight's show. I want you to know that I've never done this before and I'm frightened.

When the chairman of this affair asked me to take this job I didn't know that there would be anyone looking at me. I thought that all you people would be home where you belong. You shouldn't have come here because it just makes me feel terribly terrified.

It isn't that your presence frightens me so much. I don't mind that. It's your faces. There you are, staring at me. You look like you had all just climbed out of a barrel of flower. You're so pale and ghostly. I would like to ask you to do me a flavor. I mean, a favor.

Would you people in the first row turn around and face the other way? Please do this for me. That's fine. Now you can hear me, but you can't see me. No, that's much worse. The backs of your heads don't look much better than the front.

I have another idea. Would you mind covering your faces with your hands? Just do anything to take away that blank stare. Thank you. That's better. Only now—say, that lady in the second row has chapped hands. Madam, do you know what to do when you have a chap on your hands? There is one sure way of getting rid of him: Marry him. Please don't stare at me that way. I'm scared stiff so I'd better tell you that the first act is . . .

THE BRIDEGROOM EMCEE

By Louis J. Huber

Ladies and gentlemen, I am here tonight for two reasons. I am your emcee and it is my last night of freedom. I am to be married tomorrow. I am taking advantage of this situation and doing all the talking. After tomorrow I'll do very little of it.

I also came here because I need help. I have something I want to get off my chest and I want you folks to give me some advice. This is something that is really serious and could change my whole life. What I have on my chest is not any small matter. It so happens that I am marrying a girl named Jane and I have the name DORIS tattooed on my manly chest. So you can see my anxiety. Of course, I could go along wearing the same shirt the rest of my life but that would not be very good either. So, if anyone can tell me how to get Doris off my chest I shall be happy to listen to them.

There is another aspect to my coming marriage that has me wondering if I am on the right track. The girl I am marrying is my secretary. Do you good people think that she will take dictation from me after the big event? She won't? Oh, but she will take my pay check. Well, that's a fair exchange. I have a horrible feeling that other things will change too. As my secretary she always sat on my lap. As my wife I think she will be sitting on my lip.

I know we are going to be very happy because my wife is a smart girl. She went to college. She took shorthand and bookkeeping. She took chemistry. She also took medicine when she was sick. And then she took me. And now I take you to an evening of grand entertainment with this first act. It is the ——————.

THE TOUGH EMCEE

By Louis J. Huber

All right, you guys and gals, stop fidgeting around in those seats and put your noses in this direction. I'm here to emcee this show and I'm not going to take any fooling from any of you.

I want you to know that my men have you all covered and if there is any nonsense they will remove the cover. You know what that means? It means if they take off their cover, the undertaker will be ready to give you a wooden one.

You see this hand in my coat pocket? I'm not keeping it there so my fingers won't get cold. In that hand there is something very important to me. If and when I have to use it, you'll get the thrill of your life.

Let's get down to cases. I've had several cases lately and one of them was short several bottles and that's why I'm here. Who stole the bottles out of my cases? Oh, ho, so you won't talk, eh? Well, we got means of loosening your tongues. We have ways of making you talk. You're going to sing, my fine-feathered friends, and you're going to do it now. (Music, if possible.)

For he's a jolly good fellow, (Sings.) For he's a jolly good fellow, for he's a jolly good fellow. (Stops.) So you won't sing with me, eh? Well, then the fireworks are about to begin. Anyone got a match? I'm going to light the fuse and blow up the joint. Here, I got my own match. When I count to ten this place will be wiped off the map. (Starts counting.) One, two, three, four, five—(Stops.) Hey, what comes after five? Two? Okay, I'll try that. One, two, three, four, five, two, three, four, five, two, three, four, five—hey, I'm not getting anywhere. I might as well use this hand. (Takes his hand from his pocket.) In this hand I have the name of the first act. As I said, it will thrill you, and here it is, the (Name of the act.)

SECTION FIVE

SHORT BITS FOR THE EMCEE

In this section you will find a varied assortment of usable material for the emcee—brief introductions, appropriate short stories, clever openings, anecdotes, and puns. Although many are designed for specific situations, no attempt has been made to classify them. It is possible that the use of the material in this section will help the emcee to brighten his part in the program and start off the festivities with success.

MASSACRE OF CEREMONIES

My father told me he knew when I was just a small baby I'd grow up to be an emcee. He said I'd talk for hours and hours and say nothing. So I grew up and became a massacre of ceremonies—I murdered 'em. —Arthur L. Kaser

VACANT CHAIR

I am quite sure we will all be very sorry our secretary is not here at this meeting tonight. I cannot say we miss his vacant chair, because the vacant chair is here, but I can say we miss his vacant face. —Sidney Steele

TOURISTS

Tourists have many things in common, and a tourists' meeting of this kind should be beneficial to all concerned. One can be a tourist whether he has enough money to go to Europe, or little enough to see our own beautiful country.

Last year an acquaintance of mine toured Switzerland. I asked him what place in Switzerland he liked best. He couldn't think of the name of the town. "Berne?" I asked. "Burn?" he said. "No! Nearly froze to death."

A few years ago we hired a guide in Yellowstone Park. His right forefinger was missing. I shouldn't have asked him, but I did, how he lost his finger. "I didn't exactly lose it," he said. "It just wore off gradually pointing out places of interest to tourists." —Vance Clifford

QUICK ON THE TRIGGER

My friend Jerry is a very good master of ceremonies, but he is rather quick on the trigger. He was emceeing the other evening when one of the scheduled speakers said to him: "How long would you say I should speak?" Jerry advised him: "Watch the audience's reaction. If you haven't struck uranium in five minutes, quit digging."

—Arthur L. Kaser

SPRAINED EGO

Never say you are as good as the other fellow until you have tried what he is doing. Years ago I saw my first professional skier. I said to myself: "That's easy. I can do that as good as he." Some time later I saw my first master of ceremonies. I said to myself: "If I couldn't do as good as he, I'd jump in the lake." So I put on a pair of skis. I lost my ski and sprained my ankle. I finally got my chance as master of ceremonies. I lost my head and sprained my ego.

—Jeff Gannett

TIMES HAVE CHANGED

Times have changed somewhat for the emcee. It used to be that he would tire his listeners with his own gab before he got to the important matter of introducing the speaker. Now, the briefer the better. It is like the time the young fellow with very poor eyesight was being examined by the draft medico, and placed in 1-A. "You haven't examined my eyes," protested the draftee. "They are terrible." "Look here, you," said the doctor. "We don't examine eyes. We just count them."

—Bob Royce

CHILD DELINQUENCY

One subject that is to be covered this evening is child delinquency. It is becoming a serious problem. One of our speakers is recognized as an authority along this line. Personally, I don't know whether spanking will do a child any good or not.

When I was young I got plenty of punishment, and now look at me. Nothing but a master of ceremonies. I've had everything from slapped ears to soap mouthwashes. And I have been spanked. Where? As far back as I can remember.

Just the other day my little boy was naughty. I said to him: "I'm punishing you because I love you." He said: "I wish I was big like you so I could return your love."

It used to be that children were tanned with a razor strop. Now the little shavers get Daddy's electric shaver to play with if they promise to be good, or we turn off the television so they can't see Cowboy Hoopitup and his Topside Rangers foil some dastardly plot by the villains. So it really takes an expert to tell us what to do. Ladies and gentlemen, our speaker, Mr. **(Name.)**

—Arthur L. Kaser

LATE GETTING STARTED

Sorry, folks, that the program was a little late getting started, but if we were like Jim Haley we might use his excuse for being late. Jim worked and lived on the farm of George Hermans. Jim was late every morning getting to the sunrise chores. Finally George bounced him about it. He said to Jim: "It's strange you're late every morning, and you live right here on the farm. Now Bill gets here always on time and he lives two miles away." "Ain't nothing strange about it," retorted Jim. "If Bill's late in the morning he can hurry a little, but if I'm late I'm right here."

—Franklin Phelps

INFORMATION ON CHICKENS

Well, my chicken-raising friends, no doubt you know who our speakers are for this meeting. If you do know, you also know that you are going to get some mighty valuable information on chickens.

When my cousin in Maine heard that this meeting was to be held here he wrote me that he has a hen that laid 303 eggs last year. That smart hen realizes that an egg a day keeps the hatchet away. In the same letter my cousin says: "Don't count your chickens if you live near a toll road."

And, by the way, did you read about the bricklayer in Kansas City who can lay 36,000 bricks a day? It might be a good idea to tell this to your hens. Of course, these are rather tall tales. Here is one that really did happen when I was on the farm. We were getting ready to lay a sidewalk so all the chickens lined up to see how it was done. Ladies and gentlemen, our first chick—speaker, **(name of the speaker).**

—Vance Clifford

FOOLISH QUESTION

One evening, just before the program got under way, I was approached by a man who inquired about the scheduled speaker. "How long has he been a speaker?" he asked. I said, "Since he was two years old." "What did he do before that?" he asked me.

Every time I think of that foolish question I recall the one about two colored boys who were watching a motorcade of police cars and motorcycles escorting the President of the United States through the city. One boy said to the other: "Who dat?" "Silly," the other said, "Dat our President." The first boy's eyes bulged as he surveyed all the police equipment. "Mah, mah! What he done do?"

—Arthur L. Kaser

THOROUGH KNOWLEDGE

Members of the P.T.A., we should feel honored to have with us this evening a man who has won renown as an educational speaker. Education has made great strides in the last decade and the time is here when education is more than ever before an essential part of everybody's life.

It is getting so that an uneducated person is as out of place as a cat in a dog show. One need not know everything. This is a day of specializing. A thorough knowledge in one field will usually place a person in a very good position to live happily and comfortably.

There is the story of a man from way back in the hills whose eyes got so bad he couldn't shoot squirrels any more. So he trudged to town and went to an optometrist for glasses. After looking at criss-cross lines and circles the optometrist adjusted some glasses and placed them on the man.

"There," said the optometrist. "Now you'll be able to read without any trouble." "Gosh," said the patient, "here I been sendin' my kids to school to learn readin' and they could o' saved all that time just by gittin' glasses."

—Sidney Steele

PLAIN SPEAKERS

We like to get speakers on our programs that use simple language; use words that everybody in the audience can understand. Most forceful speeches are given in simple terms and phrases with simple words. In other words, plain speakers are preferred to lexicographers. It reminds me of my little niece, Cindy. She was in the room where the adult conversation was long and far over the head of Cindy. Finally she whispered to her daddy: "Remember me?"

—Arthur L. Kaser

THOUGHTFUL WOMAN

There are times when an emcee just can't ignore a desire to needle a speaker. However, he can temper his desire by going easier than he would like to. He should never forget the very, very polite lady who was always throwing cups of hot coffee at her husband. She was thoughtful enough to take the spoon out first.

—Jeff Gannett

WHEN THE REVOLUTION COMES

Everybody is interested more or less about the danger of subversive activities in this country. Our guest speaker is going to give you some enlightening facts that may surprise some of you. You will be surprised to learn how these termites are undermining the foundations of our freedom.

I would like to tell you about a young radical and his father. This young man didn't realize that his every move was being watched by the F.B.I. The father became very impatient with his son when the youth absolutely refused to go to work. His excuse was that he had no time to work because he had to attend so many radical meetings.

Finally his father lost all patience. "You dreaming loafer," he said, "why don't you go out and get a job and earn some money?" "But, papa," protested Icanitch, "what good will money be after we've had a revolution in the United States? This will be like Utopia where we can have everything without money."

"But," said papa, "if you would go out and earn $25,000 you could help the cause, couldn't you?" "Oh, sure, papa," said young Icanitch, "but just supposing the revolution doesn't come. I'd be stuck with $25,000."

—Arthur L. Kaser

CLOSE RACE

It certainly is going to be difficult for the judges of this amateur contest to pick the winner. It seemed to me that all the contestants were equally good. The only race I can recall that is closer is in Scotland.

—Bob Royce

PREPARED FOR AN EMERGENCY

A master of ceremonies should always have something up his sleeve besides his arm in the event of an emergency. In fact, everybody should.

There was little Orville. He learned that very same thing at an early age. Day after day he would come to school with very dirty hands. One particular morning his hands were in terrible shape. As he entered the schoolroom with his hands in his pockets the teacher said: "Orville, how are your hands this morning?" He stuck out one of his hands for inspection. "My land," gasped the teacher. "I never saw anything like it. If you can show me a dirtier hand in the entire school, I'll not say another word." He revealed his other hand, and said: "Here 'tis."

—Franklin Phelps

NEW GLASSES NEEDED

(Squinting at the program.) Some of these days I'll have to get new glasses. I'm as bad as the professional burglar who went to an optician, and said: "I need glasses." "How do you know you need glasses?" asked the optician. "I know I need 'em," insisted the burglar. "Last night I was turning the dial on a safe and out came 'Alexander's Ragtime Band.' "

—Arthur L. Kaser

RESTING ON THEIR LAURELS

(At a banquet for retiring employees.)

It is wonderful that these men, who have devoted so many years of their lives to the success of this company, will now be able to rest on their laurels.

I remember when my grandfather retired. I said to him: "Well, grandpop, what are your plans now?" "Well," he said, "for one thing I'm going to sleep every day till the sun wakes me up." "But, grandpop," I said, "you always did get up that early." He chuckled: "You forget, my boy, that I **now** sleep in a bedroom with a west window."

—Arthur L. Kaser

STRANGE LANGUAGE

Isn't it strange? One can make a grammatical mistake in private conversation and it goes practically unnoticed, but make one in public and you never hear the last of it. English is a cockeyed language, anyway.

A spectator was congratulating a diver who had just made a spectacular dive from a height of seventy feet. The spectator said: "That is a foot to be proud of." The diver said: "You mean 'feat,' don't you?" "Not unless you do it more than once," said the spectator.

—Sidney Steele

CREDIT TO WIVES

Gentlemen, do we give enough credit to our wives? Are we neglecting to give them credit for the part they play in our successes? When the news came out some time ago that Henry Ford had left an estate of over a hundred million dollars, an Arkansas farmer remarked: "Strikes me he must of had an awful savin' woman."

—Arthur L. Kaser

PLEASE BE PATIENT

You know, I presume, that a master of ceremonies is made up of ninety per cent talk and ten per cent gab, or vice versa, so if you are anxious to have me introduce the next speaker, please be patient. I'll be getting there. Thank you.

Pete Sykes had been calling on Susan for nigh onto six years, and folks were beginning to think it would never happen. Here it was June, the ideal time for a proposal. And on this particular night there was a romantic moon shining.

Something stirred within Pete and he slid a little closer to Susan. There was still quite some space between them. Time went by. Pete slid a little closer. Finally, Susan's mother called from the upstairs window. "Susan, is Pete there yet?" Susan called back: "No, Ma, but he's gettin' there."

—Bob Royce

MONEY NOT EVERYTHING

(May be used when introducing a banker.)

Tonight, ladies and gentlemen, we have as our guest speaker, Mr. Little, president of the First National Bank. He will, no doubt stress the importance of money saving. You know how these bankers are. Butchers are the same way. They say you should eat more meat. Bakers say you should eat more bread.

However, a banker has the edge on most of the others. He claims if you save money now you will be able to eat more meat and bread when you are too old to work. Maybe so, maybe so.

I was talking to my grandfather recently on the importance of hanging on to every cent possible for my old age. He said: "My boy, money is not everything. It isn't money that will mend a broken heart. It isn't money that will reassemble the fragments of a dream. It isn't money that will brighten the hearth nor repair the portals of a shattered home. You understand, my boy, I'm referring to Confederate money."

—Franklin Phelps

SNAP IT UP

Well, camera fans, let's all get into focus and see what develops. I sat in a darkroom with my girl once and see what developed. I'm married. I was working in a camera store at the time. I snipped snaps in that snappy snip shop.

I love to take snaps, but I'm always leary about looking at snaps somebody else has taken. For instance, there was the time a fellow showed me a picture of himself when he was a very small baby. I said: "You sure was a baldheaded baby." He said: "I was not. You've got the picture upside down."

Another time a girl showed me a snap of her father holding a tiny girl on his lap. I said: "I didn't know your father was a ventriloquist." How did I know the little girl was her?

And still another time. A girl acquaintance was always wanting somebody to take her picture. I told her, "Lulu Jeanie, you've had thousands of pictures taken. Why don't you have something different for a change—like having a bust made of your head?" I never could understand why she wanted so many snaps taken of her. She was anything but pretty. In fact, when she worked for Rand-McNally you should have seen her map. All right, boys, snap it—up.

—Vance Clifford

CONVERT TO GAS

Because of circumstances beyond our control, it will be necessary to make some changes in the program. However, this maneuver will not be too difficult. In fact, it will not be nearly as difficult as a change suggested by a lady customer in a television store. This lady entered the store and was immediately struck by the beauty of a very expensive television console. She asked the clerk the price. He said, "That is our most expensive set, lady. The price is $900." The lady beamed happily. "I'll take it," she said. "However, we do not have electricity so you will have to convert it to gas."

—Arthur L. Kaser

SHORT SPEECH PREFERRED

(To be used to caution a speaker about a time limit.)

It is said that Mark Twain was asked if he considered a short speech more valuable than a long, drawn-out speech. "Well," he said, "I'll answer that by telling you of an incident which might help to illustrate my views on that subject. I went to church one Sunday and listened to the preacher touchingly tell of the innumerable difficulties that the missionaries encountered in Africa. After he had spoken for five minutes I resolved to give fifty dollars to that worthy cause. After ten minutes more I reduced the amount of my prospective contribution to twenty-five dollars. Another half hour of eloquence and I cut the sum to five dollars. After the full sixty minutes that his appeal took the plate was passed and I stole two dollars."

—Arthur L. Kaser

WHEN SOMEONE SUGGESTS AN IDEA

Last month during a meeting at which I acted as emcee, I suggested an idea. A fellow in the audience got up and said: "That's idiotic!"

"What's idiotic about it?" I asked.

"The one who suggested it," he replied.

—Sylvester McGovern

OVERHEARD ON THE ELEVATOR

As I was riding on the elevator on my way up to the meeting this evening, the operator said to a passenger: "There was a horrible murder in room 502 of the hotel this afternoon."

"Is that so?" said the passenger.

"Yes," said the operator. "A paperhanger hung a border."

"Whew!" said the passenger. "It must have been a put-up job!"

—Arthur Brown

CONDUCTING A QUIZ

Last week I had the pleasure of acting as master of ceremonies at a Literary Society meeting at the high school. After the youngsters had completed a speaking program on various subjects, I was asked by the principal to conduct a quiz, testing the wit of the students.

"Young man," I said to a bright-looking fellow in the front row, "when rain falls, does it ever get up again?"

The lad jumped to his feet and cried out: "Yes, in dew time."

—Rome Roberts

QUESTIONS AND ANSWERS

Some time ago I conducted a question and answer session of the Sunday School class at our church. "Class," said I, "I am going to give you some difficult questions to answer. The first one is: 'Why is a theological student like a merchant?' "

A bright young girl waved her hand in the air, jumped to her feet and called out: "He studies the prophets" (profits).

—Hugh Lincoln

INFORMATION ABOUT GUESTS

Just before the last course was served on the dinner this evening, I turned to Bill Jones, sitting at my right, and said, pointing: "Who is that man in the far corner of the room who is eating with his knife?"

"That man," said Bill, looking, "is a very desperate character. He beats his wife up every morning!"

"You don't say!" said I, astonished.

"Yes," said Bill, "he gets up at seven, she at eight."

—Sylvester McGovern

QUESTIONS FROM THE AUDIENCE

About a month ago I was acting as an emcee for an affair such as this up at Great Neck. Right in the middle of one of my best jokes a fellow at one of the front tables jumped to his feet and said: "Can I ask you a question?"

"Certainly," I said. "Go right ahead."

"Well," said the fellow, "I notice that when you refer to our fair city, you always use the feminine form. You always call it a 'she.' Why?"

Perplexed I answered that I didn't know. Then I thought that I would stump the wag. "Do you know?" I cried out.

"Of course," said the fellow. "Because a city always has outskirts."

—Sylvester McGovern

SLOWNESS IN SERVING THE DINNER

I noted with interest the slowness with which the dinner was served this evening. However, I welcomed it, as it gave me more time to study my notes and think up fresh things to say about you fellows. Just to put up a front and show my companion on my right that I was just as peeved as he was, and I could tell that he was peeved the way he was tossing that scalped olive stone about his plate, I said to my waiter: "See here, fellow, why all of the slow motion in dishing out this dinner? All you have served at this table during the past half hour is one olive at each plate!"

The waiter reached down, picked up my plate with the one olive stone on it, and then indignantly said: "You should complain! You've got the fastest waiter in a slow group!"

—Sylvester McGovern

EVERYBODY WAS ASLEEP

It was at the last banquet I attended. The speaker had finished his speech. He had laid all the facts before them. There existed a vast silence filling the room. It was a silence pregnant with possibilities; anything could be born of a calm such as that. But, ladies and gentlemen, absolutely nothing happened. Everybody was asleep.

—Arthur L. Kaser

MY SPEECH LULLED HIM TO SLEEP

Last month I had the honor to act as an emcee at a meeting of businessmen in Center City. Just as I was in the midst of my important and what I thought my wittiest story, a man in the front row began to snore. After the meeting had adjourned, I walked down to the fellow and said: "My good friend, I see that my story put you to sleep."

The man looked up at me with sleep-filled eyes and replied: "Yah, it was a great yawn!"

—Sylvester McGovern

WHEN A LAWYER AND A DOCTOR ARE PRESENT

It is quite a distinction to have Dr. Brown and Attorney Jones present at the speaker's table this evening. Each is a representative of a great profession. I note that these gentlemen are looking each other over very closely. For a moment I am going to play mind reader and guess what each is thinking. (Studies Dr. Brown closely.) Ahem! Dr. Brown is saying to himself: "Attorney Jones makes his living out of plunder!" Now let us see what Attorney Jones is thinking about. (Studies Attorney Jones.) Ahem! Attorney Jones is saying: "Dr. Brown earns his by pillage!"

—Rome Roberts

WHEN IT'S RAINING OUTSIDE

I entered the hall this evening, drenched from the rain. As a way of a social introductory I said to the first person I met in the doorway: "It's raining cats and dogs outside."

"I know it," he answered. "I just stepped into a poodle."

—Rome Roberts

WHO TALKS FIRST?

About a month ago I acted as emcee at a celebration at Center City. Three speakers were on the agenda, one named Strange, another, Moore and another, Wright. Before the meeting began, Strange, Moore and Wright became involved in an argument over who was to talk first. Each insisted upon being the first speaker.

While I was doing my best to calm the troubled waters, in anger Moore shouted out: "There's one fool among us, and that's Strange."

"Oh, no," said Wright, "there is one Moore."

"Aha," yelled Strange, "that's Wright."

—Rome Roberts

WOMAN GUEST MISUNDERSTANDS MY QUESTION

Several months ago I presided at a meeting of a woman's organization. One of the principal speakers on the program was a Mrs. Cynthia Smith. My information about Mrs. Smith was rather sketchy, so I went around the room asking questions about the lady. Approaching a distinguished looking lady who was hard of hearing I said: "Pardon me, Madam, but could you tell me what Mrs. Smith's maiden name was?"

"Certainly," answered the lady. "Her maiden aim was to get married."

—Rome Roberts

VOCAL CHORDS

On my way to a gathering of this sort about a year ago, I had the misfortune of meeting up with an automobile accident. The local paper gave the following account of this mishap: "Bill Jones, emcee and public speaker, met with a serious accident last night when his car overturned on Highway 11, just north of town. It was feared that his vocal chords were not injured."
—Hugh Lincoln

NEED YOUR HELP

Ladies and gentlemen of the audience, this evening I would like to have you help me. We have some wonderful talent on the program and I would like to have you be very generous with your applause. Again I ask your help. I want your help as badly as the lady who called the Society for the Prevention of Cruelty to Animals. She said: "Could you send someone over immediately? There's a salesman up a tree teasing my dog."
—Vance Clifford

TIME CHANGES SITUATIONS

Well, ladies and gentlemen, if you might recall, I was master of ceremonies at your last banquet. That was quite some time ago, and many things have changed since then. It is like the case of Mrs. Dugan and Mrs. O'Reilly. Mrs. Dugan wrote a long overdue letter to Mrs. O'Reilly: "Since we saw each other last I've had my appendix taken out and a new refrigerator put in."
—Arthur L. Kaser

NOTHING SERIOUS

After my first try at emceeing, a critic said to me: "What you should learn is, talk less and say more." Years ago I was given similar advice in a different way. I complained to a friend that I was a victim of insomnia. He said it was nothing serious. A good night's sleep would cure it.

—Sidney Steele

NERVOUS

Even some of the most experienced emcees have times when their knees shake a little when standing before large audiences. So if my knees vibrate and my lips quiver, please excuse me.

A middle-aged man was telling a friend how coid it was the night before. "Cold," he said, "man, it was cold! I lay there in bed all night shivering." The other man laughingly said: "And your teeth chattered all night, too?" "I don't know," said the other. "We don't sleep together."

—Arthur L. Kaser

BE CONSIDERATE

It is part of an emcee's job to be nice and considerate of everybody. Even if one isn't an emcee it is well to be nice to everybody at all times. Some of the people you are nice to might be on a jury if you are ever in trouble, like burglary or assault and battery.

—Bob Royce

IT'S WRONG

The subject our speaker will dwell on this evening concerns the world today. This takes me back to last Christmas when I was looking for a gift for my young nephew. I ran across a toy that had me stumped. I drew the clerk's attention to it. He explained: "That is an educational toy, designed especially to adjust a child to live in the world of today. Anyway he puts it together, it's wrong.

—Jeff Gannett

PANCAKE SUPPER INSTEAD

Speaking of culture—We are not naming him, but a certain English literature professor, who was an authority on Chaucer, was negotiating for some time with a ladies' literary club in an eastern state, about a lecture on Chaucer. His price was too high, so the secretary of the club finally wrote the professor: "We have decided to have a pancake supper instead."

—Bob Royce

DON'T BURN IT UP

Welcome, conversation club members. I am told that our speaker is to stress the importance of campers to keep a camp clean and prevent any fires from spreading. Not long ago an essay was handed in that had been written by a schoolgirl in Montana. It read: "When we go camping we must keep the place neat; we must be very careful to put out fire. This is God's country. Don't burn it up and make it look like hell."

—Arthur L. Kaser

EIGHT DOLLARS DOWN

Ladies and gentlemen, we have on the program this evening one of the funniest comedians I've ever met. I was talking to him a few minutes ago and asked him where he was stopping. He said: "I'm putting up with (local) Hotel. They're peculiar. I asked the clerk about their rates and he said they were eight dollars up. 'But,' I told him, 'I'm an actor.' Then he said they were eight dollars down."

Franklin Phelps

TOO SMALL

I believe I have a story that will fit right here. Something like the salesman said to the glamour girl: "How's that sweater, miss? Too small enough?"

—Arthur L. Kaser

TOO POTENT

A doctor of world-wide renown
Was esteemed by all in his town,
  Until this M.D.
  Was appointed M.C.,
Then his doses were too
Potent to down.

—Vance Clifford

THE DIFFERENCE

There is a difference between a toastmaster and a roastmaster. The toastmaster must be tactful, diplomatic, unoffending, and genial. A roastmaster is one who conducts a meeting where anybody or everybody expects to be roasted. The roastmaster is free to use jabs, barbs, sarcasm, or most anything else to banter or ridicule anyone. All this, of course, in fun.

—Arthur L. Kaser

CAN'T REPEAT IT

Now, ladies and gentlemen, listen carefully, because I can tell this only once. I promised not to repeat it.

—Sidney Steele

TOUGH SLEDDING

Sometimes being the master of ceremonies is fun. Sometimes it is anything but. I recall the time I was to introduce a number of speakers. Half of them failed to show up. For me, it was tough sledding. There wasn't enough snow.

—Arthur L. Kaser

GOOD PRACTICE

A good way for a novice emcee to get practice is to seat himself in front of a mirror and talk to himself. Which reminds me of the goof that was in my company in the army.

One evening he was sitting on his bunk writing. Just to be neighborly, I said to him: "Writing to your girl?" "Nope," he said. "Just writing a letter to myself." "Writing a letter to yourself?" I said. "Just what can you write in a letter to yourself?" He shrugged his shoulders. "I don't know. I won't get this letter for a couple of days."

—Bob Royce

PRIVATE CONVEYANCE

When I was in the army I had the honor of emceeing a program made up of various types of entertainment. One act called for twenty-five men. I was given a list with the names of these men. I gave the list to a corporal who was to round them up and bring them to the auditorium by truck.

Just before the program began the corporal reported to me. I asked him: "Did you bring all twenty-five men?" "Yes," he said, "but there are twenty-six names on the list. I couldn't find the last one." "What's his name?" I asked. He looked over the list, and then said: "Who is Private Conveyance?"

—Arthur L. Kaser

SOUTHERN SCOTCHMAN

Uncle Billy came up from the backwoods and he came up the hard way. He earned his money by the sweat of his brow and the blisters of his hands. This made him slightly conservative. When he went to visit his nephew in the city he carried his frugality with him.

He had been introduced to a number of people and he had been made welcome. Then, while riding home on the bus his eye caught a pretty girl. And his nephew caught the old fellow looking at her.

"Uncle Billy," he interrupted the stare.

"Yes?"

"You seem interested in the lady."

"I think she's real pretty."

"I know her well. Shall I introduce you?"

"Pretty soon, lad."

"Why not now?"

"She hasn't paid her fare yet."

—Louis J. Huber

MANY THANKS

A colored gentlemen shuffled into church just as the services were about to begin. His minister saw him and greeted him. Then continued with:

"We are giving thanks, Brother Jones. Are you a thankful man?"

"Amen, I am," was the response.

"Have you much to be thankful for?"

"Amen, I do."

"Are you thankful for a good wife?"

"Amen, I do that."

"Are you thankful for good health?"

"Amen, I am."

"Are you thankful for money to pay your bills?"

"Amen, I—what did you say, Reverend?"

"Money to pay your bills. You do pay them?"

"No, sir. So I have something else to be thankful for."

"What's that, Brother Jones?"

"I'm thankful that I'm not one of my creditors."

—Louis J. Huber

NO BRIDGE TONIGHT

The army was engaged in war games in the South. The Red army had just flanked the Blue army and the Blues were desperate. In their own mythical manner they had just blown up a bridge. A native, driving a mule, approached the structure. He was stopped by a Blue soldier.

"You can't cross, sir," was the order. "The bridge has been destroyed."

"What bridge, soldier?"

"This bridge has been blown up."

"You mean the bridge you're standing on?"

"That's right. It does not exist any longer."

"I've been driving over that bridge for thirty years and it still looks the same to me. It doesn't look blown-up."

"I'm sorry but it has been destroyed."

In desperation the native turned to another soldier who was standing near the Blue lad. He had been an interested listener.

"Friend," the man asked, "is your buddy a bit balmy? The bridge is still where it has always been."

"I don't know, mister," the soldier's friend answered. "I've been a dead man for three days and I'm not allowed to answer you." —Louis J. Huber

YOUR HONOR

A traffic court judge who liked to be friendly with those who came to face him had his troubles when he tried it on one offender.

"Just a fine this time, my good man," he told the traffic violator. "Next time I'll send you to jail."

"Sort of a weather prediction, eh, Judge?"

"How do you arrive at that conclusion?"

"Fine today and cooler tomorrow, huh?"

—Louis J. Huber

SPY STORY

An Irishman, known for his willingness and ability to exaggerate, was confined to the medical ward of a veteran's hospital. The other patients soon became aware of his characteristics. One day they got him started telling stories about Ireland's mythical navy.

"We got three million sailors under arms, so we have," he bragged.

"That's a good many," someone thought.

"Come to think of it, we got four million."

"What do you do with all of them, Irish?"

"We need them for our ten thousand battleships."

"Why, that's more than all the other nations combined."

"We also have a thousand submarines."

"Where do you keep all these ships?" someone wanted to know.

This was the question that should have cornered the blarney. It didn't. The Irishman turned in his bed, glared at his tormentor, let loose with a loud and angry voice:

"Aha, you're an enemy spy, or you wouldn't be wanting me to give away my country's military secrets!"

—Louis J. Huber

SEASICK

The captain of the ocean liner approached the man who was leaning over the rail. He had seen many of his passengers in this condition and always left them with a word of comfort.

"Something I can do for you, sir?" he started.

"I'm going to die, Captain."

"No, you're not, sir. You'll be all right."

"I feel sure I'm going to die."

"I'd like to be able to help you."

"You can. How far away is land?"

"About three miles, sir."

"Three miles? Is that all? I feel better already."

"You see, sir, you're not very sick."

"In which direction is this land? I'd like to see it."

"In the direction you were just looking, sir. It's straight down."

—Louis J. Huber

COLLEGE DAZE

Old Mike had been a fixture around the college and its campus for a long time. He had seen several generations come and go. He had seen fathers send their sons and he could remember the forebears.

During this time he had learned many things that are not in the books; he had given himself an education. He had parried verbal blows with some of the best minds in the school and he had not lost too many encounters.

But the freshman who approached him one fine fall morning did not know about this. To him Uncle Mike looked like a man with whom you could trade blows and win easily.

"Hello, dad," he began pleasantly enough.

"How are you, son?" Mike returned.

"The grass you're mowing looks kind of dead and withered. Kind of a little like yourself, dad."

"Don't worry, son, in the morning it will be like you."

"Oh, new and young again."

"No, fresh and green, son, fresh and green."

—Louis J. Huber

SELF-STARTERS FOR EMCEES

By Arthur L. Kaser

I asked a well-known speaker if it ever irked him when people in the audience would keep looking at their watches. "No," he said, "I don't mind it so much—That is, until they start shaking them."

* * *

He was a very long speaker—six feet, eight inches.

* * *

Emcee's advice to young men who want practice to be public speakers: "Propose marriage to your girl over a party line."

* * *

An emcee friend of mine said he never gets nervous. He says he is not that good.

It's a wonderful gathering here this evening. So many beautiful women in so many marvelous gowns. I've often asked my wife to wear strapless gowns but she refuses. She says she would rather shoulder the responsibility.

* * *

That takes care of the build-up of our guest. Time is slithering by and it is time to introduce him. Something like this happened in a coffee bar. One girl said to another: "We'd better get back to the office or we'll be late for quitting time."

* * *

And now, ladies and gentlemen, allow me to introduce an actress who has a figure that draws more whistles than noon in a factory city.

* * *

You politicians gathered here this evening have heard a lot of funny ones, but I think one that is very apropos is about the congressman whose wife suddenly sat up in bed and whispered: "Jim, there's a robber in the house!" "Impossible," was the sleepy reply. "In the Senate, maybe; in the House, never!"

* * *

At a style show. "The latest things in men's clothing—women."

* * *

An inexperienced speaker stood in confusion after dinner and began his talk in a stumbling manner: "My—My friends, when I came here this evening only God and I knew what I was going to say. Now only God knows!"

* * *

Our comedian on this program has been unsuccessfully imitated so many times it is laughable. He has that something that he, and he alone, can put across. It is something like a sign I saw in a delicatessen store window: "Pies like your mother made—49 cents. Pies like your mother tried to make, but couldn't—59 cents."

* * *

This morning I was asked what it took to be a good master

of ceremonies. I told him I didn't know because I wasn't a **good** master of ceremonies. Reminds me of a man who asked an army officer: "What must a military man be before he is accorded a full military funeral?" "Dead," said the officer.

* * *

Emcee (at an educational function). A colored man took his battered old radio to a repair shop. The mechanic remarked: "Gone out of commission?" "Sure is," said the other. "It done graduate from commission to commotion."

* * *

Recently one of those very talkative ladies—you know the kind—the kind that has to talk just like other people have to breathe, said to me: "Oh, Mr. Blank, what in the world does a master of ceremonies do when he runs out of things to say?" I said to her: "We improvise just like the restaurant owner did when most of his help left him suddenly. He posted a sign that read: 'Courteous and Efficient Self-Service.'"

* * *

Instead of going into a lot of preliminary talk it would be much simpler for a master of ceremonies to say: "Our next speaker is—," or, "Now we hear Mr. So-and-so." An old lady watching a tug of war remarked: "Wouldn't it be simpler for them to get a knife and cut it?"

* * *

You have just heard the speech of Mr. Smith. We will now hear from Mr. Brown who has something important to say.

* * *

At this meeting of waiters and restaurant owners, I take it that most of you have heard this order called out. A customer ordered coffee, doughnuts and griddle cakes. The waiter called out to the cook: "Cylinder oil, couple of nonskid, and an order of blow-out patches."

Tonight, ladies and gentlemen, our speaker happens to be one of our city's leading lawyers. It was he to whom a lady went with her troubles. She said to him: "I've had so much trouble over the property, I sometimes wish my husband hadn't died."

Speaker (near the end of his speech.) "I believe I've spoken a little too long, but unfortunately, I forgot my watch." The emcee said to him: "I forgot to tell you there is a calendar on the wall there."

* * *

Before actually introducing a guest at a banquet the master of ceremonies praised him to the skies, telling incident after incident of the guest's achievements. Later in the evening the guest approached the emcee, and said: "Boy, can you tell 'em! If you and I were to stump the country, we could make a fortune telling lies, and I wouldn't have to say a word."

* * *

(In the following, change the name of the party to suit the occasion.) Speaker: "I wish to make it clear right now, my friends, that I was born a Democrat; I have always been a Democrat, and I expect to die a Democrat." Somebody in the audience called out: "Not very ambitious, are you?"

* * *

(When the emcee has announced the speaker at the wrong place on the program.) Please pardon my error, ladies and gentlemen. It seems I am getting the cart before the horse. In other words:

I've just found out
Why a rabbit's nose is shiny.
It's because his powder puff
Is stuck on his behin'y.

* * *

(Emcee at football banquet.) Well, fellows, you can always tell when the football season is with us. It is when the girls whistle at men in sweaters.

* * *

My friends, let us all put our hearts into this meeting. Let us get behind the project in mind with everything we have. As the lady who was dressed in black, even down to her black lingerie, said: "When I mourn, I mourn all over."

A high official of the electric company was making a stirring address. "My friends," he said: "think of the wonderful things the electric company has done for you. If I were permitted a pun, I should say: 'Honor the Light Brigade!'" A customer in the audience interrupted, "Oh, what a charge they made!"

* * *

Ladies and gentlemen, our speaker this evening is a gentleman from Texas, that tremendous state not far from Mexico. Yes, Texas, where, if you stand on a stepladder, you can see straight ahead for three days.

* * *

One must be careful how he words a phrase. In one instance the wording may fit the subject exactly, but the same wording may raise havoc with another subject. It is like the young man who entered a store in New York and saw some life-size dolls. He squeezed one and it said, "Mama." He squeezed another doll and it yelled for the floorwalker.

* * *

I was handed an announcement a few minutes ago, but due to the language used I cannot read it in public. It places me in the same boat with the minister who bought a used car. Two days later he took the car back to the dealer, and said: "I can't keep this car. To be brief, I can't drive it and stay in the ministry."

* * *

After a speech, a reporter who covered it, met his editor in the street. "Well," asked the editor, "did our eminent statesman have anything important to say?" "Nothing," said the reporter. "Then," suggested the editor, "keep it down to a column."

* * *

Timing on any program is essential. Perhaps we could learn something from the lady whose apartment was on a corner near a traffic light. She boiled her eggs to perfection by timing them with one red and two green lights.

INTRODUCING A PLAY

This has to do with the introduction of a play. It may be an amateur production. Did you know that I am writing a play? It's coming along just fine, too. It will be a three-act play. I've just finished the intermissions.

A would-be playwright submitted a play entitled, "Why Do I Live?" The play was returned with this notation: "Because you sent your play by mail."

Another so-called playwright submitted a bulky manuscript. It was immediately returned with a short note attached that read: "Am returning your paper. Somebody has written on it."

—Sidney Steele

IT'S THE TRUTH

Ladies and gentlemen, you are going to be mighty happy that you came this evening. Take it from me, a wonderful program has been planned. I wouldn't tell you this if it were not the truth. Which brings to mind a shorty about a street corner quack medicine man.

"This," he orated, holding up a bottle of brown liquid, "is the greatest of boons to mankind. Friends, in this bottle is a tonic that will add years and years to your life. Take me, for example. By using this very same medicine I have lived to be hale and hearty, though I am nearly two hundred years old."

An old codger in the crowd asked the quack's attendant: "Is he really that old?" "Can't say," said the assistant. "I've only worked for him a hundred and twenty years."

—Richard Drummond

WHERE'S EVERYBODY?

When the gathering is much smaller than was anticipated.

Once upon a time there were one hundred ostriches. Ninety-nine of them were just standing with their heads buried in the sand. Suddenly ostrich Number One Hundred came galloping up. He looked around puzzled, and then said: "Hey! Where is everybody?"

—Arthur L. Kaser

ON TOO LONG

Once, when Will Rogers was acting as toastmaster, he listened to a very long speech by a very long-winded speaker. Finally the speaker concluded his speech and sat down. "Ladies and gentlemen," said Rogers, "you have just listened to that noted Chinese philosopher, On Too Long."

—Jeff Gannett

IN A HOLE

A guest on the speakers' stand was unexpectedly called on by the toastmaster to make a speech. He stammered for a moment, then apologized for coming unprepared. Then suddenly turning to the toastmaster, he said, "I'm like Jonah and you're the whale. If you had kept your big mouth shut, I wouldn't be in this hole now."

—Richard Drummond

A PAIN IN THE EAR

Two small boys had attended a banquet the night before with their parents. Now they were endeavoring to re-enact the proceedings. One said, "You can be the mastoid of ceremonies." "Naw," said the other. "A mastoid is a pain in the ear." "Sure it is," said the other.

—Arthur L. Kaser

WITHOUT THINKING

Being rather new at this emceeing, I do not have the ability to just ramble on without thinking. I'm like the youth who had a cheap lodging near the college he was attending. He sent home an urgent air-mail letter to his parents: "Please, quick, send me rug. I need something to sweep under."

—Bob Royce

SCATTERED IDEAS

If something unforeseen happens on the program that momentarily disturbs the master of ceremonies, he might say: "It happens to everybody, I guess. A young door-to-door salesman was trying to flirt with a pretty young housewife when her husband happened to come home and hit him on the head with a club. The salesman said later that it didn't knock him out, but it sure scattered his ideas."

—Franklin Phelps

EXCUSE THE ERROR

The emcee who has caught himself mispronouncing a word: "Please excuse the error. I'm thankful I was not speaking over a nationwide hiccup."

—Vance Clifford

TO SAY SOMETHING

"Ladies and gentlemen," said the emcee, "before I start to speak I want to say something."

—Arthur L. Kaser

AFTER-DINNER SPEECH

He made a very unusually good after-dinner speech. He said, "Waiter, give me the check."

—Richard Drummond

THE RIGHT WORDS

An emcee who was momentarily stymied for want of the right words, said, "A friend of mine applied for a job as inspector in an auto plant. He filled out the application as best he could until he came to the space for 'remarks.' This puzzled him for a moment, then he wrote, 'It's a nice day, isn't it?' "

—Arthur L. Kaser

BRIEF REMARKS

Ladies and gentlemen, don't worry. I'll make my remarks very brief. In fact, I'll be as brief as the new track inspector who was instructed to keep his telegraphed reports on the condition of the railroad bed brief and to the point. His first report ran like this: "River is where railroad tracks were."

—Sidney Steele

BABY'S NIGHT OUT

For a substitute master of ceremonies

I am sorry to announce that your regular emcee could not be here this evening. It's the baby's night out and he had to stay home with the sitter.

—Jeff Gannett

MOSTLY IN FUN

An audience should never take too seriously everything an emcee says. It's mostly in fun.

After the sixteenth was born to the Skites family someone suggested to Mr. Skites that he should throw rocks at the stork. "Aw," said Skites, "he ain't doin' much harm. He's just kiddin'."

—Richard Drummond

THERE'S ALWAYS A WAY

Sometimes it is difficult to approach a subject from one angle, but it can be accomplished by another angle. Jed Hawkins was a little peeved with his neighbor, Dave Dikes. However, Jed saw Dave getting ready to go to town. "Goin' to town, Dave?" asked Jed. "Yep," said Dave. "Mind takin' my coat along?" asked Jed. "Sure, I'll take it," said Dave, "but where'll I leave it?" "Don't worry about that," said Jed. "I'll be in it."

—Arthur L. Kaser

HELP OTHERS

It is often necessary for an emcee to put in a word or two extra when there is a delay in the progress of the program. This comes in the category of "help others." One of my uncles needed help just about once every month. Periodically, the police department would phone us to come to the police station. "Jim has another tankful. Come and bail him out." If anybody had ever taken a pot shot at him, there would have been a flood.

—Bob Royce

LIMITED VOCABULARY

Some people have the idea that to be a master of ceremonies one must possess a very large vocabulary. This isn't true. His available words may be limited if he has the ability to use them over and over in different arrangements.

Recently I met an acquaintance who had made application for a job as house detective in a hotel. He seemed to think along the same lines as I. It wasn't necessary to have many of anything to get by. I said to him: "Why did you apply for the job as house detective when you have only one eye?" He said: "Why not? You can use only one eye to peek through a keyhole."

—Arthur L. Kaser

TALKING TOO MUCH

Sometimes talking too much is disastrous, and I don't want to cause a disaster. As one girl said to another: "I can only stand him for an hour. He gets tired of listening after that."

—Richard Drummond

WHAT CIRCUS?

The same day that I was informed that I was to emcee this program a young man approached me and asked if I could use my influence to let him put on an act. I asked him about his act. He said: "I have a wonderful act. It is the same I used in the circus." I asked him: "What circus?" He looked at me as if he resented my question. "What circus?" he sputtered. "My good man, if you were in England and you heard someone say, 'God save the Queen,' would you ask him what queen?"

—Arthur L. Kaser

A SLIP OF THE TONGUE

An emcee, whose tongue slipped on a word, quickly apologized and said: "Olsen and Schultz entered a bar. 'I tink,' said Schultz, 'I haf a leedle shin.' Olsen laughed, and said: 'My goodness, Schultz, you ban een dis country ten year now and you can't yet say yin.' "

—Vance Clifford

OUT OF PLACE

I feel as out of place emceeing this program as the man from Oklahoma who was on his way to the inaugural ball in top hat and black tie. He said if he was seen in these clothes back home they would bury him.

—Arthur L. Kaser

BIG SURPRISE

When the entertainment is a surprise for the audience

Ladies and gentlemen, there is a wonderful surprise in store for you this evening. However, it isn't anything like the surprise a friend of mine got in the hospital this morning. When he saw the nurse come out of a certain room he rushed up and said excitedly: "Quick, nurse! Tell me, is it a boy?" The nurse said: "Well, the one in the middle is."

—Franklin Phelps

WHO KNOWS?

When an emcee starts off with "Ladies and gentlemen—" what is he going to say? Who knows? You might as well try to figure out what a woman driver is going to do when she holds out her hand. Does it mean she is going to turn—right or left, shake the ashes from her cigarette, reverse or stop, or is she pointing to a pretty hat in the window?

—Arthur L. Kaser

OUTLYING PROVINCE

Not long ago I had the honor of being selected to emcee a banquet in Houston. There were many at the banquet from Oklahoma. A professor from the University of Texas was speaking. When the professor mentioned the neighboring state of Oklahoma as an "outlying province of Texas," an Oklahoman leaped to his feet and shouted: "Man, there ain't no state can out-lie Texas!" —Richard Drummond

FAMOUS

Our speaker of the evening woke up one morning and found himself famous. That is so much better than staying up all night and find oneself notorious. —Arthur L. Kaser

SPARE THE ROD

Gentlemen, this meeting of adherents to the science of piscatology will enjoy, I am sure, some of the advice our speakers will pour forth this evening. It used to be spare the rod and spoil the child. Now it's spare the rod and spoil the fishing.

Our minister went fishing one sunny day last summer and was horrified to hear a youngster who was fishing using words that were dyed a dark, deep electric blue. "My boy," said the minister, "don't you know you can never catch fish if you swear like that?"

The lad said: "Yeah, I know I'm not much good at it, but I thought maybe I could catch some little ones on the few words I do know. Here, you take my pole and try it. See what you can do." Then the boy said suddenly: "Say, how many did you catch?"

Of course the minister couldn't lie about it, so he said, "Well, if I catch the one I'm after and then two more, I'll have three."

—Richard Drummond

TWICE AS FAST

The emcee at a sports banquet

I might start off by telling the one about the champion runner who received the cup, and then was called on for a speech. He was a little bashful, but finally said: "Gentlemen, I have won this cup by the use of my legs. I trust I may never lose the use of my legs by the use of the cup."

I asked one of your boys this morning what he thought of a certain pole vaulter, and he said: "That guy a pole vaulter? Why, he can't even clear his throat." Then I asked him about a certain one of your runners. "Oh, him? Say, he's fast. He can run so fast that all the others in the race have to run twice as fast as he does to keep up with him."

—Arthur L. Kaser

PAINFUL EXPERIENCE

When the emcee anticipates a smooth-running program

I feel assured this program will go much smoother than the last one at which I was the master of ceremonies. Everything seemed to go wrong, and whenever I look back on that painful experience I think of the two old timers who had come to town to celebrate.

The two rode to town on one horse. It might have been that it was a one-horse town. Anyway, they did a good job celebrating and when they started home in the wee dark hours they were quite befuddled. After some maneuvering they got astride their horse. It was so dark they depended upon the horse to take them home.

They rode for awhile without incident until the man in front fell off, and landed with a splash in a creek alongside the road. The second man fished him from the creek. The dunked man shouted: "Stop the horse, Jim. Something fell off." The other man said: "Shut up, you fool. It was you fell off." "Nope," muttered the other, "it wasn't me. I'm all right."

Still arguing, they climbed the bank and searched for the horse in the dark. With his hands in front of him and groping blindly, Lem touched the horse's rump. "I got him," he shouted. "It was his head that fell off. Nothin' left here but his mane." The fact was, he had found the horse's tail. "We don't need his head," said Jim, "we can steer him by pulling his mane."

They climbed on the horse but were seated backwards. Getting a grip on what they thought was the horse's mane, Jim said: "Giddyup." As the horse began to move, Jim muttered: "Now the dang crittur is going backwards."

—Vance Clifford

WHAT'S YOUR SCORE?

For a golf get-together

Golf is invading every field. I went to a dentist yesterday. He said: "I'm sorry I can't take you this afternoon. I have eighteen cavities to fill." He went out with his golf bag.

I like golf, but I'm no whiz at it. Saturday, when I got home after playing golf, my wife asked: "What was your score?" I told her it was seventy-two. She said: "Seventy-two? That's good." "It's not so bad," I said. "Tomorrow I hope to do better on the second hole." —Arthur L. Kaser

GOOD-NATURED EMCEE

A speaker on a program said jokingly at the beginning of his speech, "We speakers are always glad to have a good-natured master of ceremonies. Whatever goes wrong we can blame on him." When the speech was finished the emcee said: "Well, I've learned something. From now on, if anything goes wrong I'll blame it on the speakers."

This brings to mind the one about a practical joker who was riding on a train opposite a pair of spinsters. The train suddenly entered a very dark tunnel. The joker made some loud kissing noises. As the train pulled out of the tunnel into daylight he stood and bowed low to the ladies, and said: "I don't know which one of you ladies to thank for those exceedingly pleasant moments." —Franklin Phelps

LAUNDRY BUSINESS

Speaking of business, a census taker approached a lazy-looking individual and found out his name, age, etc. Then he inquired: "What business are you in?" "I'm in the laundry business," said the lazy one. "Where is your business located?" asked the census taker. "There she comes now," said the other. —Arthur L. Kaser

ENTIRELY DIFFERENT

Our program this evening is so much different from the usual run of programs I hardly know how to announce it. And speaking of differences, I visited a very small town not long ago and dropped into the only general store there.

I said to the proprietor: "This town is only a few miles from the next town, but seems so entirely different in every way." "Yes," said the proprietor, "I know what you mean, but I think the biggest difference is, that in that other town in the winter the girls sit around and hug the stove and the men smoke. Here, the men sit around and hug the girls and let the stove smoke." —Richard Drummond

DOWN TO BUSINESS

At a businessmen's meeting

Gentlemen, this is a meeting of businessmen, so we will get right down to business. I ran across a business card of an enterprising youngster in our neighborhood. It goes as follows: Mr. Harold Cross, Jr., Manager and President. Personal escorter. Young fry took to school and returned, prompt in perfect condition, if received that way. Strick disapline. Rates, 30 cents a week in advance. Refined conversation. No extra for nose wiping. Don't trust your kids to anybody. Ask me."

Business enters into every phase of life in some way or another. The owner of a southern plantation was discussing the hereafter with one of his colored help. "Pete," he said, "let's make a bargain. If you die first, I want you to come back and tell me about it. If I die first, I'll come back and tell you." "Dat suits me, sah," replied Pete, "but dey's one stippelation in de contract. If you dies fust, Ah wants you to promise me dat you'll come back in de daytime." —Arthur L. Kaser

SUITABLE SECRETARIES

No doubt all you businessmen know that one of the most difficult tasks of an office manager is to get suitable secretaries —that is, suitable to the manager and suitable to the manager's wife. One of these managers was telling me the other day that he hired a new secretary and she spent two hours the first day on the phone trying to get "Established 1-8-8-5." Then he continued: "When I had finished dictating my first letter to her, she said, 'Now what did you say between Dear Sir and Sincerely Yours?' She's the latest thing in stenographers. She was late one hour that day." —Bob Royce

REAL THRIFT

I am happy to be master of ceremonies at this meeting of the Thrift Club. Nowadays to practice thrift one must have a club. Wasn't it Franklin who said, "To modern Americans a penny saved is a pocket burned"? Real thrift was shown by a Scotsman who came to this country and immediately went out west and became a cowboy. He got himself a horse but bought only one spur. He figured that if one side of the horse went the other side was sure to follow.

—Arthur L. Kaser

HUNTING LICENSE

At a meeting of the gun club

In this state, I believe, a hunting license entitles you to one deer and no more. It's just like a marriage license. I was hunting with my cousin not long ago. We had no success whatever. I said to him: "It's getting dark, and we haven't hit a thing." My cousin said: "Let's miss two more and then go home."

—Sidney Steele

MIGHTY GOOD GRAVY

Ladies and gentlemen (mostly ladies), the speakers this evening have some wonderful messages for everyone interested in home economics. I don't care much about the rest of the house, but I do get interested in good food recipes.

Perhaps I am like an acquaintance of mine who was host to a gentleman from Virginia. The guest was telling the host the best way to prepare ham. The host had called in his cook to take notes on the recipe.

"Place the ham in a deep pan," said the guest, "and for a whole day soak it in rye whiskey. The second day add a bottle of Jamaica rum, and cook for an hour. The third day add a bottle of port wine and on the fourth day a bottle of bourbon."

The host turned to his cook, and said: "What do you think of that?" "Well," said the cook, "Ah doan know 'bout de ham, but it sho' do sound like de makin's of mighty good gravy."

—Franklin Phelps

I DON'T KNOW EITHER

Well, boys, you are about to leave this institution of learning and cope with a sad and troubled world.

I had the same idea of some day graduating and coping with the world when I was younger. There was only one drawback; I didn't graduate. I was kicked out. Yes, sir, kicked out. Landed flop right on my Alma Mater, but I guess it didn't matter.

The reason I was kicked out was because the dean thought I called him a fish. I didn't call him a fish. All I did was say: "That's our dean," real fast. He didn't like me anyway. He asked me once what German chieftain captured Rome. I said: "It was Hannibal, wasn't it?" He said: "Don't ask me. I'm asking you." So I said: "I don't know either."

—Arthur L. Kaser

MONOLAFFS

The Army likes to keep its men sport-minded. This morning I passed the parade ground and saw twenty-two enlisted men tossing the **old pigskin** around. What a horrible way to treat a Second Lieutenant!

Florida is famous for its many resorts. There's Miami, Palm Beach, Coral Gables, and of course, Hialeah—That's always the last resort!

If I am elected to Congress, I promise to clean up all the mess in Washington. I intend to start my campaign direct from the Senate floor—All I need is your support and a gallon of Johnson's Glo Coat!

Last election I voted for a Congressional Candidate who promised to reduce personal income taxes fifty per cent—The lousy skunk introduced a bill requesting all wages be cut in half!

According to statistics, seventy-five per cent of the tax payers in this country try to cheat the government—The other twenty-five per cent use the short form.

A dollar goes a long way today. I know—After tax deductions, I sent five hundred of them all the way to Washington.

I've just returned from a very strange and unusual place—I found a parking space on (mention busiest street in town.) It took me three hours to park between two cars—Of course, they were bumper-to-bumper!

The stars have much to tell. The other day I read the horoscope of a poor, unfortunate peasant who lives behind the Iron Curtain. Ivan was born under the sign of Taurus, the Bull—

It's true, because they've been bullying him ever since. He is ruled by the Planet Venus, known as the Planet of Emotion. That's the reason why Ivan loves his country—He'd love to get out of it! His lucky number is six. Six years from today Ivan will no longer toil and sweat twenty-two hours a day in the mines. Why? Because, six years from today Ivan will be executed! His lucky color is red. Actually, it's blue, but under the circumstances, why quibble? Ivan's lucky months are May and July. This is vacation time. Twice a year all the peasants rush to the seashore. Last year Ivan almost succeeded in drowning himself.

How do you like the suit I'm wearing tonight? My tailor made it for me right after seeing one of those movies about interplanetary travel. It's a regular space suit—There's space enough here for two other guys.

—A. Guy Visk

GOLF VS. BUSINESS

A businessman is one who talks golf all morning at the office and business all afternoon on the links.

—Arthur L. Kaser

SHALL WE PROCEED?

There were many at the banquet. They had broken up into small groups and all seemed to be having a very good time. The emcee turned to one of the speakers of the evening, and said: "Shall I let them enjoy themselves a little longer, or shall I introduce you?"

—Bob Royce

NOTHING TO SAY

Pity the poor emcee who runs out of things to say. He has to keep going nevertheless. It is like the dance floor that was so crowded with dancers. Everybody fainted but kept right on dancing because there was no room to fall down.

—Sidney Steele

DON'T BOTHER ME

Even a master of ceremonies has his moments when he would like to needle someone on the program, but it being un-ethical, he must refrain. Most everyone at some time gets needled at home, anyway. A friend of mine said to me: "My wife is always needling me." I said: "Just ignore it." He said: "Even if she uses needles?" —Arthur L. Kaser

THE USE OF TACT

A policeman was detailed to inform a wealthy and prominent lady that her dog had been run over and killed, but he was cautioned to use tact when telling her because she loved the dog very much. The officer called at the mansion and said to the lady: "Sorry, lady, but part of your dog has been killed."

It was during the Wall Street panic. Again tact came in mighty handy. A certain husband lost all his money. He wanted someone else to break the news to his wife. "Break the news of my entire loss gently to my wife. Tell her I'm dead."

Sometimes a man can be tactful even if he is a little gin-bleary. This particular man was belligerently daring anyone in the crowd to knock a chip off his shoulder. "I'll fight any man in the crowd," he shouted. "Come on, one at a time." Just then he saw Joe Louis who had stepped over to see what was going on. "Come on," repeated the noisy one. "I'll fight any man here, provided that Joe Louis referees."

Yes, my friends, tact is one of the essential ingredients in an emcee's makeup. One day the secretary of a golf club came across a tramp sleeping behind the bunker on the golf course, and kicked him none too gently. "Hey," said the tramp, "who are you?" "I'm secretary of this club," was the answer. "Humph!" grunted the tramp. "That's no way to get new members."

An emcee, among hundreds of other things, must possess tact.

On one of the South Pacific islands, our turkey dinner, as we know it in this country, is almost unheard of. A group of Americans were seated around the table when the servant entered with an oversize baked turkey on a platter. As he entered the room he stumbled, spilling the bird on the floor. The hostess, calmly, but tactfully, said: "Never mind, Zimbo. Take that back and get the other turkey."

Tact pays off in a lot of ways. A lad from the deep South had been in Chicago only a few weeks when he began to feel ill. He went to a doctor for an examination. The doctor advised him to see a dentist. The dentist informed the lad that an impacted wisdom tooth had to come out.

As the lad looked about the room the ominous-looking instruments appeared much bigger and more dangerous than they really were. The young man was really scared.

Finally he said to the dentist: "You-all a Yankee, sah?" The dentist said: "Oh, yes, I'm a full-fledged Yankee." The lad turned to the assistant. "You-all a Yankee?" "Nothing else," said the assistant. The scared lad hesitated a moment and then said: "Ah'm a Yankee, too."

—Richard Drummond

ONE BONE

Our speaker this evening is going to talk on finance. That is a big word nowadays—finance. I have some fine aunts—wonderful women they are. But speaking of finance, aren't things changing? For instance, now, when a young man wants to marry a girl he has to buy a diamond ring, spend lots of money on entertainment, money for this, for that—money, money, money. My, my, what a difference between the young folks of today and Adam and Eve. All Eve cost Adam was one bone."

—Jeff Gannett

CHICKEN ON HIS KNEE

A friend of mine recently asked me: "Would you rather be a master of ceremonies or one of the speakers on your program?" I told him that depended a lot on how good I was at emceeing, as well as how good the speaker might be. When I was in the army I asked a buck private if he would like to be a Colonel with an eagle on his shoulder? He said he would rather be a private with a chicken on his knee.

—Bob Royce

DUE CREDIT

Next we have on the program (name). Let's welcome him with a great big hand. I always believe in giving credit where credit is due. A certain amount of credit was passed up recently in Hollywood. A small boy had suddenly skyrocketed to fame as a child actor. At a get-together of movie folk, the director and the father of the boy were having some very nice things said about them. One of the guests interrupted with: "Isn't someone going to say something nice about the goose that laid this golden egg?"

—Arthur L. Kaser

LITTLE ROCK

And now, ladies and gentlemen, it is time to bring on the speakers who will explain the importance of this Community Chest Drive. You are urged to give for this most worthy cause. Give till it hurts. It is about the only hurt that will make you feel better. I was hurt once because I gave, but it didn't make me feel better. When I gave my wife a diamond engagement ring, she said: "You know, dear, this diamond reminds me so much of the capital of Arkansas—Little Rock."

—Franklin Phelps

GREAT FUN

Well, folks, it is certainly gratifying to see such a turn-out at this get-together. These parties — I think we could call them that — are always great fun if not overdone. I was to a party not long ago that hung on, and on, and on. Finally I heard one guest say: "Boy, I'm all in! I'm going to flirt with some good-looking dame so my wife will take me home." At the same party when the last of the guests were leaving, the host said: "We should get together again soon. Have a nice summer."

—Vance Clifford

WISE HECKLER

If there is anything that can spoil an evening of good speaking it is some wise heckler in the audience. A professional speaker friend of mine put an end to one of these nuisances in a hurry. The speaker, being much irritated by the heckler's persistent interruptions, said: "I hope the audience appreciates the foresightedness of the management in supplying two speakers this evening; one for **this** end of the hall, and one for **that** end."

—Sidney Steele

REQUEST FOR CONTRIBUTIONS

The publishers of this volume contemplate that "Humorous Introductions for Emcees" will be so well accepted that there will soon be a demand for a companion volume.

In anticipation of the publication of a second volume, the publishers invite the readers and users of this book to submit original introductions for possible inclusion. Payment will be made for accepted introductions and appropriate stories for emcees with the understanding that such material becomes the exclusive property of the publishers. Rejected material will be returned promptly.

T. S. Denison & Company
321 Fifth Ave. South
Minneapolis 15, Minn.